Gasconade County Missouri

Marriage Records
Books A-C
1821-1873

Teresa L. Blattner

HERITAGE BOOKS, INC.

Copyright 1995 by
Teresa Blattner

Other books by Teresa Blattner:
Divorces, Separations, and Annulments in Missouri, 1769 to 1850

People of Color: Black Genealogical Records and Abstracts from Missouri Sources, Volume 1

Published 1995 by

HERITAGE BOOKS, INC.
1540-E Pointer Ridge Place, Bowie, Maryland
20716
(301) 390-7709

ISBN 0-7884-0174-2

A Complete Catalog Listing Hundreds of Titles
on Genealogy, History, and Americana
Available Free on Request

DEDICATION

This volume is dedicated to the memory of Andreas and Elizabeth (WEHRLI) BLATTNER, who along with their three children, Henry, Sophronia, and Frederick, left Switzerland in 1843, bound for America. The family first made their way to Gasconade County, before finally settling in Warren County.

TABLE OF CONTENTS

Book A, 1822 - 1848 1
Book B, 1848 - 1855 29
Book C, 1855 - 1873 50
Index 117

PREFACE

Gasconade County was organized on November 25, 1820 from Franklin County. Original boundaries included all of present-day Crawford County, which was created in 1829; Pulaski County, created in 1833; Osage County, created in 1841; Maries County, created in 1855; and Phelps County, created in 1857, along with parts of Dent, Miller, Laclede, and Camden counties. The earliest settlers in this region were old-stock Americans, but the 1830's heralded the mass migration of thousands of Germanic people.

Every attempt has been made to ensure accuracy, but early Gasconade County public servants were usually American born, and were unaccustomed to the new languages being introduced to the area. This created major obstacles in recording marriages for those of foreign birth, so please keep this in mind, and check for all possible spelling variations.

Abbreviations have been used in place of the officiate's title:

      M. G. - Minister of the Gospel,
            or Preacher,
      J. P. - Justice of the Peace,
      Fr. - Father, or Catholic Priest.

Good luck!

ACKNOWLEDGEMENTS

A very special thank you to the staff of the Callaway County Public Library. A more dedicated, concerned, and sometimes hilarious group, is hard to find. Thanks for keeping things interesting!

BOOK A
1822 - 1848

Jonathan HOLLIWAY to Elizabeth FREEMAN - May 2, 1822, by William W. REDMAN, M. G..

Jonathan CAIN to Narcissa HINSON - July 4, 1822, by John DUNCAN, Jr..

Amos NICHOLAS to Mary MURRAY - August 17, 1822, by John DUNCAN, Jr..

John HUMPHRIES to Nancy SLAGGS - September 5, 1822, by Henry STUART.

Benjamin JONES to Sarah HINSON - August 12, 1822, by John DUNCAN, Jr..

John PRYOR to Patsey EDMONDSON - March 23, 1823 by Abraham D. BERRY.

William CHRISMON to Margaret WRATTLES - January 1, 1824, by Joseph M. MORROW.

Jacob FOULK to Polly SIMON - January 1, 1824, by Joseph M. MORROW.

John M. LAUGHLIN to Magdalene ALKIRE - March 6, 1823, by Joseph M. MORROW.

Peter WELLS to Nancy SIMON - April 2, 1823, by Joseph M. MORROW.

William LAUGHLIN to Mary Alice Polly EADDS - September 30, 1823, by Joseph M. MORROW.

John DAY to Martha HUMPHREY - March 29, 1823, by Henry STUART.

Jesse LIVELY to Sarah WRATTLES - September, 1824, by Robert SHOBE.

Jonas SHOBE to Elizabeth HUGH - December 26, 1824, by Joseph M. MORROW.

William MERTEER to Caty OVINSON - Jan 2, 1825, by William BUMPASS.

Joel STARKEY to Francis WYATT - July 10, 1825, by William BUMPASS.

James ESTES to Sarah LAUGHLIN - August 6, 1825, Joseph M. MORROW.

John HOBACK to Dice HOBACK - December 6, 1825, by James HARRISON.

James WILLAIMSON to Rebecca HOUSINGER - February 5, 1826, by James M. HARRISON.

James CRIDER to Mukey OWENS - January 1, 1826, by David HOOPS.

Obadiah KEE to Mary Ann CARTER - January 1, 1826, by J. Robert CLINTON.

Col. Daniel WALDO to Malinda LUNDSFORD - March

13, 1825, by James HARRISON.
John B. WALDO to Avanela TURPIN - April 23, 1826, by David Waldo, Probate Judge.
Joel STARKEY Jr. to Frances WYATT - March 19, 1826, by David WALDO.
David LEMON to Elizabeth BROWN - May 18, 1826, by James HARRISON.
Hiram ROBERTSON to Elizabeth COYLE - April 9, 1826, by James HARRISON.
Samuel James HARDISTER to Elizabeth HELMS - June 5, 1826, by James HARRISON.
William CORNELIUS to Permela SULLENS - March 12, 1826, by J. Robert CLINTON.
James D. WATKINS to Vicy COPPEDGE - March 24, 1826, by J. Robert CLINTON.
Samuel SINKLER to Nancy SWAFORD - June 22, 1826, by J. Robert CLINTON.
Joseph HOLBERT to Mahala BALDRIDGE - February 12, 1826, by J. Robert CLINTON.
George POINTER to Ruth BUTLER - May 14, 1826, by Philip JACKSON.
Daniel CRIDER to Elizabeth REED - August 24, 1826, by David WALDO.
Joseph AUD to Hannah SHOBE - October 8, 1826, by Anthony MARGRAVES.
Farmer DOYLE to Polly NEWBERRY - October 6, 1826, by William COPPEDGE.
Leonard REED to Rhoda VEACH - January 11, 1827, by William BUMPASS. Bride of Franklin county.
Samuel BURCHARD to Barbara BARBARICK - January 4, 1827, by David WALDO.
Lewis WELTON to Mary (sic) HULL- February 1, 1827, by Anthony MARGRAVES.
Charles MARRIE to Luiza ROWARD - February 15, 1827, by William BUMPASS.
David MILLER to Elizabeth HELTON - February 11, 1827, by William BUMPASS.
Nathan HUMPHRIES to Latetia PAMISON (sic) - March 27, 1827, by William MONTGOMERY.
John BURGOYNE to Mary BYONSIDES - March 27, 1827, by William MONTGOMERY.
Albion LOGSTON to Sarah SIMON - March 8, 1827, by Anthony MARGRAVES.
John POINTER to Eveline CAPEHART - April 8, 1827, by William Brown.

John NANCE to Peggy HOWARD - August 9, 1827, by William BUMPASS.
Bilberry HINCHY to Belinda WARDEN - August 4, 1827, by William BROWN.
John EDDS to Meron CALDWELL - July 19, 1827, by Anthony MARGRAVES.
Jacob STUART to Elizabeth BRISTO - July 11, 1827, by James HARRISON.
Eliga BENTON to Artamus MIDLOCK - February 10, 1827, by J. Robert CLINTON.
James BALL to Anna SINCLAIR - September 27, 1826, by J. Robert CLINTON.
Adam SMITH to Sary HOGAN - April 4, 1827, by J. Robert CLINTON.
Thomas CAPHARTE to Agnes PRYOR - July 19, 1827, by William BROWN.
James GIBSON to Peggy MORROW - October 11, 1827, by Anthony MARGRAVES.
Ezekiel HINCHY to Sarah SHIVERS - August 20, 1827, by William BUMPASS.
Wilson LENOX to Susannah BROWN - October 2, 1827, by William COPPEDGE.
John HOSINGER to Matilda GILLESPY - October 17, 1827, by Isaac N. DAVIS.
Joniah TYGERT to Elizabeth WALDEN - January 17, 1828, by Isaac N. DAVIS.
Henry I. HULL to Mary Ann ALKIRE - January 10, 1828, by Anthony MARGRAVES.
William MASSIE to Elizabeth HILL - January 10, 1828, by David WALDO.
Samuel PEARCE to Sarah BAKER - January 15, 1828, by J. Robert CLINTON.
Abraham HEWS to Mary BAKER - January 29, 1828, by J. Robert CLINTON.
Henry HOLDER to Honor REED - April 10, 1828, by William BUMPASS.
Isaac N. BRADFORD to Martha DUNCAN - June 26, 1828, by William BRADFORD.
John HARRISON to Cintha COPPEDGE - May 6, 1828, by William BRADFORD.
Green WILLIAMS to Ruth BALLEW - July 10, 1828, by Isaac N. DAVIS.
George TACKETT to Mary PRYOR - August 14, 1828, by Anthony MARGRAVES.
Isaac HELTON to Elizabeth HUGHES - October 2, 1828, by Anthony MARGRAVES.

Cyrus PATTERSON to Elizabeth MOONEY - August 8, 1828, by Spencer O'NEAL.
George SALLY to Alley BROWN - October 12, 1828, by William COPPEDGE.
John DUNCAN to Nancy BRADFORD - September 25, 1828, by Wiliam BRADFORD.
John STARK to Rachel CASEBOLT - November 27, 1828, William CASEBOLT.
John P. CAMPBELL to Beddy L. TIGERT - November 20, 1828, by Spencer O'NEAL.
Samuel STUART to Nancy THROCKMORTON - January 12, 1829, by William BRADFORD.
Joseph BUTLER to Barbara TACKETT - January 29, 1829, by William BRADFORD.
Thomas SHOCKLEY to Rachel CRIDER - March 26, 1829, by Samuel BURCHARD.
Benjamin YATES to Amelia CRIDER - April 9, 1829, by Samuel BURCHARD.
Michael CROW to Nancy STRINGER - June 18, 1829, by William BUMPASS.
James MILLER to Margaret FLETT (sic) - June 18, 1829, by Anthony MARGRAVES.
George REVIS to Mary REED - August 6, 1829, by William BUMPASS.
John TACKETT to Sally HENSLEY - July 30, 1829, by Anthony MARGRAVES.
Rodney A. WALKER to Rachel WYATT - September 6, 1829, by Anthony MARGRAVES.
Abraham CRIDER to Mary OWENS - November 5, 1829, by Samuel BURCHARD.
Madison POE to Eliza BACKUS - January 14, 1830, by Hugh BARCLAY.
William SHIVERS to Nancy PERRY - January 10, 1830, by Hugh BARCLAY.
James KERLEY to Mary FLATT (sic) - January 7, 1830, by Anthony MARGRAVES.
N. Hardin ROBERTSON to Lydia HENSLEY - January 14, 1830, by Anthony MARGRAVES.
Joseph GRAHARD to Mary DENOE - May 27, 1830, by Jesse EVANS.
Thomas OWEN to Sally POINTER - March 11, 1830, by Hugh BARCLAY.
Lewis VINCENT to Margaret GRAHARD - July 28, 1830, Jesse EVANS.
Baptist GRAHARD to Cecil VINCENT - May 27, 1830, Fr. L. F. P. GERREYDH.

Davis MASSEY to Temperance PETTY - April 22, 1830, by David HOOPS.
Uriah SHOCKLEY to Matilda BARBRAKE - May 6, 1830, by Joshua COX.
John WYATT to Jane WILSON - May 23, 1830, by Joshua COX.
_____ HOODENPYL to Sarah BRIGES - April 4, 1830, by Joshua COX.
John CAPEHART to Louisa HUGHS - April 8, 1830, by William BROWN.
Henry STEWART to Rachel EDES - September 30, 1830, by Thomas TAYLOR.
Isaiah RAY to Julia CAPTAIN - October 4, 1830, by Jesse EVANS.
Richard SHOCKLEY to Elizabeth BURGESS - October 14, 1830, by Joshua COX.
Edward PRICE to Hannah BROWN - July 22, 1830, by David HOOPS.
James STUART to Hannah PHILIPS - July 29, 1830, by David HOOPS.
William CURTIS to Hannah DAVID - December 5, 1830, by William BRADFORD.
Drury RIGHT to Elizabeth SHOBE - December 3, 1830, by Thomas TAYLOR.
Barnet BOLWARE to Elizabeth WALKER - February 3, 1831, by William BUMPASS.
James WYATT to Mary CRAIG - April 10, 1831, by William BUMPASS.
George BOLWARE to Frances WALKER - May 23, 1831, by William BUMPASS.
James HOBOUGH to Ludice POE - June 19, 1831, by Hugh BARCLAY.
Sampson PUMMEL to Deborah MORROW - June 23, 1831, by Anthony MARGRAVES.
James HELTON to Mary HILL - June 21, 1831, by William BROWN.
Hugh HETHERLY to Isabella McBRIDE - September 20, 1831, by Hugh BARCLAY.
John G. HUFFMAN to Agnes PRIOR - June 23, 1831, by Thomas TAYLOR.
James CAPHART to Juda CRISMAN - September 15, 1831, by William BROWN.
William VINEYARD to Stacy COWEN - October 23, 1831, by Joseph BRASHEAR, M. G..
James Matson DOWNS to Perlina CALLAWAY - November 14, 1831, Elder John BURGESS.

Richard RICHARDSON to Charlotte COOPER - November 20, 1831, by Elder John BURGESS.
William WYATT to Elizabeth McGOUR - November 24, 1831, by Elder John BURGESS.
Jacob HOLLIWAY to Amiable Elizabeth ISBELL - July 7, 1831, David HOOPS.
Robert BOWER to Anna MORROW - December 22, 1831, by Anthony MORROW.
Robert JEWEL to Mary GALLAWAY - December 18, 1831, by Elder John BURGESS.
Joseph MYERS to Mary BAYLES - January 5, 1832, by Anthony MARGRAVES.
William COX to Margaret BARBARICK - January 26, 1832, by Elder John BURGESS.
Thomas ROGERS to Margaret GALLIWAY - May 3, 1832, by Elder John BURGESS.
Samuel WYATT to Jane WYATT - March 11, 1832, by William BUMPASS.
William MILLER to Nancy HOWARD - February 16, 1832, by Anthony MARGRAVES.
Rev. Edward REED to Miss Delitha SHIVERS - April 19, 1832, by David HOOPS.
John THOMPSON to Mary HOLLIWAY - May 2, 1832, by James G. WALKER, M. G..
Valentine BRANSON to Sealy BECK - April 1, 1832, by Thomas SMITH, M.G..
Leonard REED to Rebecca BRANSON - March 29, 1832, by Thomas SMITH. M. G..
David BRANSON to Sally DAVID - June 14, 1832, by William BRADFORD.
John PATTY to Polly McNIGHT - July 31, 1832, by Samuel HARRISON.
Lawrence OWEN to Fanny BRUMLEY - January 22, 1832, by Joseph BRASHER, M. G..
Samuel BRASILL to Feby TABOUR - May 20, 1832, by Joseph BRASHER, M. G..
Stephen MASON to Rebecca ROBERTSON - May 24, 1832, by Joseph BRASHER, M. G..
Samuel LAUGHLIN to Sally AGEE - October 18, 1832, by Anthony MARGRAVES.
John LOGSDON to Annastasia SIMON - August 24, 1832, by Fr. S. F. L. NEMYDT.
Thomas VEACH to Sarah REED - September 11, 1832, by Hiram PINNELL.
Henry McGEE to Rosannah REED - February 10, 1833, by Samuel HARRISON.

John PRIOR to Patsy HUGHS - February 14, 1833, by Thomas Taylor.
Ratio RENFRO to Malinda SABERFIELD - March 19, 1833, by Thomas SMITH, M. G..
Henry KERLEY to Elizabeth DANIEL - March 14, 1833, by Hugh BARCLAY.
Uriah HENCHY to Elizabeth CUTBIRTH - May 9, 1833, by Hugh BARCLAY.
John HENCHY to Charlotte CUTBIRTH - May 2, 1833, by Hugh BARCLAY.
John MURPHY to Lucretia VAUN - February 10, 1833, by William BROWN.
James N. McCORD to Elizabeth E. LANE - February 28, 1833, by William BROWN.
Edward REED to Noncy BITTICK - May 30, 1833, by Samuel HARRISON.
Ephriam PERKINS to Louisa STRIEN - June 2, 1833, by Samuel HARRISON.
Daniel PRYOR to Cintha Ann MASSIE - May 5, 1833, by Anthony MARGRAVES.
William SHOCKLEY to Rebecca COPELAND - August 15, 1833, by Joseph BRASHER, M. G..
David HOOPS to Louisa Ann WALTON - August 22, 1833, by Joseph BRASHER, M. G..
Thomas BUTLER to Elizabeth TACKET - August 29, 1833, by Hugh BARCLAY.
Benjamin SMITH to Martha HOOPS - September 24, 1833, by Joseph BRASHER, M. G..
Harris CALDWELL to Jane VINEYARD - October 22, 1833, by Samuel W. PARKS.
James HELTON to Bursella VAUGHAN - October 10, 1833, by David HOOPS.
Henry COWINS to Patsy WILLIAMS - July 7, 1833, by Hiram PINNELL.
John M. TOWNLY to Perima ALKIRE - September 26, 1833, by Thomas TAYLOR.
William CLARK to Ann NICKLES - November 27, 1833, Thomas TAYLOR.
Stephen HUGHS to Jane HELTON - September 19, 1833, by William BROWN.
John CHRISMAN to Meltina BRASHEAR - December 15, 1833, by William BROWN.
John BARTLETT to Sally BARCLAY - December 19, 1833, by William BROWN.
George MASSIE to Margaret BRANSON - December 29, 1833, by John B. HARRISON.

James COIL to Mary Jane BRASHEAR - February 3, 1834.
James POINTER to Sarah MILLER - February 12, 1834, by Anthony MARGRAVES.
Leroy McGOWAN to Sarah BRANSON - March 14, 1834, by John B. HARRISON.
Thomas MASON to Mary SAMPSON - February 12, 1834, by Samuel BURCHARD.
Green TERRY to Elizabeth CHILDERS - January 8, 1834, by Thomas SMITH.
Henry SHOCKLEY to Mahaly CHRISMAN - February 20, 1834, by Samuel W. PARKS.
William JARVIS to Jane POYNTER - May 11, 1834, by Anthony MARGRAVES.
David CALDWELL to Elizabeth COWAN - March 12, 1834, by Jpseph BRASHEAR, Elder.
Moses SIMPSON to Nancy DODDS - April 3, 1834, by William BRADFORD.
Jesse GALLAWAY to Sally SCAGGS - May 11, 1834, by Samuel W. WOODS, J.P..
James HALL to Matilda COURTRIGHT - June 19, 1834, by Joseph BRASHEAR, Elder.
Samuel SIMPSON to Sarah PRYOR - July 6, 1834, by William BUMPASS.
Hugh ESTES to Sarah HUFFMAN - May 29, 1834, by Joseph M. MORROW.
Seth CASON to Sally MOODY - September 26, 1833, by Charles BOLTON.
James HALL to Kisiah (sic) Matilda CARTRIGHT - July 20, 1834, by Charles BOLTON.
Augustin HAWKINS to Sarah HUTTON - August 7, 1834, by Joseph HAWKINS.
Levi ROGERS to Morning HAINS - February 18, 1834, by John B. HARRISON.
Peter HELTON to Emelin ANDERSON - September 30, 1834, by Samuel W. WOOD, J. P..
Amos A. SHEMY to Susannah COLLENS - July 28, 1834, by William WEIR.
David P. HUFFMAN to Jane AGEE - April 14, 1834, by Thomas TAYLOR.
Thomas PIPER to Sally Hannah STUART - October 10, 1834, by Hugh BARCLAY.
John MURPHY to Mary Ann SHAW - July 19, 1834, by Elder George Morris.
William BRANSON to Matilda SHOCKLEY - October 21, 1834, by Thomas SMITH.

Jacob CARROLL to Milly BRANSON - November 29, 1834, by Thomas SMITH.
Balsar GROFF to Sally BACKUS - January 1, 1835, by Sanuel W. WOOD, J. P..
Robert ORME to Elizabeth SHOBE - December 16, 1834, by Joseph M. MORROW.
William POINTER to Vecinda DANIEL - January 8, 1835, by William BUMPASS.
Exekiel BALDUS to Sarah NAPEAR - January 15, 1835, by Hiram PINNELL.
James THOMPSON to Nancy DANFORTH - March 12, 1835, by William WEIR.
William JOHNS to Matilda SHOOKMAN - February 23, 1835, by Thomas SMITH.
Valentine BRANSON to Alpha SHURLS (sic) - January 22, 1835, by Joshua COX.
Westley SHOCKLEY to Betsey CURTIS - January 25, 1835, by Joshua COX.
Reuben McFARLAND to Martha BENTON - February 15, 1835, by Joshua COX.
Jesse MILLER to Matilda ORMES - March 1, 1835, by Joshua COX.
William MILLER to Lucy Ann OWENS - March 19, 1835, by Joshua COX.
John PRYOR to Ann STRINGER - April 30, 1835, by William BUMPASS.
Andrew ROYE to Margaret DUNICA - May 4, 1835, by Charles BOLTON.
Thomas LADD to Sarah LOYD - May 18, 1835, by Mortimer M. BRASHEAR.
Jacob MENAS to Emelin EVANS - February 27, 1835, by Elder George MORRIS.
Stephen COLVAN to Nancy POINTER - April 5, 1835, by Anthony MARGRAVES.
David McKINNEY to Maria L. MASSIE - May 21, 1834, by James McBRIDE.
John FLATT to Polly POINTER - May 24, 1835, by Anthony MARGRAVES.
Milton HYATT to Rosannah ADAMS - April 16, 1835, by Gran. RUTHERFORD. Groom of Franklin county.
William H. VAUGHAN to Nancy WASHAM - March 13, 1835, by Samuel W. WOOD, J. P..
McKamy HUGHS to Elnora (sic) DAVIDSON - June 11, 1835, by Samuel W. WOOD, J. P..
William WEATHERFORD to Leamay SAGE - June 18,

1835, by Charles BOLTON.
William KIRLEY to Margaret COLVIN - July 23, 1835, by Thomas SMITH.
Tarleton MASSIE to Caroline WARD - September 3, 1835, by William BUMPASS.
Mathew MILLER to Jane COLVAN - October 10, 1835, by Thomas SMITH.
William MASON to Celia SIMPSON - September 27, 1835, by Jesse LIVELY, M. G..
Ripley M. WILSON to Dorcas DAVENPORT - August 27, 1835, by S. R. SHURRELL.
John BRANSON to Julian DAVENPORT - January 7, 1836, by S. R. SHURRELL.
Thomas BRANSON to Lucinda HAINS - January 10, 1836, by S. R. SHURRELL.
John K. SEALS to Thuresy CHASE - January 5, 1836, by William BUMPASS.
Elisha RODGERS to Susannah WALLACE - December 17, 1835, by William WEIR.
George MARTIN to Polly COWIN - January 17, 1836, by Samuel W. WOOD, J. P.
Madison THOMPSON to Eliza ANDERSON - May 15, 1835, by Hiram PINNELL.
Alford SMITH to Mary Ann HOOPS - August 20, 1835, by John SCOTT.
Capt. Davis WOODY to Partheany ISBEEL (sic) - July 23, 1835, by Charles BOLTON.
Capt. James DAVIS to Elizabeth MOODY - July 12, 1835, by Charles BOLTON.
James POINTER to Nancy BRANSON - January 10, 1836, by Joshua COX.
Lewis DAVID to Jane SMITH - February 7, 1836, by Joshua COX.
Jesse EVINS to Martha SURRATT - December 29, 1835, by John THOMPSON, M. G..
William HENDERSON to Charlotte MALONE - January 28, 1836, by John AVERY.
Andrew Jackson ROBERTSON to Polly McGEE - December 27, 1835, by John AVERY, M. G..
James JONSTON to Elvina HUGHS - January 28, 1836, by John AVERY, M. G..
Daniel SIMPSON to Elizabeth PRYOR - May 23, 1836, by William BUMPASS.
Thomas MIDDLECALF to Sarah HARRIS - June 28, 1836, by William BUMPASS.
Drury HUGHS to Violet LAVEN - August 7, 1836,

by John SCOTT.
George HOOPS to Amanda WALTON - June 23, 1836.
Harvey HAWKINS to Elizabeth CAMPBELL - August 18, 1836, by Elder John BURGESS.
John TENNERSON to Honor HOLDEN - August 9, 1836, by William WEIR.
William THOMPSON to Martha MORMAN - September 8, 1836, by William WEIR.
Robert R. LAUGHLIN to Elizabeth McNIGHT - November 29, 1836, William BUMPASS.
William WARD to Elenor GRIFFY - September 19, 1837, by John B. HARRISON.
J. B. HARRISON to Maria GRIFFY - November 8, 1836, by William BUMPASS.
James BELL to Tempy ROY - December 15, 1836, by John MILLER.
Robert McKINNEY to Elizabeth BRIGS - March 19, 1837, by Elder John BURGESS.
Pleasant CROUCH to Nancy COFFETT - February 9, 1837, by William BUMPASS.
William COX to Precious CAMPBELL - March 23, 1837, by John B. HARRISON.
Thomas BRANSON to Hanner SIMPSON - May 11, 1837, by Joshua COX.
John WEIR to Masey BRANSON - May 21, 1837, by William BRADFORD.
Moses SIMPSON to Elizabeth VINSON - March 30, 1837, by John W. JOHNSON.
Luster HAINS to Susannah BRANSON - June 1, 1837, by Thomas SMITH.
Jesse HARRIS to Elizabeth DAVID - July 29, 1837, by William BUMPASS.
John PERKINS to Eliza BURGESS - August 31, 1837, by William BUMPASS.
Jesse EVANS to Patsy SANARTT (sic) - September 4, 1837, by John AVERY, M. G..
Daniel BOON to Judah HELTON - July 9, 1837, by Samuel W. WOOD, J. P..
William BROWN to Ruth MARKUM - September 21, 1837, by William BUMPASS.
John PRYOR Jr. to Mary Ann GRIFFEY - October 3, 1837, by Elder John BURGESS.
Isaiah SHOCKLEY to Malinda CAMPBELL - November 23, 1837, by Elder John BURGESS.
George BURCHARD to Nancy AGEE - September 21, 1837, by John W. JOHNSON.

Thomas ANDERSON to Mira Ann WISEMAN - November 12, 1837, by John AVERY.
David BARBARICK to Elizabeth WEST - December 14, 1837, by Joseph HAWKINS.
Thomas SMITH to Elizabeth NICOLES - November 30, 1837, by Thomas TAYLOR.
William OWENS to Amanda DUCKWORTH - November 23, 1837, by Mark D. SPAIN.
Abner HOPTON to Margaret FLACK - December 14, 1837, by Thomas SMITH.
Joseph RODGERS to Pasha RATTLER - December 14, 1837, by Joseph HAWKINS.
Isom POINTER to Elizabeth McMANNUS - September 28, 1837, by Hobson WHITLEY.
Charles McMANNUS to Susan Charlotte POINTER - August 12, 1837, by Hobson WHITLEY.
Isaac MILLER to Narcissa SHOCKLEY - November 1, 1837, by Hobson WHITLEY.
John RICHEY to Delitha McNITE - December 24, 1837, by Joseph HAWKINS.
Bartley MATTEWS to Minerva BAKER - January 11, 1838, by Joseph HAWKINS.
Charles SELBY to Polly PHILLIPS - November 11, 1837, by Thomas ROWARK.
William TACKET to Sariann CHAPPLE - October 8, 1837, by Thomas ROWARK.
Henry KIRLEY to Nancy MILLER - January 14, 1838, by Hobson WHITLEY.
William THOMSON to Mary RAMSEY - January 2, 1838, Hobson WHITLEY.
Pleasant COFFETT to Clacy RICHIE - November 27, 1837, by William BUMPASS.
Samuel H. CLUBB to Belinda B. PYATT - December 7, 1837, by Camm SEAY.
Hosea H. BRIDGES to Rebecca J. PYATT - December 7, 1837, by Camm SEAY.
Thomas BUTLESS (sic) to Liza CAPEHART - March 8, 1838, by Roysden ROBINSON.
Seaden POSEY to Sary CAMPBELL - March 20, 1838, by Solomon TABOR, M. G..
Samuel W. HORN to Catarin BRANSON - March 30, 1838, by Elder John BURGESS.
James BRANSON to Mary HAINS - April 22, 1838, by Elder John BURGESS.
James BELK to Emaline HELTON - April 23, 1838, by Elder George MORRIS.

John KIRN to Elizabeth BRAKEHOFF - July 5, 1838, by Thomas T. ASHLEY. Both of Westphalia Settlement.
John Bernard REPHTO (sic) to Mary AIKEN (sic) - July 8, 1838, by Thomas T. ASHLEY.
William RATTLES to Polly REED - July 3, 1838, by Mark D. SPAIN.
Thomas JACKSON to Mary BAKER - May 30, 1838, by Alfred MOORE.
Alexander VAUGHN to Nancy DAVIS - August 5, 1838, by Thomas T. ASHLEY.
Samuel WARRIN to Mary Ann MORRIS - September 18, 1838, by John McEWIN.
John ROBINSON to Jane BRAY - October 25, 1838, by Jesse AGEE.
Roland H. PATTY to Nancy McNIGHT - November 1, 1838, by Jesse AGEE.
George BLISH to Irene YOUNG - August 12, 1838, by Hobson WHITLEY.
Samuel COWAN to Polly MILLER - July 15, 1838, by Hobson WHITLEY.
Elza TURNER to Margaret THOMPSON - August 5, 1838, by Jesse BOUNDS. Groom of Crawford county.
T. E. PATTIE to Sarah McKNIGHT - November 27, 1838, by Jesse AGEE.
John COPELAND to Mary America WISEMAN - December 30, 1838, by Wm. SHOCKLEY.
William McKNIGHT to Mahaly LAUGHLEN - January 1, 1839, by Jesse AGEE.
Thomas BACKUS to matilda KENNY - December 20, 1838, by John SCOTT.
John R. BITTICK to Syntha WALLACE - January 10, 1839, by Mark D. SPAIN.
Terry GOODALL to Nancy SHIVERE - December 27, 1838, by Mark D. SPAIN.
Hiram NAPIER to Winny MORMAN - February 16, 1839, by Mark D. SPAIN.
Nathan R. REED to Sealy REED - March 10, 1839, by Mark D. SPAIN.
Thomas MARTIN to Elizabeth BOON - November 12, 1838, by Elder George MORRIS.
David GILMORE to Elizabeth PHILLIPS - August 16, 1836, by John B. HARRISON.
Daniel LAMBETH to Nancy MILLER - October 30, 1838, by John B. HARRISON.

Washington BRANSON to Joanna JETT - March 24, 1839, by John B. HARRISON.
Benjamin SIMPSON to Ann BRANSON - April 14, 1839, by John B. HARRISON.
Joseph SMITH to Mary C. NICHOLS - February 24, 1839, by Thomas TAYLOR.
Andrew BURCHARD to Elizabeth AGEE - April 1, 1839, by William B. PANNELL.
David LOWERY to Susannah WEIR - January 25, 1839, Jesse BOUNDS, M. G..
Eli GEERLER to Charlotte SCAGGS - March 28, 1839, by William HENDERSON.
Lewis RIDEN to Rachel SERCY - January 6, 1839, by Hobson WHITLEY.
William SHERMAN to Ammarrian ENFIELD - April 14, 1839, by William HENDERSON.
Sanford AMMERMAN to Susan AWBERRY May 23, 1839, by William HENDERSON.
Gideon P. WYATT to Matilda WEIR - April 18, 1839, by Jesse BOUNDS, M. G..
John SMITH to Sarah WEATHERFORD - July 7, 1839, by Calvin MAXWELL, M. G..
Alexander HILL to Lucinda EDMISTON - July 21, 1839, by Roysden ROBINSON.
William WALLACE to Sarah RIDENHOUR - May 2, 1839, Mark D. SPAIN.
William Frederick W. SCHULSE to Catharine W. WESTHOBS (sic) - August 18, 1839, by Herman GAXLICKS (sic).
Austin RITCHIE to Mahala LOFTON - March 2, 1839, by John MILLER.
William Andrew MORELAND to Eleanor NOBLET - August 8, 1839, by William HENDERSON.
Robert JEWEL to Elvira SHIVERS - July 14, 1839, by L. L. L. LANE.
William Calvin THOMPSON to Elizabeth LOVING - July 7, 1839, by L. L. L. LANE.
David STILES to Rutha RUTHERFORD - August 15, 1839, by Calvin MAXWELL, M. G..
Henry BAKER to Mary HANDON - October 27, 1839, by Joshua COX.
John GRAZIER to Debby QUICK - August 21, 1839, by Thomas JACKSON, M. G..
James JUMP to Rebecca GIBSON - October 31, 1839, by Camm SEAY.
Thomas A. JACKSON to Margaret SMITH - November

10, 1839, Thomas JACKSON, M. G..
John Herman KEMPER to Angel Caroline Dorothea MEYOR - December 25, 1839, by Julius LEOPOLD.
Micle (sic) KENNEY to Scenull (sic) BACKUS - December 26, 1839, by John SCOTT.
Silas POSEY to Mary CAMPBELL - January 2, 1840, by Mark D. SPAIN.
Valentine RODGERS to Malinda DURBIN - November 29, 1839, by Mark D. SPAIN.
William TERILL to Virginia SORRELL (sic) - October 15, 1839, by Mark D. SPAIN.
Thomas HALLAWAY to Nancy BAUL (sic) - December 19, 1839, by John B. HARRISON.
James COFFETT to Elizabeth FINLEY - January 2, 1840, by Mark D. SPAIN.
Phillip GOOCH to Rosannah PRYOR (sic) - January 6, 1840, by John B. HARRISON.
James BRANSON to Sarah BUMPASS - December 14, 1839, by John B. HARRISON.
John McAFEE to Mrs. Caroline MASSIE - January 16, 1840, by Eli McTILTON.
Franklin JINKINS to Sophrony MATTHEWS - February 20, 1840, by John B. HARRISON.
Vardey BURGER to Malinda COX - February 6, 1840, by Elder John BURGESS.
William MARGRAVES to Mahaly BAKER - March 27, 1840, by Joshua COX.
Fred William PAUSAULL to Caroline VALLET - April 20, 1840, by Julius LEOPOLD.
Perry D, WILLIAMS to Rachel GRAFF - April 16, 1840, by David STITES, M. G..
Daniel KELLIAN to Mary SMITH - March 10, 1840, by Reuben LEME.
James CLEMENS to Elizabeth WILSON - April 14, 1840, by James L. PORTER.
Nelson MILLER to Elizabeth HUFFMAN - March 24, 1840, by Eli McTILTON. Groom of Pulaski county.
John WOODY to Mary JACKSON - March 17, 1840, by Thomas JACKSON, M. G..
Cornelius HAINS to Moranda BRANSON - April 16, 1840, by Eli McTILTON.
James WILSON to Amy DAVIS - April 19, 1840, by John SCOTT.
James FINLEY to Susan STEIN - May 14, 1840, by Meredith SHOCKLEY.

Conrad BANTO to Elizabeth TROUTMAN - May 19, 1840, by Julius LEOPOLD.

John BACKUS to Ann MARGARETTA SCOEMER - July 11, 1840, by Julius LEOPOLD.

Moses POWERS to Lucy Ann CASON - July 2, 1840, by Mark D. SPAIN.

Henry ECKYMEYER to Angela PEITZMEYER - May 19, 1840, by Eli McTILTON. Bride of Westphalia.

William KENNEY to Rosann BACKUS - August 20, 1840, by John SCOTT.

Thomas DOGETT to Margaret HIBLER - June 20, 1840, by George McDANIEL.

John STOVEALL to Mary BRANSON - July 16, 1840, by James M. MATHEWS.

Lazarus STEWART to Jane FINDLY - August 13, 1840, by John SCOTT.

James M. SMITH to Rachel HOOPS - July 18, 1840, by John SCOTT.

John HUGHES to Mary HELTON - July 29, 1840, by John SCOTT.

Peter STRADER to Nancy THOMPSON - May 6, 1840, by Thomas TAYLOR.

John JOHNS to Rosanna BUTCHER - April 30, 1840, by Thomas TAYLOR.

Isom POINTER to Polly HENSLEY - July 20, 1840, by Thomas TAYLOR.

John CHAPPEL to Libby TACKET - August 9, 1840, by Thomas TAYLOR.

Linzy CORRIGAN to Sarah SMITH - August 16, 1840, by Thomas SMITH.

John T. WYATT to Cristian DUCKWORTH - October 3, 1840, by Meredith SHOCKLEY.

Herman BACK to Mary McCRACKEN - October 3, 1840, by Julius LEOPOLD.

Alfred PICKERING to Ann GREENSTREET - August 30, 1840, by Joshua COX.

Thomas DAVID to Matilda BRANSON - August 20, 1840, by Joshua COX.

William SCRIBNER to Nancy BRANSON - August 21, 1840, by Joshua COX.

William COX to Elizabeth WALLACE - October 29, 1840, by Elder John BURGESS.

George MARTIN to Mary VAUGHN - October 11, 1840, by John SCOTT.

John WATSON to Eliza MOORE - October 8, 1840, by Meredith SHOCKLEY.

Adam FISHER to Frances PARSONS - November 17, 1840, by Elder Samuel RODGERS. Groom of Warren county.
Joseph HAWKINS to Mary RODGERS - recorded November 25, 1840, by Calvin MAXWELL, M. G..
Daniel BARBARICK to Nancy DURBIN - November 5, 1840, by Eli McTILTON.
George W. BOWIN to Frances Ann DAVIS - October 22, 1840, by Huey SMITH.
William PATTY to Elizabeth COFFEE - August 13, 1840, by L. L. L. LANE.
James PARSON to Sarah STITES - October 20, 1840, by David STITES.
Rufus E. BURCHARD to Lelah SMITH - December 17, 1840, by Thomas JACKSON, M. G..
Anthony Benchard BARTMAN to Ann Margaret BOSSEN - January 5, 1841, by Huey SMITH.
Wright CRAWFORD to Matilda COX - January 24, 1841, by John SCOTT.
Jacob SCHUFER to Wilhelmina ROHREBACKER - February 14, 1841, by Julius LEOPOLD.
George HOLT to Elizabeth ROGERS - February 27, 1841, by Benjamin LEECH.
Daniel PRYOR to Tibitha CRAWFORD - February 25, 1841, by John B. HARRISON.
John HENSLEY to Elizabeth KERLEY - March 12, 1841, by William BUMPASS.
Andrew BRANSON to Nancy MARGRAVE - January 14, 1841, by Joshua COX.
James WOODY to Nancy BAKER - January 14, 1841, by Alfred MOORE.
John STREIN to Polly SHOEMAKER - December 31, 1841, by Samuel BURCHARD.
Reuben COX to Ann NAPIER - December 31, 1841, by Reuben TERRILL.
Samuel GUYLER to Hannah HEATH - December 16, 1840, by Alec B. SNITHEN.
Belmeus Augustus BUTCHER to Mary Ellen RECKETS - June 3, 1841, by Joshua COX.
Richard SEARCY to Polly RATTLES - June 3, 1841, by William B. PANNELL.
Francis LANGENDOEFFER to Frederika GRASMAN - May 2, 1841, by Julius LEOPOLD.
John Geo. PRAGERS to Ann Cath. SCULDTHEIST - February 20, 1841, by Julius LEOPOLD, J. P..
Daniel STRECKER to Richarde BAUER - March 21,

1841, by Julius LEOPOLD.
Claus MERTENS to Margaretta LUKEKINGS - April 2, 1841, by Julius LEOPOLD, J. P..
Thomas B. HOWARD to Sarah PRICE - December 6, 1840, by Mark D. SPAIN.
Reuben COX to Rachael EADS - May 20, 1841, by Elder John BURGESS.
Jackson BROWN to Rebecca PLUMMER - June 12, 1841, by Thomas SMITH.
Robert GILMORE to Roda BRANSON - June 25, 1841, by William BUMPASS.
Frederick WEYMANN to Martha Ann Lewsey SHONNGERS - March 10, 1841, by H. BOCK..
Frederick BEYERSDORFF to Mrs. Mona GADDEN - August 1, 1841, by Julius LEOPOLD.
John J. FURGISEN to Mary BALLARD - August 22, 1841, by John G. HEATH, J. P..
John MASON to Edna BROCK - December 19, 1841, by Thomas SNELSON, M. G..
Michael FISHER to Elizabeth Ann SHOBE - September 9, 1841, by James M. WRIGHT, M. G.. Groom of Boone county.
William STREIN to Lavicy BOLES - October 21, 1841, by Benjamin LEECH, M. G..
Samuel G. TROWER to Mary Ann DOUGLASS - July 24, 1841, by B. F. WILLIAMS, J. P..
John SHAW to Sarah ENDECOTT - July 17, 1841, by Samuel BURCHARD, J. P..
Richard BAXTER to Mickey KINGCADE - September 9, 1841, by Mark D. SPAIN.
Edward LUCAS to Mary Ann BURGESS - September 9, 1841, by Burton COOPER, J. P..
Rudolph GOTZ to Catherine KLEINDIERST - November 30, 1841, by Julius LEOPOLD.
Adam BETZOLD to Susannah BAUER - December 19, 1841, by Julius LEOPOLD.
Henry SMITH, Esq., to Mary Ann SORRELS - January 2, 1842, by Samuel BURCHARD, J. P..
Thomas SMITH to Nancy WEIR - November 20, 1841, by Samuel BURCHARD, J. P..
William AKERS to Sarah TAYLOR - October 14, 1841, by Samuel BURCHARD, J. P..
William COX to Cassey Jane BOUNDS - October 10, 1841, by Elder John BURGESS.
Joel STITES to Elizabeth Ann HOWARD - October 21, 1841, by Jesse LIVELY, M. G..

John HOLLANDSWORTH to Sarah Ann SMITH - December 2, 1841, by Jesse LIVELY, M. G..
Joseph CRIDER to Margarett DURBORN (sic) - December 12, 1841, by Thomas L. VEACH, J. P..
Richard BAXTER to Meaky KINKEAD - October 10, 1841, by Henry SMITH, J. P..
Joseph VOGT to Ann Christian PETERSON - December 26, 1841, by Julius LEOPOLD, J. P..
Andrew GROH to Caroline HUTTENRAUCH - December 26, 1841, by Julius LEOPOLD, J. P..
William R. DOUGLASS to Herreat (sic) E. WALTON - December 19, 1841, by David STITES, M. G..
James NEPYEAR to Rebecca COX - December 16, 1842, by Elder John BURGESS (recorded April 8, 1842).
Charles VOGT to Barbara HULLION - March 6, 1842, by Julius LEOPOLD, J. P..
Theodore VOGT to Josephine DIEBOLD - March 6, 1842, by Julius LEOPOLD, J. P..
Henry HINCKE to Louisa RODEN - February 18, 1842, by Julius LEOPOLD, J. P..
Andrew LANGENDORFER to Sophia SCHRIEBER - March 14, 1842, by Julius LEOPOLD, J. P..
Jacob MAUPIN to Rhody HOLT - January 20, 1842, by David STITES, M. G..
James Mat____ to Mary Ann ELLER - January 6, 1842, by Henry SMITH, J. P..
Thomas F. GROFF to Elvira B. WILLIAMS - September 1, 1842, by David STITES, J. P..
Joseph DUGAN to Catherine BAYER - April 12, 1842, by Julius LEOPOLD, J. P..
George SIMPSON to Lavina MILLER - February 13, 1842, by Samuel BURCHARD, J. P..
Henry J. FINN to Barbara NEWMANN - March 23, 1842, by Julius LEOPOLD, J. P..
Frederick MATHIE to Mrs. Amelia TRAUTWEIN - June 15, 1842, by Julius LEOPOLD, J. P..
George W. LOFTON to Elizabeth NORTHCUT - April 3, 1842, by Henry SMITH, J. P..
Silas HALL to Charlotte KATTLEMEYER - March 2, 1842, by Thomas ROARK, J. P..
G. M. FARRIS to Margaret BAXTER - March 28, 1842, by Henry SMITH, J. P..
William SIMPSON to Sarah (no last name) - April 14, 1842, by David STITES, M. G..
Martin R. DOUGLASS to Martha WILLIAMS - April

3, 1842, by David STITES, M. G..
Cornelius SCHUBERT to Louisa BETHMAN - July 23, 1842, by Julius LEOPOLD, J. P..
George SCHAFER to Catherine HULLION - July 24, 1842, by Julius LEOPOLD, J. P..
Henry GRAINERMAN to Maria VON BEHREN - August 27, 1842, by Julius LEOPOLD, J. P..
Isaiah COX to Mary Ann DAVID - June 30, 1842, by Elder John BURGESS.
Henry WISEMANN to Rebecca STITES - October 20, 1842, by Thomas HIBLER, J. P..
Mathias MacChisney to Olive McCRACKEN - September 27, 1842, by Julius LEOPOLD, J. P..
Andrew GROH to Barbara KIEBETZ - November 3, 1842, Julius LEOPOLD, J. P..
Samuel S. GIBSON to Martha SIMPSON - October 20, 1842, by Jesse LIVELY, M. G..
William KENKEAD (sic) to Sarah SMITH - September 8, 1842, SAmuel BURCHARD, J. P..
Jacob H. FISHER to Jemima SHOBE - December 29, 1842, by Samuel ROGERS, M. G..
Simon F. V. WEST to Mary STENDRIDGE (sic) - January 4, 1843, by William B. PANNELL, J. P..
John C. FOWLER to Olivia HEATH - January 15, 1843, by Julius LEOPOLD, J. P..
James BROWN to Mrs. Sarah IVERS - January 18, 1843, by Julius LEOPOLD, J. P..
Drury HOLLAND to Martha MAXWELL - November 3, 1842, by David STITES, M. G..
Gottfried GHBERT (sic) to Rosina M. KRAG - January 29, 1843, by Julius LEOPOLD, J. P..
George BAXTER to Ann G. MILLER - December 8, 1842, by Henry SMITH, J. P..
Robert SORRELL to Margaret RICHARDSON - January 19, 1843, by Robert LUCAS, J. P..
John W. GLOVER to Martha WARD - February 19, 1843, by James STREIN, J. P..
Pleasant MOLAND to Mary E. BAYER - March 20, 1843, by John AVERY, J. P..
John L. TENNURE to Sarah L. WINN - February 23, 1843, by Thomas HIBLER, J. P..
Augustus LEONHARDT to Catherine KLEINDIERST - May 11, 1843, by Julius LEOPOLD, J. P..
James BEST to Susannah ELLIS - June 22, 1843, by Julius LEOPOLD, J. P..

John ROBERTSON to Emily PINNELL - March 29, 1843, by Isaac HINKLE, J. P..
William WILLCOX to Cindy YEATS - March 29, 1843, by Robert LUCAS, J. P..
John H. BOHLKEN to Jacoline GROSSMAN - August 20, 1843, by Julius LEOPOLD, J. P..
Henry FRECKMANN to Margaret ROTTHOFF - August 28, 1843, by Julius LEOPOLD, J. P..
John B. JARVIS to Sarah KERBY (sic) - July 14, 1842, by Samuel CROW, M. G..
George BERNARD to Margaret BUSCH - September 1, 1843, by Julius LEOPOLD, J. P..
Henry HEINRESHS to Mary PAULMAN - October 5, 1843, by Julius LEOPOLD, J. P..
William PHARLY to Catherine CARROLL - September 1, 1843, by Elder John BURGESS.
John C. ROGERS to Elizabeth WILAMS - October 8, 1843, by Thomas HIBLER, J. P..
Coleman D. SMITH to Emma BIGALOW - October 22, 1843, by William STEVENS, M. G..
John WALTERS to Mary STEEN - September 14, 1843, by Samuel BURCHARD, J. P..
Henry UHALL to Fredericke STOEKE. widow - November 12, 1843, Joseph LESSELL, J. P..
Jacob CARROLL to Jane JENKINS - August 16, 1843, by Franklin JENKINS, M. G..
Henry AMELING to Sophia WARNARE - December 7, 1843, Burton COOPER, J. P..
Amon McHUTTON to Mary A. MAXWELL - November 5, 1843, by Calvin MAXWELL, M. G..
George ROOK to Jemima Ann LIVELY - December 21, 1843, by Thomas HIBLER, J. P..
Willis BRUMLEY to Mary JOHNS - February 25, 1844, David C. HEATH, J. P..
James HENSLEY to Patience POYNTER - February 25, 1844, by David C. HEATH, J. P..
Green L. GRIFFITH to Mary RADDEN - January 15, 1844, by Henry SMITH, J. P..
Winthrop H. HOPSON to Rebecca G. PARSONS - April 30, 1844, by Elder M. P. WILLS.
John G. BARTZ to Mrs. Cathrine WAGNER - December 23, 1843, by Julius LEOPOLD, J. P..
Michael BAUER to Mariann FRITZ - April 21, 1844, by Julius LEOPOLD, J. P..
Charles D. EITZEN to Jean KEHR - April 23, 1844, by Julius LEOPOLD, J. P..

Nic. STUEHLINGER to Catherine BOTTLER - April 27, 1844.
William KNGKADE (sic) to Sally KINGKADE - February 22, 1844, by Robert LUCAS, J. P..
Jacob RIDENHOUR to Elizabeth STUMP - May 8, 1844, by Francis SULLIVAN, J. P..
John JACOB MANN to Rebecca EBELER - April 5, 1844, by Frederick HUNDHAUSEN, German Protestant.
Henry THEYES to Maria BRANDHORST - June 12, 1844, by Frederick W. POMMER, J. P..
Joel STITES to Nancy COMBS - March 25, 1844, by David STITES, M. G..
Christian MULLER to Catherine Wilhelmine MULLER - June 16, 1844, J. F. KOWING, M. G..
Ferdinand KAEMPFF, M. D. to Elisabeth DOESS - July 4, 1844, by Julius LEOPOLD, J. P..
Jean Jacques LABAUBE to Andele LABAUBE - August 2, 1844, by A. J. MINOR, J. P..
Joseph Chas. KOHL to Mrs. Magdalena Caroline BARTIGAM - August 11, 1844, by Julius LEOPOLD, J. P..
Andrew BRANSON to Harriet SHOCKLEY - June 2, 1844, by Burton COOPER, J. P..
John Fred. TENGE to Mrs. Elizabeth BALLBACK - August 24, 1844, by Julius LEOPOLD, J. P..
Luke Adam RODGERS to Emily GREENSTREET - September 1, 1844, by Benjamin LEECH, M. G..
Jacob MENGES to Louisa PAULMAN - September 25, 1844, by Frederick W. POMMER, J. P.. Witnesses were E. C. STAFFHORST and J. H. WITTMAN.
Alfred SHOBE to Mary Ann McMANNIS - October 7, 1844, by Julius LEOPOLD, J. P..
Adam FISHER to Jemima PARSONS - September 10, 1844, by Elder Winthrop H. HOBSON.
John H. HAYNES to Sally REED - September 19, 1844, by Thomas HIBLER, J. P..
John J. BRANSOM to Ruth SHOKLEY - October 25, 1844, by Thomas HIBLER, J. P..
Rudolph GOETZ to Dorothea KATTLEMANN - December 2, 1844, by C. I. JAMES, M. G..
Adam WAGNER to Caroline ROESKE - recorded December 10, 1844. Married by Julius LEOPOLD, J. P..
Francis GABLER to Johanna NAGLIN - December 13,

1844, by Julius LEOPOLD, J. P..
John FRECKMANN to Magdalena CLAUS - December 15, 1844, by Julius LEOPOLD, J. P..
Pleasant CRISMAN to Sarah HALL - January 12, 1845, by Daneil CAMPBELL, J. P..
Charles KNEISEL to Margaret SCHODEL - January 18, 1845, by Julius LEOPOLD, J. P..
Thomas MCKINEY to Elizabeth SCOTT - December 5, 1844, by Lewis DAVID, J. P..
Richard SULLENS to Malinda SHELTON - October 7, 1844, by David STITES, M. G..
Samuel PHILLIPS to Clary McHANY - November 16, 1844, by David STITES, M. G..
Levi STITES to Martha J. RUTHERFORD - December 18, 1844, David STITES, M. G..
Zachaus VORK to Elizabeth GRUBER March 13, 1845, by Julius LEOPOLD, J. P..
Henry F. LUCAS to Rebecca Elizabeth SORRELS - February 5, 1845, by Robert LUCAS, J. P..
Fields BRADSHAW to Mary Jane LUCAS - February 6, 1845, by Robert LUCAS, J. P..
Dowswell ROGERS to Julia Ann CRIDER - December 12, 1844, by Robert LUCAS, J. P..
James BURGES to Ruth COX - March 16, 1845, by Calvin MAXWELL, M. G..
Fred SEMKIN to Pauline POMMER - April 10, 1845, by Julius LEOPOLD, J. P..
Fred HUFFMAN to Susannah BOEING, alias METZ - April 3, 1845, by Daniel CAMPBELL, J. P..
Philip SCHNEIDER to Agnessa GROSSMANN - recorded April 26, 1845, by Frederick HUNDHAUSEN, M. G..
Magnus WELL to Maria WEINLAND - January 26, 1845, by Julius LEOPOLD, J. P..
Absalom WHITE to Susannah WINN - February 13, 1845, Solomon KIMZEY, J. P..
William BLACKWELL to Parthena PALMER - January 26, 1845, by Henry SMITH, J. P..
Diedrich Wilhelm STONNER to Rebecka Maria BUSHMANN - March 10, 1845, J. F. KOWING, M. G..
Gabriel SHAEFER to Rosina HUBER - April 20, 1845, by Julius LEOPOLD, J. P..
Jerry HOLT to Nancy BROWN - April 21, 1845, by James GREENSTREET, J. P..
Joseph A. REED to Sarah Ann HENSON - July 2,

1845, by James GREENSTREET, J. P..

William L. MATTOCKS to Arabella WILLIAMS - July 6, 1845, by Thomas HIBLER, J. P..

James Nicholas BLEVENS to Nancy RICHARDSON - June 1, 1845, by Henry SMITH, J. P..

Edward J. HUSMANN to Henrietta TOFARN - September 8, 1845, Frederick HUNDHAUSEN, M. G..

William S. LEACH to Lucile A. MASSIE - September 5, 1845, by A. J. MINOR, J. P..

Gabriel SHAEFER to Mrs. Rosine HUBER - April 20, 1845, by Julius LEOPOLD, J. P..

Frederick STIEF to Mrs. Caroline HILSMAN - September 15, 1845, by Julius LEOPOLD, J. P..

Jacob SCHMITT to Margaret WALKER - September 27, 1845, by Julius LEOPOLD, J. P..

William RICHIE to Elizabeth Elenor PRIEL - September 28, 1845, by Robert LUCAS, J. P..

Simeon L. BIDICKS to Parmelia HAWKINS - September 7, 1845, by Robert LUCAS, J. P..

Oscar MONNIG to Amalia SETZER - October 29, 1845, by Frederick HUNDHAUSEN, M. G..

Christian JACOB to Friederica KELLER - November 23, 1845, by Frederick HUNDHAUSEN, M. G..

Johann Gerdes SIEPS to Mrs. Anna Maria VOLLERTSON - November 30, 1845, by Elder John BURGESS.

Franklin DOTSON to Nancy CHAREL - November 10, 1845, by Elder John BURGESS.

Peter C. DAVIS to Matilda BOWEN - December 16, 1845, by Henry SMITH, J. P..

Drury LEE to Matilda SHOCKLEY - December 25, 1845, by Abner HOPSON, J. P..

John T. BRANSON to Rebecca Jane DOTSON - November 13, 1845, by James GREENSTREET, J. P..

Alton H. HIBLER to Mary Ann BAXTER - November 18, 1845, by Thomas HIBLER, J. P..

Henry W. KEISCHER to Charlotte WITTEN - December 13, 1845, by J. F. KOWING, M. G..

John JOHNS to Matilda AYERS - June 28, 1845, by Daniel CAMPBELL, J. P..

Jonathan LEE to Catharine PINNEL - January 11, 1846, by J. R. BURK, M. G..

James O. SITTON to Susannah G. HIBLER - February 18, 1846, Thomas HIBLER, J. P..

John STRAIN to Jane McKINNEY - January 1, 1846,

by Shamwell PARHAM, J. P..
Johann Georg CHRISTEL to Christina Johanna BENKER - February 18, 1846, by Frederick HUNDHAUSEN, M. G..
Ludwig NAEGELIN to Johanna Friederica BRANDIGAM - March 18, 1846, by Frederick HUNDHAUSEN, M. G..
Joseph G. POGUE to Ann MONCA - February 19, 1846, by Robert LUCAS, J. P..
Alexander BARBRICK to Mary COX - February 19, 1846, by Elder John BURGESS.
John MOTSCHENBACKER to Marie KLEIN - April 21, 1846, Julius LEOPOLD, J. P..
Johann Friedrich POCH to Mrs. Johanna Barbara OTTLEB - April 27, 1846, by Frederick HUNDHAUSEN, M. G..
Julius LEOPOLD to Mathilde BEHNE - December 13, 1845, by A. J. MINOR, J. P..
William L. DODDS to Lucinda DORNE - November 25, 1845, by Wm. L. STAFFORD, M. G..
Frederick Christian GROSS to Juliane ECKBLATT - August 13, 1846, by Frederick HUNDHAUSEN, M. G..
Mathias HEINRICH VOGT to Catherine Wilhelmina EBERS - September 3, 1846, by Frederick HUND-HAUSEN, M. G..
William COOPER to Mary E. BURGESS - September 12, 1846, by Abner HOPSON, J. P..
Robert M. BURNS to Emily FITZGERALD - July 26, 1846, by J. R. BURKS, M. G..
Anthony MILLER to Catharina GOETZ - November 4, 1846, by Julius LEOPOLD, J. P..
Washington CHARESINBERRY (sic) to Matilda SHOCKLEY - October 28, 1846, by Benjamin LEACH, M. G..
Stephen BRUMLY to Jamima MILLER - September 27, 1846, by David C. HEATH, J. P..
Lucas PILLAT to Ursula KRETTI - November 26, 1846, by A. EYSVOGEL, M. G..
Clark BOWLWARE to Jane C. BURGES - September 13, 1846, Isaac WHITE, M. G.. Groom of Osage county.
William D. FARIS to Mary Ann C. SMITH - January 7, 1847, by James GREENSTREET, J. P..
James D. PRYOR to Rachel Jane SIMPSON - December 27, 1846, by James GREENSTREET.

Andreas MONZEL to Catherine ROSENBERGER - January 19, 1847, by Frederick HUNDHAUSEN.

Alexander SMITH to Mary Elizabeth POGUE - November 17, 1846, Robert LUCAS, J. P..

Garret VIEMANN to Martha RIDENHOUR - December 6, 1846, by Robert LUCAS, J. P..

David WITTMANN to Uraine GRUBER - December 9, 1846, by Julius LEOPOLD, J. P..

Robert BILES to Malinda WALTON - November 26, 1846, by Benjamin LEACH, M. G..

Charles KNEISEL to Caroline WAGNER - February 27, 1847, by Julius LEOPOLD, J. P..

Charles Christopher Friedrich LANDENBURGER to Catherine Scharlott FRICKER - November 30, 1846, by Frederick HUNDHAUSEN, M. G..

Alfred BEHR to Catherine FAZER (sic) - December 9, 1846, Frederick HUNDHAUSEN, J. P..

William BRUMLEY to Ruth Kane KERLEY - February 18, 1847, by John G. PIGMAN.

Jacob P. SHOCKLEY to Nancy HEBBER - March 25, 1847, by Benjamin LEACH, M. G..

Garrett MYERS to Delina ROBERTSON - March 21, 1847, by Burton COOPER, J. P..

Nicholas S. ADAMS to Martha S. MOSEBY - May 11, 1847, by James ARNOTT, Jr., J. P..

Langston B. MILLER to Jane SEWEL - April 1, 1847, by N. ELDREDGE, J. P..

Jesse WELTON to Mary P. CLARK - May 20, 1847, by Winthrop H. HOPSON, J. P..

Frederick BERTINKAMP to Anna Maria Charlotte STRICKER - June 1, 1847, by Frederick HUNDHAUSEN, M. G..

John M. STITES to Juliann FAIRBANK - April 18, 1847, Benjamin LEACH, J. P..

George WERLY (sic) to Catharine PHILIPS - April 28, 1847, by Frederick HUNDHAUSEN, J. P..

Samuel ALEMANN to Christina Barbara FELY - August 2, 1847, by Frederick HUNDHAUSEN, J. P..

Charles C. PERKINS to Roxana PIGMAN - February 21, 1847, by Wm. STAFFORD, M. G..

Augustus MULENHAHN (sic) to Eleanora SCHRADER - June 28, 1847, by Julius LEOPOLD, J. P..

Igantius BLEILE to Welhelmine MICHEL - July 21, 1847, by Julius LEOPOLD, J. P..

William C. WHITE to Patsy BRANSON - July 29,

1847, by Solomon KIMZEY, J. P..
Hiram REED to Lucy DEARBIN - August 9, 1847, by Peter RICHARD, Bishop of St. Louis. Groom was the son of Henry REED and Rachael ROBISON, bride was the daughter of Phillip DURBIN and Lucy LOGSTON.
John CALDWELL to Mary HENSLEY - June 17, 1847, by James ARNOTT, Jr., J. P..
Francis SCHIRER to Diana ESSING - September 11, 1847, by Julius LEOPOLD, J. P..
George VANDERGRIFF to Catherine McGOWN - October 3, 1847, by Solomon KIMZEY, J. P..
George SHERALD to Louisa Lane (sic) SWANSON - October 7, 1847, by Solomon KIMZEY, J. P..
Henry KAISER to Marianna BAER - January 7, 1848, by Francis H. KEINEY, J. P..
Reuben S. SHOCKLEY to Elizabeth KIMZEY - January 11, 1848, by Thomas HIBLER, J. P..
John HENSLEY to Margaret KERLEY - December 17, 1847, by J. H. HUFFMAN, J. P..
Reuben SPALDING to Lousey BRANSON - December 30, 1847, by Solomon KIMZEY, J. P..
James SIMPSON to Elizabeth BARBARICK - March 5, 1848, by Samual BURCHARD, J. P..
Gottlieb RUGGESICK to Christine GUMPER - February 10, 1848, by J. F. KOWING, M. G..
John Frederick AUSTERMANN to Freiderike Florentine SUNKEL - July 25, 1847, by J. F. KOWING, M. G..
James MERRY to Lucretia ELDRIDGE - April 25, 1848, by H. N. WATTS, M. G..
Nathan SOUDER to Nancy Ann TAYLER - April 17, 1848, by H. N. WATTS, M. G..
William BOILS to Rebecca WALTON - May 16, 1848, by Benjamin LEACH, M. G..
Elizah M. JOOD (sic) to Mary WARE - May 27, 1848, by Francis SULLIVAN, J. P..
John MITCHEL to Elizabeth WARREN - January 30, 1848, by Isaac HINKLE, J. P..
Wiley COX to Matilda COFFELT - May 11, 1848, by Burton COOPER, J. P..
Reuben SORRELL to Martha BRANSON - May 6, 1848, by Burton COOPER, J. P..
William C. HOLT to Lucinda VANDERGRIFF - April 27, 1848, by James GREENSTREET, J. P..
James SMITH to Evaline ROGERS - March 26, 1848,

by Thomas HIBLER, J. P..

John Henry BRINKMAN to Ann Catharine SCHRODER - April 7, 1848, by J. F. KOWING, M. G..

Bernhard APEL to Conradine SHIES - April 5, 1848, by Frederick HUNDHAUSEN, M. G..

Christoph EITEL to Catherine PLENZINGER - May 28, 1848, by Frederick HUNDHAUSEN, M. G..

Gerhart PROLLER to Wilhelmina Elizabeth SHURMANN - June 20, 1848, by Frederick HUNDHAUSEN, M. G..

Carl TEUPNER (sic) to Maria Josephine HUSMANN - September 20, 1847, by Frederick HUNDHAUSEN, M. G..

Joseph SCHRACK to Margretha HOFFMAN - October 2, 1847, by Frederick HANDHAUSEN, M. G..

Robert MELON to Sarah STEEN - May 3, 1848, by James GREENSTREET, J. P..

BOOK B,
1848 - 1855

Mark RENFROW to Martha J. MARKSFIELD - April 9, 1848, by Green B. LEE, J. P..
Heinrich SPICHTING to Barbara JUST - July 21, 1848, by Frederick HUNDHAUSEN, M. G..
Martin WEBER to Barbara HENNEBERGER - July 27, 1848, by Frederick HUNDHAUSEN, M. G..
Christian LANGENDORFER to Ernestina Wilhelmina BEIERMANN - August 3, 1848, by Frederick HUNDHAUSEN, M. G..
James SCHINDLER to Mary Ann SCHANOT - July 24, 1848, by Fr. Joseph BLAARER.
George PHILIPP to Ursula LUDWIG - July 24, 1848, by Fr. Joseph BLAARER.
Friederich LAMS to Friederica FIX - August 31, 1848, by Frederick HUNDHAUSEN, M. G..
Julius HUNDHAUSEN to Frederica MORELOCK - September 10, 1848, by Frederick HANDHAUSEN, M. G..
Frederick Wilhelms POMMER to Anna Schella SCHIEFER - September 12, 1848, by Frederick HUNDHAUSEN, M. G..
Nelson JARVIS to Margaret HAPTON (sic) - September 3, 1848, by E. M. KIMZEY, J. P..
Conrad BREHE to Amalia BUCKER - June 24, 1848, by Phillip J. HEYER, M. G..
Casper GREIS to Josephine KELESCHMANN - September 28, 1848, by Frederick HUNDHAUSEN, M. G..
William A. FOSTER to Laney G. HALL - October 4, 1848, by Francis H. KEINEY, J. P..
James EDSELL to Margaret G. HEATH - July 23, 1848, by Elder John H. STEPHENS.
James PARSONS to Mary SHOBE - September 10, 1848, by Elder John H. STEPHENS.
Carl Frederick ROLAND to Caroline Louisa HUSMAN - October 31, 1848, by Frederick HANDHAUSEN, M. G..
Jacob BECKER to Rogena VOLK - November 7, 1848, by Frederick HANDHAUSEN, M. G..
John George BECK to Johanna VOLK - October 12, 1848.
Ferdenand SHONGER to Anna HARNESH - November 28, 1848, by Frederick HANDHAUSEN, M. G..
John Michael SHAMBURG to Anna Christina HAMBURG

- December 16, 1848, by Frederick HANDHAUSEN, M. G..

John H. WITMANN to Magdaline MESCHLER - February 24, 1849, by Julius LEOPOLD, J. P..

Daniel McMILLIAN to Eliza Jane BURCHARD - January 4, 1849, Isaac HINKLE, J. P..

Thomas TUCKER to Jane MILLER - December 24, 1848, by Solomon KIMZEY, J. P..

Robert SORRELL to Polly Ann BROWN - November 26, 1848, by Solomon L. LICKLIDER, J. P..

George CARL to Anna PHILIPS - March 9, 1849, by Frederick HANDHAUSEN, M. G..

Wendelin (sic) DEIBOLD to Margaretha KLENG - February 8, 1849, by Fr. Joseph BLAARER.

Joseph H. BARBARICK to Manerva SHOCKLEY - February 22, 1849, by Elder John BURGESS, M. G..

August KATTLEMANN to Caroline BERKHARD - March 25, 1849, by Julius LEOPOLD, J. P..

Conrod NAEGLIN (sic) to Christine GROSS - April 15, 1849, by Frederick HANDHAUSEN, M. G..

Frederick FRICK to Marie VERAGUT - April 9, 1849, by Frederick HANDHAUSEN, M. G..

Christian SCHMIDT to Sophia BRINGMANN - April 22, 1849, by Frederick HUNDHAUSEN, M. G..

John Nicholas SEIDLER to Margaretha PFEIFER - April 22, 1849, by Frederick HUNDHAUSEN, M. G..

Reinhard ERBSCHLOE to Babette WITZSTEIN - September 22, 1849, by Francis H. KEINEY, J. P..

Patrick GIBSON to Julian JAMESON - September 27, 1849, by C, I. JAMES, M. G..

Benjamin MOSS to Maria REED - August 6, 1849, by Joseph LESSELL, J. P..

John G. BURTZ to Catharine AREND, widow - August 8, 1849, by Joseph LESSELL, J. P..

Augustus NEVENHAHN to Regina REUTTER - September 22, 1849, by Julius LEOPOLD, J. P..

Charles P. STREHLY to Sophia SCHLENDER - April 15, 1849, by Frederick SEMKEN, J. P..

Jacob PHILLIP to Cathrine BOESCH - May 11, 1849, by Frederick SEMKEN, J. P..

Fredrick Wm. STOEPPERMANN to Catrine MILLER - June 9, 1849, by Frederick SEMKEN, J. P..

Louis POMMER to Johanna REHNE - June 16, 1849,

by Frederick SEMKEN, J. P..
Augustus RICK to Mary DOWLING - June 17, 1849, by Frederick SEMKEN, J. P..
Henry OXNER to Helene CLAUSS - August 26, 1849, by Frederick SEMKEN, J. P..
Frederick Wilhelm NURRENBERG to Barbara SPICHTING - October 22, 1849, by Frederick SEMKIN, J. P..
Joseph Benedict MEIER to Josephine MELLER - Oct 22, 1849, by Julius LEOPOLD, J. P..
August PENNING to Ema Floretine SPANHAUZEN - August 20, 1849, by Julius LEOPOLD, J. P..
Green B. WILLIAMS to Mary RODERS - October 25, 1849, by Benjamin LEACH, M. G..
Claborn STADFORD to Mary CERLEY (sic) - October 22, 1849, by John BURGESS, M. G..
Gotlieb WEBER to Mary Sophia GOETTE - December 25, 1849, by Francis H. KEINEY, J. P..
Thomas REYNOLDS to Delilia COX - December 29, 1849, by Soloman KIMZEY. J. P..
William LEWIS to Margaret McKENNEY - December 9, 1849, by Soloman KIMZEY, J. P..
William R. McMILLON to Rebekah ROBINSON - September 20, 1849, by John GILES, M. G..
Elisha HENSLY to Lucinda MOPPIN - April 19, 1849, by Green B. LEE, J. P..
John CARTER to Elvina NUSBIT - June 8, 1849, by Green B. LEE, J. P..
James CARTER to Mary CONEL - April 22, 1849, by Green B. LEE, J. P..
Irvin HENSLEY to Barbra Ann KERLEY - December 28, 1847, by Green B. LEE, J. P..
Frederick SWEICHAUSER to Anna Maria HAAK - July 4, 1849, by Frederick HUNDHAUSEN, M. G..
Christian MANGENMEYER to Catherine BECK - July 15, 1849, by Frederick HUNDHAUSEN, M. G..
Johann BARIS to Regina F. WICKER - July 24, 1849, by Frederick HUNDHAUSEN, M. G..
Augustus MULLER to Anna Maria STRICKER - January 20, 1849, by J. F. KOWING, M. G..
Isaiah BOWIN to Mary Ann CULBERSON (sic) - April 12, 1849, by Solomon L. LICKLIDER, J. P..
Christoph KESKER (sic) to Christinne BRUNS - January 11, 1849, by J. F. KOWING, M. G..
E. M. KIMZEY to Elizabeth COX - November 18,

1849, by John BURGESS, M. G..

Andres PFOUTENHOUR to Margretha PHILIPP - December 21, 1849, by Frederick HUNDHASEN, M. G..

Edward MACKFEE to Zelda WILSON - December 17, 1849, by Lawrence KUPPER, J. P..

Henry HONIG to Elizabeth MARROTT - November 1, 1849, by Julius LEOPOLD, M. G..

Philipp NAGEL to Kunegunde HONIG - February 5, 1850, by Julius LEOPOLD, M. G..

Jobe MAHONEY to Manerva STITES - March 21, 1850, by Benjamin LEECH, M. G..

John DUNCAN to Elizabeth McKENNEY - April 21, 1850, by John GILES, M. G., at the house of Thomas McKENNEY.

Benjamin F. CARTER to Ruth SHOCKLEY - May 15, 1850, by Benjamin LEECH, M. G..

Mathew William KEMZEY to Margarett Ann BURCHARD - May 16, 1850, by R. V. ELDREDGE.

George Washington WOODS to Mary GARNER - March 19, 1850, Solomon L. LICKLIDER, J. P..

William TACKET to Nancy WINN - April 21, 1850, William O. SHOCKLEY, M. G..

Rudolph MULLER to Emilia HELD - June 29, 1850, by Francis H. KEINEY, J. P.. Witnessed by John KAISER and Josephine ZELLS.

James A. RICHE to Isabel Jane BRANSON - April 30, 1850, by Robert LUCAS, J. P..

John ROARK to Julianna ZUMWALT - January 16, 1850.

John Michael VON ART to Magdalena KAISER - September 24, 1849, by Lawrence KUPPER, J. P..

Fredrick DALTER to Wilhelmina PAULMANN - May 20, 1850, by Frederick HUNDHAUSEN, M. G..

Samuel STARLING to Eliza MEREDITH - January 20, 1850, by Robert LUCAS, J. P..

Edmond HALE to Mary Ann BURGESS - July 2, 1850, by John BURGESS, M. G..

Pleasant PANKEY to Matilda DODSON - January 21, 1850, by Francis SULLIVAN, J. P..

Engelbert DREKES to Anna Christina PETERSON - June 23, 1850, by Frederick HUNDHAUSEN, M. G..

John MULLER to Anna Marie HUSVALDEN - July 6, 1850, by Frederick HUNDHAUSEN, M. G..

Ernst NUREMBERGER to Christine Emelie SCUBNER – July 5, 1850, by Frederick HUNDHAUSEN, M. G..
C. WILL to W. FRITZ – August 12, 1850, by A. EYSVOGEL, M. G..
Henry F. LUCAS to Ruth HARLIN – August 11, 1850, by Solomon L. LICKLIDER, J. P..
John Gottlieb ROESCHELL to Christina KAHUND – June 7, 1849, by Frederick HUNDHAUSEN, M. G..
Jacob SALADIN to Catherine BERNARD – September 10, 1849, by Lawrence KUPPER, J. P..
Heinrich BLACK to Louisa HAMIER – August 4, 1850, by Lawrence KUPPER, J. P..
Reuben RIDENOUR to Esther SHOCKLEY – February 24, 1850, by Robert LUCAS, J. P..
John HERSCH to Regina WELLER – September 16, 1849, by Frederick HANDHAUSEN, M. G..
Christopher SOUDER to Miss HAMBY – June 3, 1849, by Solomon LICKLIDER, J. P..
Isaac HAMBY to Elizabeth STREIN – June 3, 1849, by Solomon LICKLIDER, J. P..
Henry MITCHEL to Mary Jane STRUMP – December 15, 1849, by Benjamin LEACH, M. G..
John WILLIAMS to Harriet SPAULDING – December 15, 1849, by Benjamin LEACH, M. G..
John T. STITES to Mary SPAULDING – December 15, 1849, by Benjamin LEACH, M. G..
Gottlieb FIRN (sic) to Susannah BETZHOLD – May 3, 1850, by Frederick HANDHAUSEN, M. G..
Thomas TUCKER to Jane MILLER – December 24, 1848, by Solomon KIMZEY, J. P..
Henry T. FISHER to Mary Ann SMITH – July 18, 1849, by William C. STITES, M. G..
Ludwig RUDEGER to Cathrina OTT – April 7, 1850, by Frederick HUNDHAUSEN, M. G..
Carl HECK to Henretta GUNTNER – April 7, 1850, by Frederick HUNDHAUSEN, M. G..
H. REYNOLDS to Martha E. BURGESS – February 24, 1850, by John BURGESS, M. G..
John F. W. TANEKE to Anna Catherine PRAGER – May 21, 1850, by Frederick HANDHAUSEN, M. G..
Michael NEFF to Elizabeth REITH – May 11, 1850, by Julius LEOPOLD, J. P..
John George SCHNEIDER to Maria Elizabeth HOFFMAN – August 25, 1850, by Frederick HANDHAUSEN, M. G..
William POESCHEL to Theodora NEITHARDT – Septem-

ber 15, 1850, by Frederick HANDHAUSEN, M. G..
Lewis NEIWALD to Sophia LINKE - September 5, 1849, by Phillip J. HEYER, M. G..
Adolph RECKER to Henretta WELLNER - September 11, 1849, by Phillip J. HEYER, M. G..
Jacob OTT to Henrietta HOFFMAN - August 27, 1850, by Phillip J. HEYER, M. G..
Amstead E. MYERS to Mary J. HIATT - August 8, 1850, by John GILES, M. G..
George PFOUTCH to Rosina HUBER - September 7, 1850, by A. EYSVOGEL, M. G..
Christian Frederick KLEIN to Johanna Frederica PEBION - May 14, 1850, by Frederick HANDHAUSEN, M. G..
Wilhelm REMMERT to Welhelmina SCHMIDT - November 5, 1850, by Frederick HANDHAUSEN, M. G..
John G. RECKERS to Mona SCHAEFER - November 22, 1850, by Joseph LESSELL, J. P..
Christian KOTTHOFF to Bertie PELTER (sic) - August 17, 1850, by Joseph LESSELL, J. P..
Frederick GEILMANN to Elizabeth BISCHOFF - October 31, 1850, by Frederick HANDHAUSEN, M. G..
Anton GROSS to Henrietta HECK - November 31, 1850, by Frederick HANDHAUSEN, M. G..
Charles VOGT to Louise ECKELHAFT - December 6, 1850, by Joseph LESSELL, J. P..
Jacob SOUDERS to Ellen RIDENHOUR - November 17, 1850, Solomon L. LICKLIDER, J. P..
Henry B. GROFF to Susan MORGAN - Dcember 12, 1850, by Benjamin LEACH, M. G..
Christian ONCKEN (sic) to Elizabeth JEAGER - December 21, 1850, by Benjamin LEACH, M. G..
Frederick RUDEMEYER to L. WINTERS - November 22, 1850, by J. F. KOWING, M. G..
John LUCAS to Mary Jane READER - December 1, 1850, by Robert LUCAS, J. P..
David LUCAS to Mary Adaline McMILLIAN - December 18, 1850, by Robert LUCAS, J. P..
John DURBIN to Isabella CRIDER - November 7, 1850, by Fr. Edward HAMILL.
Adolph REMMERT to Fredrica OBERMIER - January 11, 1851, by Frederick HANDHAUSEN, M. G..
Simon NULLMIER to Louisa BURTE - December 16, 1850, by Phillip J. HEYER, M. G..
James Alexander HEARST to Malinda M. DAVID -

Simon BAER to Catherine MOUSEHUND - January 12, 1851, by Frederick HANDHAUSEN, M. G..
Frederick FRICKE to Augusta GARTMANN - January 15, 1851, Frederick HANDHAUSEN, M. G..
Otto G. MARKEL to Julia Henretta SCHENKER - February 1, 1851, by Joseph LESSELL, J. P..
Phillip ROUSCH to Maria Dorothe MICHELS - November 24, 1850, by Charles BEHNE, J. P..
Francis Wm. MARX to Mina BUSCH - November 10, 1850, by William L. STAFFORD, M. G..
Otto YEAGER to Charlotte RANSELL - January 7, 1851, by William L. STAFFFORD, M. G..
William WALLACE to Rutha Grammer MERRELL - December 29, 1850, by Solomon LICKLIDER, J. P..
Henry SHOCKLEY to Julian DURBIN - February 20, 1851, by Robert LUCAS, J. P..
Isaac TUCKER to Neony (sic) MEEKS - March 13, 1851, by Benjamin LEACH, M. G..
Francis William SANDERS to Loesa HOMIER - February 28, 1851, by J. F. KOWING, M. G..
Nathan BURCHARD to Martha Ann SORREL - May 1, 1851, by I. M. BURKS, M. G..
Ferdinand POMMER to Louisa RIEFENSTAHL - May 6, 1851, by Joseph LESSELL, J. P..
Mathias SCHAEFER to Sophia BERGMANN - June 8, 1851, by Joseph LESSELL, J. P..
Joseph KEPLER to Poline SEMKER - April 10, 1851, by Charles BEHNE, J. P..
Simeon HELD to Welhelmina DAUBE - July 10, 1851, by J. F. KOWING, M. G..
Jasper KAMMERLAUDER to Rosina PEHR - June 7, 1851, by A. EYSVOGEL, M. G..
John KLOSNER to Malinda SHOCKLEY - August 3, 1851, by Burton COOPER, J. P..
Mark MATLOCK to Nancy SMITH - May 8, 1851, by Solomon L. LICKLIDER, J. P..
Rudolph HUBER to Johanna SEP - July 29, 1851, by Solomon L. LICKLIDER, J. P..
Julius NEUBAUER to Maria LABAUBE - June 19, 1851, by Solomon LICKLIDER, J. P..
William KRECH to Matilda GROH - August 17, 1851, by G. A. DETHARDING, M. G..
William R. JOHNSON to Hannah Eveline BARTLETT - April 1, 1851, by J. B. HARRISON, M. G..
John C. BURHLE to Elin WINN - April 20, 1851, by

Thomas CLAREY, J. P..

Christian OCLASCHLAGER to Mary KRATTLE - August 10, 1851, by J. F. KOWING, M. G..

William MAGGE to Amelia BACHER - September 30, 1851, J. F. KOWING, M. G..

Samuel SMITH to Sarah MARSH - October 16, 1851, by James LEE, M. G..

S. M. FRAKER to Caroline MOSSES - September 18, 1851, by Francis H. KEINEY, J. P..

Barna TUCKER to Ruth Elendor PENNINGTON - November 18, 1849, by Fielding JENKINS, M. G..

Martin SCHAUENBERG to Margaretta SCHAEFER - August 23, 1851, by Joseph LESSELL, J. P..

Jacob SUTTER to Johanna SENN - August 24, 1851, by Joseph LESSELL, J. P..

Ludwig RUEDEGER to Marie CLAUS - August 24, 1851, by Joseph LESSELL, J. P..

Washington SEVERS to Manerva ROBISON - October 19, 1851, by John H. STEPHENS, Elder.

Jarred E. BRANSON to Theodora TALBERT - October 8, 1851, by John BURGESS, M. G..

J. R. OWENS to Isabella R. COOPER - October 9, 1851, by John BURGESS, M. G..

Otto JEAGER to Charlotte RAMSELL - January 7, 1851, by Joseph LESSELL, J. P..

Elisha STERLING to Elizabeth REED - December 24, 1849, by William R. BRANSON, J. P..

William ROGERS to Paulina Jane SKINNER - March 9, 1848, by Benjamin LEACH, M. G..

Solomon ZUMOLT to Rebecca REED - September 7, 1848, by James GREENSTREET, J. P..

Hermann B. JUTTHOUSE to Anna Marie FEHNER - December 6, 1851, by J. F. KOWING, M. G..

Seeman WINTER to Johanna W. EPKER - December 12, 1851, by J. F. KOWING, M. G..

Henrich HAYEMEYER to Anna Marie STONER - December 18, 1851, by J. F. KOWING, M. G..

Samuel FOSTER to Elizabeth OVERSTREET - October 28, 1847, by James ARNOTT, Jr., J. P..

August GATZAMEIER to Josephina BEHNEY - November 8, 1851, by A. EYSVOGEL, M. G..

Jacob FUGGER to Rosetta GUNTHER - January 13, 1852, by Francis Wm. BOING, J. P..

William SUTHERLAN to Phebe Ann STUMP - December 14, 1851, by Robert LUCAS, J. P..

Dr. Johann FELDMANN to Therese STEIGER - January

10, 1852, by Francis Wm. BOING, J. P..
Adam KLEIN to Fredericke LENK - February 11, 1852, by Francis Wm. BOING, J. P..
Frederick KEMPLE to Catharine BUDDEMIER - March 12, 1852.
Francis K. BUSHMANN to Maria DUTSCHES - February 6, 1852, by J. F. KOWING, M. G..
Jacob BOSCH to Elsbert KREATLY - March 23, 1852, by J. B. HARRISON, M. G..
William HIBLER to Mrs. Arabella MATTOCKS - March 16, 1852, by Benjamin LEACH, M. G..
Phillip HENRICKS to Drusey CRIDER - February 19, 1852, by Robert LUCAS, J. P..
Colestin DEIBOLD to Susanna KLARING - April 29, 1852, by Francis Wm. BOING, J. P..
Lewis MATTIX to Charity HIBLER - April 21, 1852, by Benjamin LEACH, M. G..
Henry SOUDERS to Sarah Ann GIBSON - March 14, 1852, by John L. BURCHARD, M. G..
August Ludwig SCHAEFER to Margarette BURLE - May 2, 1852, by H. BOCK, J. P..
John SCHUSTER to Anna Maria BAUER - April 25, 1852, by Fr. George TUERK.
Joseph Thomas BRAND (sic) to Elisabeth FRITZ - May 20, 1852, by Fr. George TUERK.
Rudolf KLUMAS, of Prussia, to Mrs. Angeline LEE, a widow, born DILLERD (sic) - June 5, 1852, by F. BIRKNER, M. G..
John G. MOORE, of Osage County, to Rebecca Jane PERKINS - May 23, 1852, by John L. BURCHARD, M. G..
William SOUDERS to Ann Amelia CRAVEN - April 1, 1852, by Solomon LICKLIDER, J. P..
Theodore VOGT to Maria BEIBER - April 25, 1852, by Joseph LESSEL, J. P..
Ernst ROSER to Maria Sophia WEBER - May 30, 1852, by Joseph LESSELL, J. P..
Henrich JOHNS to Virginia RIEFENSTAHL - June 28, 1852, by Joseph LESSELL, J. P..
Hiram ROBINSON to Adeline HYATT - June 15, 1852, by James H. SHELTON, J. P..
George BERNARD to Anna Maria Alvira SPIELMAN - June 6, 1852, by Fr. George TUERK.
Joseph FRITZ to Maria Anna HALTER - July 18, 1852, by Fr. George TUERK.
Henry Wilhelm SOUDERWERT (sic) to Maria BRINKMAN

- May 7, 1852, by J. F. KOWING, M. G..
John H. TAYLOR to Elizabeth CLARK - July 24, 1852, by A. EYSVOGEL, M. G..
Jacob LUTY to Anna RATGEB - August 7, 1852, by Francis Wm. BOING, J. P..
Carl BOHL to Henrietta BRISCH - September 1, 1852, by Francis Wm. BOING, J. P..
Jacob WICK to Henrietta LENENBERGER - September 6, 1852, by Frederick HUNDHAUSEN, M. G..
Henriech WOHLT of Bosinzfeld, Lippe Detmold, to Christina BORCHARDT - September 15, 1852, by F. BIRKNER, M. G..
J. W. RITCHEY to Martha Adeline REED - July 11, 1852, by J. M. RITCHEY, M. G..
Washington BRAMBLE to Louisa A. COLE - August 26, 1852, by James H. SHELTON, M. G..
Charles WHITACER to Polly HOFFMAN - July 25, 1852, by James H. SHELTON, M. G..
George B. SKILES to Bertha A. McAFEE - July 22, 1852, by James H. SHELTON, M. G..
Ludwig OTT, of Rothenberg, Kingdom of Wurtemberg, to Charltte WISEMAN, of Lippe - October 22, 1852, by F. BIRKNER, M. G..
Heinrich FRITZEMEIER to Maria Magdalena SCHEIDECKER, of Otten, Canton Sototteum, Switzerland - October 24, 1852, by F. BIRKNER, M. G..
John G. ELLIS to Martha Ann MILLER - October 7, 1852, by R. S. D. CALDWELL, M. G..
Thomas MILLER to Esther A. LACEY - November 4, 1852.
Walter O. LOCKHART to Susan SOUDERS - September 30, 1852, by Solomon L. LICKLIDER, J. P..
Henry PARSONS to Elizabeth PANNELL - September 30, 1852, by John H. STEPHENS, Elder.
George W. ROOK to Rebecca RUNELS - September 20, 1852, by Benjamin LEACH, M. G..
Elisha HOLLANDSWORTH to Julian REED - November 13, 1852, by Francis SULLIVAN, J. P..
Joseph B. ARTHUR to Irene H. RUSSEL - October 20, 1852, by Francis H. SULLIAVAN, J. P..
Henry JOHNS to Virginia RIEFENSTAHL - June 28, 1852, by Joseph LESSELL, J. P..
Frederick BOCK to Anna MEIER - September 3, 1852, Joseph LESSELL, J. P..

Carl William RUDOLF to Maria A. FRICKE - November 25, 1852, by Joseph LESSELL, J. P..
Jacob SCHNEIDER to Margaretha MEIER - December 14, 1852, by Francis Wm. BOING, J. P..
Nicholas WOLZ to Barbara NECKERMANN - October 19, 1852, by Fr. George TUERK.
Clastingter (sic) RAMSON to Mrs. Caroline CORDRAY - January 29, 1852, by Wm. L. STAFFORD, M. G..
Jacob SCHINDLER of Canton Glarns, to Margaretha BISCH of Canton Granbandter, Switzerland - December 27, 1852, by F. BIRKNER, M. G..
William WITTICH to Sophia Wilhelmina STOEHR - January 1, 1853, by Francis Wm. BOING, J. P..
Samuel DUNCAN, M. D. to Culprenany McKENNEY - August 29, 1852, by John GILES, M. G..
August SCHARF to Marie E. STOCKLIN - January 15, 1853, by Francis Wm. BOING, J. P..
Joseph CHRISEMANN to Elizabeth Ann STINES - December 16, 1852, by Benjamin LEACH, M. G..
Cornelius HENSON to Malinda WEST - December 23, 1852, by Benjamin LEACH, M. G..
Gerard Anton POLL to Julia DEMWOLF (sic) - December 30, 1852.
Frederick Wilhelm KEHLINBRINK to Wilhelmina TROMER, widow, born SCHURMANN - January 29, 1853, by F. BIRKNER, M. G..
Lorenz RAUSS (sic) to Rosaline HICKMAN - January 4, 1853, by F. BIRKNER, M. G..
Henry EITZEN to Theresa RIEFENSTAHL - February 6, 1853, by Francis Wm. BOING, J. P..
Shadrick S. GIBSON to Martha A. CALDWELL - December 2, 1852, by Jacob HOLLMAN, M. G..
Simon BUDDE to Anna Marie MANSUR - January 12, 1853, by J. F. KOWING, M. G..
John F. BUNTAE to Friderike DECKHANER - December 15, 1852, by J. F. KOWING, M. G..
Robert M. RICHARDSON to Frances Elizabeth PALMER - December 12, 1852, by Robert LUCAS, J. P..
John Jefferson MEREDITH to Mary BLACKWELL - December 19, 1852, by Robert LUCAS, J. P..
Hermann Henrich BRINKOTTER to Anna Maria Elizabeth BOCKSTIC - January 20, 1853, by Peter Herman OBENNABRENBROCK, Evangelical Lutheran.
Charles TRAUTWEIN to Elizabeth ROGERS - February 3, 1853, by H. BOCK, J. P..
Lorenzo DUVALLS to Anna SELLERS - December 18,

1852, by Jacob CARROLL, J. P..
Daniel HUG to Magdelena KAISER - February 14, 1853, Joseph LESSELL, J. P..
Friedrick HAHN to Maria MOUSEHUND - February 12, 1853, by Joseph LESSELL, J. P..
Bolivar C. ROOK to Mary WILLIAMS - January 6, 1853, by James SMITH, J. P..
John BREWER to Rebecca CARROLL - February 13, 1853, by Jacob CARROLL, J. P..
William HENSLEY to Mary Ann CRIDER - January 9, 1853, by Joseph H. BARRARICK (sic), J. P..
Jacob G. KINGLEY to Elizabeth CHILDERS - February 27, 1853, by James H. SHELTON, J. P..
David TAYLOR to Emily Jane SOUDERS - January 13, 1853, by Solomon L. LICKLIDER, J. P..
Christopher L. DURBIN to Elizabeth SHOCKLEY - February 12, 1853, by Joseph H. BARRARICK, J. P..
Joseph HAMBY to Martha Maria FULKS - February 24, 1853, by Solomon L. LICKLIDER, J. P..
Christian ISLER to Jahanna Maria RUPRECHT - March 13, 1853, by Francis Wm. BOING, J. P..
Martin Matthias SCHNELL to Louisa HECKMAN - March 22, 1853, by Francis Wm. BOING, J. P..
Heinrich RINWORD (sic) to Charlotte HANKE (sic) - February 4, 1853, by J. F. KOWING, M. G..
Nikolaris DYKMAN to Adelreid ALDERS - March 6, 1853, by Fr. George TUERK.
Gerard ALDERS to Catherine FELLING - March 14, 1853, by Fr. George TUERK.
Wilhelm HOLTWICK to Adeleida HEYING - April 2, 1853, by Fr. George TUERK.
Henrich TEHOTTE (sic) to Gertrude HOLTWICK - April 2, 1853, by Fr. George TUERK.
Amon N. ROOK to Nancy STRADFORD - January 2, 1853, by Thomas HIBLER, J. P..
William COX to Julian STANTON - February 6, 1853, by E. M. KIMZEY, J. P..
John KISO to Charlotte MEGAN - April 14, 1853, by J. F. KOWING, M. G..
Nicholas FISHER to Susan WILSON - April 30, 1853, by H. BOCK, J. P..
Isaac HOLLANDSWORTH to Cyntha HOLLANDSWORTH - April 10. 1853, by Francis SULLIVAN, J. P..
John BROWN to Syrena THOMSON - April 21, 1853, by Benjamin LEACH, M. G..

Ambros KRAMER to Leopoldine LANQUILLION - May 23, 1853, by Frederick HUNDHAUSEN, M. G..
Albert BRANNAM to Martha ROOKS - February 19, 1853, by Fielding JENKINS, M. G..
John MEYER to Catherine GRABOR - June 8, 1853, by Francis Wm. BOING, J. P..
William LEE to Dorris SCHMIDT - May 23, 1853, by Charles KONOKE.
Marion LUSTER to Elizabeth WALTON - June 23, 1853, by Benjamin LEACH, M. G..
Andreas ALBER to Theresia SCHMIDT - July 14, 1853, by Fr. George TUERK.
Gustav MITZEL to Auguste FISCHER - September 7, 1853, by Francis Wm. BOING, J. P..
Allen M. HAIN to Louisa CARROLL - July 17, 1853, by Jacob CARROLL, J. P..
John HORNER to Maria CORTES - July 13, 1853, by Joseph LESSELL, J. P..
Henry HALL to Lusiva (sic) HARNER - August 11, 1853, by Joseph LESSELL, J. P..
William HENGE to Rosine SCHRAM - September 11, 1853, by Joseph LESSELL, J. P..
Alonzo POTTER to Mrs. Eliza GAMBLING, bride of Crawford County - August 7, 1853, by Solomon L. LICKLIDER, J. P..
Albert TUCKER to Mina PENNINGTON - July 17, 1853, by E. M. KIMZEY, J. P..
Frederick HECK to Lucy GROSS - September 25, 1853, by Francis Wm. BOING, J. P..
James JONES to Sarah A. BARNS - September 1, 1853, by James B. BRALY, M. G..
Mathew ROBERTSON to Mary KOTTES - October 30, 1853, by Frederick HUNDHAUSEN, M. G..
James JOHNS to Sarah C. KERLY - July 4, 1852, by Thomas F. CLAREY, J. P..
Jesse NAPIER to Mary Ann TACKEITT - August 19, 1852, by Thomas F. CLAREY, J. P..
Tinch MAHANEY to Hannah SPALDIN - September 22, 1853, by Benjamin LEACH, M. G..
Frederick Welhelm VOLLMAN to Louise Wilhelmina SCHRAKE - November 4, 1853, by J. F. KOWING, M. G..
Joseph WOOLLAM to Mary Ann STITES - November 9, 1853, by Benjamin LEACH, M. G..
Isaac CREEK to Sarah MACKDADE, both of Crawford County - October 31, 1853, by R. S. D. CALD-

WELL, M. G..
George W. SEWELL to Sirena Clementine PRYOR - November 17, 1853, by R. S. D. CALDWELL, M. G..
Lunsford W. PRYOR to Serena SATTERFIELD - September 29, 1853, by R. S. D. CALDWELL, M. G..
John STRAIN to Lucy A. KEFFER - November 16, 1853, by James B. BRALY, M. G..
George ZEUGGEN (sic) to Caroline KLEE - November 19, 1853, by Joseph LESSELL, J. P..
Joseph MUNDWILLER to Catherine SPILLMAN - November 21, 1853, by Joseph LESSELL, J. P..
Simon SUNKEL to Elisa SCHLOMANN - October 26, 1853, by Charles KONEKE.
Christopher SCHAFER to Thereesa UMRATH - December 27, 1853, by Joseph LESSELL, J. P..
Conrad MEYER to Maria SCHMIDT - January 9, 1854, by Joseph LESSELL, J. P..
Jacob KLOTT to Katherine NEUMAN - December 1,1853, by Fr. George TUERK.
Peter McCANN to Ellen MULLIGAN - December 4, 1853, by Fr. George TUERK.
John JOHNS of Franklin County, to Dorothea MICHEL - January 5, 1854, by Charles BEHNE, J. P..
Larkin HENSON to Mary TODD - December 23, 1853, by Benjamin LEACH, M. G..
John H. GRUBER to Margaretha KRATTLEY - February 6, 1854, by Joseph LESSELL, J. P..
August STROKMEIER to Johanna KRAUP (sic) - February 6, 1854, by F. BIRKNER, M. G..
Frederick TAPPMEIER to Anna Maria MEIER - December 21, 1853, by F. BIRKNER, M. G..
Isaac M. BLEVENS to Elizabeth Jane LACEY - December 22, 1853, by R. S. D. CALDWELL, M. G..
Harmon HOWARD of Ozark County, to Priscilla FOLLEY - February 4, 1854, by R. S. D. CALDWELL, M. G..
Andrew Jackson RIDENHOUR to Jane HINKLE - December 25, 1853, by Solomon L. LICKLIDER, J. P..
Samuel T. RICHIE to Mary L. RICHARDSON - January 26, 1854, by Robert W. REED, M. G..
Solomon L. LICKLIDER to Elizabeth LUCAS - January 19, 1854, by Robert LUCAS, J. P..
Havier C. DURBIN to Belinda REED - February 12, 1854, by Robert LUCAS, J. P..

F. W. MIEGEL to Catharina BURNE - December 7, 1853, by J. F. KOWING, M. G..
Simon SPINDLER of Maisprach?, to Mary ERNI of Rothfluh, Switzerland - January 1, 1854, by A. J. MINOR, J. P..
William HENSON to Cyntha SHOEMAKER - January 15, 1854, by Francis SULLIVAN, J. P..
Jasper N. STEEN to Leothe MATHEWS - February 9, 1854, by Thomas HIBLER, J. P..
John SCHMIDT to Margaretha BATTAGER - March 13, 1854, by H. BOCK, J. P..
Heinrich SCHOENIGOETZ to Ana Elizabeth NOLDE - February 14, 1854, by Fr. George TUERK.
Jacob LUPPOLD to Christina WINDOLF - March 5, 1854, by Fr. George TUERK.
William WELSH to Elisabeth HEID - March 27, 1854, by Joseph LESSELL, J. P..
Jacob LANGENDORFER to Anna Maria LAMS - January 15, 1854, by Joseph LESSELL, J. P..
Herman SCHMIDT to Sophie SCHAFER - March 20, 1854, by H. BOCK, J. P..
George D. RICHIE to Sarah E. POPE - March 30, 1854, by Robert W. READ, M. G..
John LOOBY to Elizabeth BOUGHAN - April 15, 1854, by Frederick HANDHAUSEN, M. G..
George TUCKER to Elizabeth MURPHY - March 19, 1854, by E. M. KIMZEY, J. P..
Joseph REYNOLDS to Nancy VAUGHAN - March 22, 1854, by E. M. KIMZEY, J. P..
Jackson TUCKER to Matilda MILLER - April 1, 1854, by E. M. KIMZEY, J. P..
George Rudolf STENTER to Mary FILLINS (sic) - April 17, 1854, by Jacob SCHWARTZ, M. G..
John CRIDER to Mary JOHNSON - February 26, 1854, by Robert LUCAS, J. P..
Herman SCHMIDT to Sophie SCHAEFER - March 20, 1854, by H. BOCK, J. P..
Charles PALKOWICH to Margaretha KLEIN - May 3, 1854, by H. BOCK, J. P..
James RICHARDSON to Mary TENISON - April 3, 1853, by William R. BRANSON, J. P..
Ancel SATTERFIELD to Julia Ann AGEE - May 7, 1854, Robert W. READ, M. G..
Louis RUHLE to Augusta LEONHARDT - May 9, 1854, by Joseph LESSELL, J. P..
Christian TOCHAPPLE (sic) to Eva DANUSER - May

25, 1854, by William R. BRANSON, J. P..
Samuel FUNCH to Mrs. Matilda WYATT - March 2, 1854, by Solomon L. LICKLIDER, J. P..
Charles USLER to Jane SCHNAPPERS - May 29, 1854, by H. BOCK, J. P..
Phillip EBERSTEIN to Elizabeth REITH (sic) - June 2, 1854, by Francis Wm. BOING, J. P..
John HANNEGAN to Mary BUTCHER - April 30, 1854, by Fr. George TUERK.
John MURPHY to Briget MORRISY - April 30, 1854, by William R. BRANSON, J. P..
Benedict JACOB to Frederika KELLNER - June 13, 1854, by Frederick HANDHAUSEN, M. G..
Frederick VALETTE to Minka ISLY - April 18, 1854, by F. BIRKNER, M. G..
Florian JUST to Agnes RUFFNER - June 18, 1854, by Francis Wm. BOING, J. P..
Johann HARTUNG to Hana Frederica MULLER - June 27, 1854, by Joseph LESSELL, J. P..
Charles STANGE to Wilhelmina MARX - July 1, 1854, by H. BOCK, J. P..
Samuel ADAMS to Polly SOUDERS - May 11, 1854, by Solomon L. LICKLIDER, J. P..
Lewis Jefferson RINEHART to Eliza Ann MILLER - May 21, 1854, by Solomon L. LICKLIDER, J. P..
Wilhelm HILDEBRANDT to Anna LEE - July 3, 1854, by Charles KONOKE.
Edward FRANKE to Elizabeth GIELMAN - July 23, 1854, by Francis Wm. BOING, J. P..
Frederick W. KATTLEMAN to Frederica Caroline KRABEN - July 29, 1854, by Joseph LESSELL, J. P..
Isaac JOHNSON to Elizabeth CRIDER - May 21, 1854, by Robert LUCAS, J. P..
George HUSMANN to Louise Caroline KIELMAN (sic) - July 13, 1854, by F. BIRKNER, M. G..
Bernard HELD to Amelia BRANDT - June 26, 1854, by Herman RAHN, M. G..
John KELLNER to Albertine MAIER - June 18, 1854, by Fr. George TUERK.
Absalom COALTER to Ellen JONES - December 15, 1853, by James H. SHELTON, J. P..
Wesley MASSIE to Martha MAUPIN - March 16, 1854, by James H. SHELTON, J. P..
Herman EICKERMAN to Caroline DOPPE - August 11, 1854, by Herman RAHN, M. G..

Zachariah SMITH to Narcisis CANON - July 9, 1854, by Jonathan S. ROOK, J. P..
Ferdinand SCHONING to Wilhelmina HOMAN - August 30, 1854, by Charles KONOKE.
Casper KOTHOFF to Minna MULLER - August 17, 1854, by Charles BEHNE, J. P..
George HOFFNER to Catharine MOSHEL - August 26, 1854, by Joseph LESSELL, J. P..
George FRANK to Marie Mary MONY - August 26, 1854, by Joseph LESSELL, J. P..
Charles SUMTAG (sic) to Mary SCHIERMAN - September 18, 1854, by Charles NESTEL, M. G..
Ernst MELLIER to Wilhelmina AUFDERHEIDEN - September 13, 1854, by Thomas HIBLER, J. P..
William A. EMERSON to Susan M. HARRISON - September 28, 1854, by Thomas HIBLER, J. P..
Furman STITES to Louisa Jane BANAM - September 27, 1854, by Benjamin LEACH, M. G..
Jacob KRECKER to Margaretha SCHMIDT - September 24, 1854, by Frederick HANDHAUSEN, M. G..
Gabriel Jackson WOOD to Sophia PERKINS - August 17, 1854, by Burton COOPER, J. P..
Louis G. MORRIS to Jane McMILLEN - August 16, 1854, by Samuel BURCHARD, M. G..
Andrew H. HAMBY to Amie E. FULKS - August 10, 1854, by N. ELDREDGE, J. P..
John HIRSH to Felina STRAUB - September 3, 1854, by Joseph LESSELL, J. P..
Samuel SCHWEIGHAUSER to Margaret JAEGER - October 7, 1854, by Joseph LESSELL, J. P..
Paul PETERSON to Rebecca LEE, married at the house of Greenberry LEE - September 24, 1854, by Hiram C. RICH, M. G..
Johann FALTEY to Marie MULLER - October 23, 1854, by Francis WM. BOING, J. P..
John G. GUTTMAN to Elizabeth FREIDAG (sic) - November 14, 1854, by Joseph LESSELL, J. P..
John SULLIVAN to Sarah THOMSON - October 5, 1854, by Benjamin LEACH, M. G..
Benjamin M. MAHANEY to Martha SPAULDING - November 17, 1854, by Benjamin LEACH, M. G..
Enick DOUGLAS to Elizabeth M. MOOR - October 18, 1854, by Samuel TROWER, J. P.. Witnesses were Jemima MOOR, Tarlton ESTES and Morgan MISON.
William Henry MEYER to Charlotte STOLLON - July 25, 1854, by E. M. KIMZEY, J. P..

Phillip DEITS to Eliza WARD - November 21, 1854, by Thomas HIBLER, J. P..
Thomas HIBLER to Jane HARRISON - November 21, 1854, by James A. MATTHEWS, J. P..
Andrew J. REED to Sarah Jane BURLEY (sic) - October 29, 1854, by Robert W. READ, M. G..
Matthias MUTH to Augusta Julia KUSCHEL - October 10, 1854, by A. J. MINOR, J. P..
Thomas TINNAL to Melissa D. PRYOR - August 7, 1854, by Owen SHOCKLEY, M. G..
Phillip TACKETT to Elizabeth WILSON - December 14, 1854, by Owen SHOCKLEY, M. G..
Conrad RUGGE to Friederika BUNTE - December 13, 1854, by William HOMEIER, M. G..
John KUNZELMANN to Louisa GRAF - November 1, 1854, by Frederick HUNDHAUSEN, M. G..
Samuel CRIDER to Isabell A. BURGESS - August 25, 1854, by John BURGESS, M. G..
John HESS to Gertrude SCHMITZ - December 31, 1854, by Francis Wm. BOING, J. P..
Franz FOELLING to Margaretha WOHLGEMUTH - December 21, 1854, by Fr. George TUERK.
John McMAHAN to Katherine SCLATTERY - December 6, 1854, by Fr. George TUERK.
Henry Jackson SMITH to Sarah M. PRISE - January 18, 1855, by Benjamin LEACH, M. G..
Joseph SIMPSON to Annie SMITH - November 10, 1854, by Fr. John J. SULLIVAN.
John DUNN to Margaret CONNORS, alias RYAN - December 26, 1854, by Fr. John J. SULLIVAN.
Frederick GABLER to Caroline GUETNER (sic) - February 4, 1855, by Francis Wm. BOING, J. P..
August KRETER to Wilhelmina SANDERS - February 12, 1855, by William KLEINSCHMIDT, M. G..
Carl PETERSON to Charlotte KOPS - February 12, 1855, by William KLEINSCHMIDT, M. G..
Frederick SCHRODER to Amalia MEIER - December 4, 1854, by William KLEINSCHMIDT, M. G..
Francis L. MENNYPENNY to Esther C. SHURMAN - November 30, 1854, by Elder John H. STEPHENS.
Nelson WOOD of Crawford County, to Martha FOLEY - January 4, 1855, by R. S. D. CALDWELL, M. G..
Jacob LAMANCE to Mary GREVY - July 5, 1854, by Thomas L. POWELL, J. P..
Ezra STITES to Sarah A. CHILDERS - October 14, 1854, by Thomas L. POWELL, J. P..

William J. PERKINS to Eliza Ann WILLIAMS - December 5, 1854, by Thomas L. POWELL, J. P..

Clemens SCHNIDEKER (sic) to Wilhelmina THOFERN - March 15, 1855, by Sebert WEISS, M. G..

Timothy McCARTHY to Anna HEART - January 3, 1855, by Fr. George TUERK.

John McGOWEN to Mary Ann SHIVERS - January 4, 1855, by John BURGESS, M. G..

Frederick KLOCKENBERGER to Maria BOHM - April 12, 1855, by Francis Wm. BOING, J. P..

Michael POESCHAL to Catherine WAGNER - March 18, 1855, by Frederick HUNDHAUSEN, M. G..

N. B. BROWN to Elizabeth THOMSON - April 5, 1855, by Benjamin LEACH, M. G..

Michael SMITH to Ursula REEDLER - October 6, 1854, by Thomas L. POWELL, J. P..

Henry LUEBBE, son of Christopher LUEBBE and Dorothia HASENHOLZ from Eilenstadt Circuit Oscherslobon, Kingdom of Prussia, to Sophia BERKLING, daughter of Frederick BERKLING and Dorothia SCHICKERLING, also from Eilenstadt Circuit Oscherslobon - April 5, 1855, by Charles BEHNE, J. P..

David SHOCKLEY to Jane NELSON - April 8, 1855, by Joseph H. BARRARICK, J. P..

Samuel DERBIN to Nancy Ann NELSON - April 12, 1855, by Joseph H. BARRARICK, J. P..

Cornelius HAINS to C. Rebecca REED - February 19, 1855, by Jacob CARROLL, J. P,..

M. J. WROTON to Victorine ELDREDGE - May 10, 1855, by Anderson J. GAITER.

Daniel REED to Caroline REED - March 11, 1855, by Solomon L. LICKLIDER, J. P..

Jacob STROBEL to Rosalia BATES - May 28, 1855, by Francis Wm. BOING, J. P..

William T. HIBLER to Nancy Ann COOPER - May 23, 1855, by Benjamin LEACH, M. G..

Simon TRACHT to Florentina WIEMAN - June 15, 1855, by H. RANSCHENBUSCH, M. G..

Ludwig NIEWALD to Sophia RUEGGE - March 27, 1855, by H. RANSCHENBUSCH, M. G..

Theodore SCHNEIDER to Wilhelmina OVERKROME - April 14, 1855, by H. RANSCHENBUSCH, M. G..

Marquiis DeLafayette BALLARD to Elizabeth M. JAMISON - May 12, 1855, by R. S. D. CALDWELL, M. G..

Ernie STEINHAUSER to Rosalie BAYER - June 21, 1855, by Francis Wm. BOING, J. P..
Clifford THERIEN to Magdalene VOHLGEMOUTH - April 30, 1855, by Frederick HUNDHAUSEN, M. G..
David A. WATER to Mary PRIOR - June 4, 1855, by Joseph H. BARRARICK, J. P..
Jacob BOONE to Rosina ROGERS - June 4, 1855, by Joseph LESSELL, J. P..
Christoph SIMMONS to Welhelmina RAHNS - November 28, 1854, by Joseph LESSELL, J. P..
Casper SCHUBERT to Maria Sophia STOHR - December 17, 1854, by Joseph LESSELL, J. P..
Charles RIEK to Freniece Emilie TEUBNER - December 31, 1854, by Joseph LESSELL, J. P..
August HAMMEL to Appolonia VOGEL - January 3, 1855, by Joseph LESSELL, J. P..
Christopher KOTTHOFF to Theresa SCHNEIDER - January 8, 1855, by Joseph LESSELL, J. P..
John FRUBER to Frederica LAMS - January 26, 1855, by Joseph LESSELL, J. P..
Fritz KRAMER to Maria KASENS - March 4, 1855, by Joseph LESSELL, J. P..
Frederick NOE to Sophia KAISER MAGDALENE (sic) - March 26, 1855, by Joseph LESSELL, J. P..
Andreas BOMET to Anna M. VOGEL - April 1, 1855, by Joseph LESSELL, J. P..
Urick WEISS to Rosina HOTTINGER - April 23, 1855, by Joseph LESSELL, J. P..
Heronimus THOMAS to Maria W. MOSCH - May 4, 1855, by Joseph LESSELL, J. P..
Jacob SCHMIDT to Elizabeth W. WOLLSCHLAGER - May 19, 1855, by Joseph LESSELL, J. P..
David LAIN to Anna KERLEY - June 18, 1855, by James H. AIKEN, J. P..
George LUCAS to Amelia BUESH - July 3, 1855, by James H. AIKEN, J. P..
John D. POPE to Mary RICHARDSON - June 24, 1855, by Daniel A. RICHIE, J. P..
James COOPER to Ann BURRITT - July 29, 1855, by Benjamin LEACH, M. G..
Fieldin JENKINS to Elizabeth JENKINS - July 1, 1855, by Alonzo POTTER, J. P..
Hezekiah CARROLL to B. SMITH - July 15, 1855, by Alonzo POTTER, J. P..
Eli HAYNES to Fanny SMITH - July 22, 1855, by Alonzo POTTER, J. P..

Lester ANDERSON to Olive BRANSON - August 30, 1855, by Alonzo POTTER, J. P..

Christian KUHFUSS, of Boesenfeld, Lippe Detmold, Germany, to Caroline DRAWE, of Percebeck, Lippe Detmold - July 14, 1855, by Charles BEHNE, J. P..

Hugh LAYTON, of Norfolk, England, to Mary L. SULLIVAN, of Virginia - August 2, 1855, by Charles BEHNE, J. P..

John George PLATTNER to Dorothy KRETTLE - June 30, 1855, by Charles NESTEL, M. G..

William R. DOUGLAS to Nancy SHOCKLEY - September 6, 1855, by Robert W. READ, M. G..

John CUTHBERTSON to Isabella DOWLER - September 13, 1855, by R. S. D. CALDWELL, M. G..

John M. FERRELL to Elvira FITZGERALD - July 26, 1855, by T. J. SHELTON, J. P..

Jacob RUEGGER to Maria ROESCHER, widow of George Roescher, bride and groom of Niedermye, Canton Argon, Soffingen, Switzerland - September 10, 1855.

James M. SHOCKLEY to Caroline HOFFMAN - July 26, 1855, by Thomas L. POWELL, J. P..

William Emitt GABLER to Eugenia SENN - October 21, 1855, by Francis Wm. BOING, J. P..

Florian JUST to Mrs. Ursula BORSCH - August 24, 1855, by Frederick HUNDHAUSEN, M. G..

Anthony VALENDORN to Mrs. Rosina WAFRI - October 27, 1855, by Frederick HUNDHAUSEN, M. G..

BOOK C
1855 - 1872

Heinrick BIEKER to Wilhelmina BIRKEMEIER - October 3, 1855, by John G. SCHAIBEL, M. G..
Jacob SOUDERS to Adolpha FULKS - April 12, 1855, by Preston H. COLLIER, J. P..
Solomon KEEFER to Elenda STRAIN - October 25, 1855, by Preston H. COLLIER, J. P..
Daniel PLOUGHMAN to Martha Jane GARNER - November 15, 1855, by Preston H. COLLIER, J. P..
Julius BEUERMAN to Ursala VOGEL _ November 8, 1855, by Sebastian WEIP, M. G..
William NORWOOD to Roda HOWARD - October 21, 1855, by Daniel A. RITCHIE, J. P..
John Paul HOCHEN (sic) to Carolina DRESWELL - November 27, 1855, by Francis W. BOING, J. P..
Henry SCHUREMANN to Carolina KUSCHEL - October 12, 1855, by Charles NESTEL, M. G..
Christopher KEMPER to Anne Fredricke BERGER - September 20, 1855, by Charles NESTLE, M. G..
Frank Henry FIELDMANN to Fredricke GEPPE - September 21, 1855, by Charles NESTEL, M. G..
Franz KEHR to Barbara STRICK - October 24, 1855, by Kasten BUSHMAN, J. P..
Joseph M. VAUGHAN to Annie C. LEACH - November 1, 1855, by Thomas HIBLER, J. P..
Burgess A. MATHEWS to Mary Ann MASON - October 15, 1855, by Thomas HIBLER, J. P..
George SCHAEFFER to Dorthea SCHAFER, born BESE - January 2, 1856, by Fr. George TUERK.
Jacob KLOTT to Franzesca KLOTT, born FALLENS - November 6, 1855, by Fr. George TUERK.
John DIEDRICK to Regina DICTRICK, born MORIK - November 4, 1855, by Fr. George TUERK.
Diedrick HEIMSER to Julia AUSTERMAN, widow, by birth Julia MEYOR - December 7, 1855, by John George SCHAIBLE, M. G..
William COLTER to Julian JOHNS - October 7, 1855, by H. M. SKYLES, J. P..
David C. PRICE to Anis (sic) LEACH - January 18, 1856, by Benjamin LEACH, M. G..
Henry THOFERN to Virginia SCHEIDECK - January 9, 1856, by John George SCHAIBLE, M. G..
Henry WALDECKER to Henriette HOLMER - January 11, 1856, by John George SCHAIBLE, M. G..

Edmon SORREL to Nancy WALTON - December 6, 1855, by R. W. READ, M. G..
Lansford W. PRYOR to Francis FITZGERALD - November 20, 1855, by R. W. READ, M. G..
Julius BECKMEISTER to Mary BECK - December 6, 1855, by James M. AITKEN, J. P..
Franz DOCEMANN to Carolen STOLTMANN - December 21, 1855, by Herman RAHN, M. G..
John BARREIA to Margaretha SCHMIDT - February 14, 1856, by Charles NESTEL, M. G..
William DOUGLAS to Sarah SITTON - January 30, 1856, by Benjamin LEACH, M. G..
Reuben F. DOTSON to Tabitha REED - January 1, 1856, by Daniel RITCHIE, J. P..
Henry RUDIGAR to Louise WEBER - February 4, 1856, by Julius HUNDHAUSEN.
John W. WINN to Nancy M. MATTOCK - February 21, 1856, by James SMITH, J. P..
William CRIDER to Elizabeth GATTS - filed March 10, 1856, by Jos. H. BARBARICK.
William MOTHER (sic) to Sarah SHOCKLEY - February 28, 1856, by Burton COOPER, J. P..
Charles M. MATHEWS to Jane FITZGERALD - February 21, 1856, by R. S. D. CALDWELL, M. G..
R. W. MAHANEY to Easter SMITH - February 28, 1856, by Benjamin LEACH, M. G..
John COLVIN to Margaret EASTUS - February 28, 1856, by Benjamin LEACH, M. G..
William R. VAUGHAN to Sarah Catharine LEACH - December 27, 1855, by Thomas HIBLER, J. P..
Casper LEIMKUHLER to Polly ATKINS - February 28, 1856, by Burton COOPER, J. P..
Franz KUHLEM to Maria LABERS - February 1, 1856, by Kasten BUSHMAN, J. P..
William KRUGER to Abigal BETHE - March 10, 1856, by Francis W. BOING, J. P..
William MORRIS to Rhode MATHIS - March 10, 1856, by Francis W. BOING, J. P..
Bartholomaus SCHULER to Barbara BRAUNNORTH - April 11, 1856, by Francis W. BOING, J. P..
George SCHAEFFER to Dorothea BEDE - January 2, 1856, by Fr. George TUERK.
Joseph BAJER to Josepha GAU - January 22, 1856, by Fr. George TUERK.
Chrisylostomus (sic) WILE to Maria Ana STOLLER - January 29, 1856, by Fr. George TUERK.
William FORSYTH to Katharina NEISON - March 5,

January 29, 1856, by Fr. George TUERK.
William FORSYTH to Katharina NEISON - March 5, 1856, Fr. George Tuerk.
John E. WARD to Louisa Elizabeth Susan PRIOR - April 20, 1856, by Kasten BUSHMAN, J. P..
Isaac L. LOWS (sic) to Mary SATTERFIELD - March 27, 1856, by Robert W. READ, M. G..
Benton H. SHELTON to Mary S. ROBERSON - April 9, 1856, by Benjamin LEACH, M. G..
Thomas LEMMONS to Isabella SMITH - March 16, 1856.
Ferdinand George OGESCHKI to Auguste Dorothea BOCK - March 30, 1856, by Charles NESTEL, M. G..
John Henry HAGEN to Catharine BAER, widow, born BESCHOFF - April 10, 1856, by Charles NESTEL, M. G..
Christian FULLMAN to Lisette BRUNGRABER - April 18, 1856, by Charles NESTEL, M. G..
Heinrich RUDIJER to Louise WEBER - May 4, 1856 (this marriage was also recorded as having taken place on February 4, 1856).
Wm. SOUSE to Anna BOWEN - April 3, 1856, by R. S. D. CALDWELL, M. G..
George BAXTER to Amanda M. E. F. CUTHBERTSON - April 27, 1856, by R. S. D. CALDWELL, M. G..
William A. MILLER to Eliza C. COLLIER - January 17, 1856, by William MINER, M. G..
Andrew WALKER to Mathilda GUEDEN (sic) - April 6, 1856, by Joel HUNDHAUSEN, J. P..
John Henry Anton OBERKROM to Anna POLLE (sic) - April 8, 1856, by Joel HUNDHAUSEN, J. P..
Phillip CAPELLA to Mrs. Catharine TSCHAEPLER - April 27, 1856, by Joel HUNDHAUSEN, J. P..
Anton WALKER to Henrietta RONNEBERGER - May 4, 1856, by Joel HUNDHAUSEN, J. P..
Michael BUNKHARDT to Christine KUPE - May 18, 1856, by Joel HUNDHAUSEN, J. P..
Pleasant F. PRICE to Prudence Marilus SPALDEN - May 22, 1856, by C. H. MITCHEL, M. G..
Herman IHRE (sic) to Sophia BERNICKE - May 15, 1856, by J. G. SCHAIBLE, M. G..
Emil MENZ to Marie HICKE - June 1, 1856, by Francis W. BOING, M. G..
Rudolph C. SCHLEUDER to Maria Margaretha MERTENS - June 6, 1856, by Francis W. BOING, J. P..

William C. BOING to Adelhird KNOCHE - June 8, 1856, by Francis W. BOING, J. P..
August HEILERT to Caroline NULLMEYER - June 25, 1856, by John G. SCHAIBLE, M. G..
Feany (sic) Xavier SCHNEIDER to Maria Ana KOCH - May 12, 1856, by Fr. George TUERK.
Herman NORE to Anna Maria BUNKER - May 26, 1856, by Fr. George TUERK.
Martin FREUKBIP (sic) to Clara SCHARFENBERGER - May 25, 1856, by Fr. George TUERK.
William ATKINS to Mary SMITH - April 4, 1856, by H. M. SKYLES, J. P..
Burrel LAIN to Mary M. SMITH - May 11, 1856, by H. M. SKYLES, J. P..
Franklin R. MATTOCKS to Nancy REED - July 20, 1856, by Joshua A. ROOK, J. P..
Louis KROMER to Henriette HANS - June 22, 1856, by Herman RAHN, M. G..
James RICKETTS to Louisa WARDEN - July 13, 1856, by Kasten BUSCHMAN, J. P..
Allen M. HAINES to Elender WHITE - July 27, 1856, C. H. RATLIFF, M. G..
Christopher RITTERBUSH of Osage County, to Louise RETKIN - August 15, 1856, by John George SCHAIBLE. Witnesses were Friedrick BLANKE and Christian SCHAIBLE.
Peter DILTHEY to Joan FRANKE - August 10, 1856, by Charles NESTEL, M. G..
John HELLER to Friedricke BLANKE, widow, born SOUNTAG - August 13, 1856, by Charles NESTEL, M. G..
Frederic William RUHLMAN to Sophia MILLER - September 11, 1856, by Charles NESTEL, M. G..
Theopholis BIEBUSCH to Dorothy BECK - July 6, 1856, by Charles NESTEL, M. G..
John HAFER to Nerene SCHNORF - July 9, 1856, by A. BALTZER, M. G..
Robert WHITE to Sina BRANSON - July 11, 1856, by Alonzo POTTER, J. P..
Gottleb KOCH to Frederika KLEIN - October 18, 1856, by Francis W. BOING, J. P..
James REED to Margaret SCRIBNER - September 28, 1856, by Francis SULLIVAN, J. P..
John BOILS to Marian FANCE - October 16, 1856, by Benjamin LEACH, M. G..
John SATTERFIELD to Rachael Roan BLEVIN - Septem-

ber 16, 1856, R. S. D. CALDWELL, M. G..
Lewis TACKETT to Amarilla STRADFORD - October 20, 1856, by Joseph H. BARBARICK, J. P..
David CRIDER to Barbara SCHOCKLEY - October 12, 1856, by Joseph H. BARBARICK, J. P..
George SOUDER to Emily RIDENHOUER - June 5, 1856, Preston COLLIER, J. P..
Frederick WALLENSTEIN to Julian MUSCAT - September 25, 1856, by Preston COLLIER, J. P..
Herman PRINCE to Charlotte HONSFIELD - October 19, 1856, by Preston COLLIER, J. P..
John Christopher ISREAL of St. Louis, to Caroline BUCKER - November 18, 1856, John George SCHAIBLE, M. G..
Ludwig FEITZEL to Maria SCHACK, HOFFMAN by birth, - December 4, 1856, by Joel HUNDHAUSEN, J. P..
George GEAR to Anna Maria YELLY (sic) - November 24, 1856, by Joel HUNDHAUSEN, J. P..
William T. WILLIAMS to Osage County, to Elizabeth C. McAFEE - December 11, 1856, by Vardry (sic) BURGESS, M. G..
Augustus WILMS,"called by Americans, WILLIAMS" to Susan LAMBERT - October 14, 1856, by August RAUSCHEUBUSCH.
Bernhart SCHAFFNER of Franklin County, to Litea SPINDLER - November 13, 1856, by John C. HOECK, M. G..
Carl Heinrich BRANDHORST to Wilhelmina Louise ROTHMEIER - December 29, 1856, by John George SCHAIBLE, M. G..
Johann Michael HOFFMAN to Mrs. Christine Frederike OTT, widow, born SCHAFER - October 21, 1856, by Charles NESTEL, M. G..
William HEITKAMP to Lesette KORF - November 23, 1856, by Charles NESTEL, M. G..
George KRATZHELLER to Wilhelmina Charlotte POHLMAN - January 17, 1857, by Francis W. BOING, J. P..
Eimert WILTING to Ana Maria KEBE - December 8, 1856, by Fr. George TUERK.
Peter MICHELS to Mary STRAUB - December 30, 1856, by Fr. George TUERK.
Carl KAISER to Johanna OCHSNER - November 27, 1856, by Fr. George TUERK.
John STOVEAK to Nancy TACKETT - October 13, 1856, by John BURGESS, M. G..

Alfred P. BRANSON to Elizabeth HAINES - January 8, 1857, by John BURGESS, Elder.
Frederick HEIDBRINK to Johanna F. W. RABENS - February 8, 1857, by John G. SCHAIBLE, M. G..
Philip George Anton WEBER to Ernistine Julie BURCKHARDT - January 31, 1857, by Francis W. BOING, J. P..
Thomas E. PIENIER to Rachel STRAIN - December 14, 1856, by Benjamin LEACH, M. G..
William BALEY to Lisey McMEAN - December 18, 1856, by Jonathan S. ROOK, J. P..
John W. JENNINGS to Mrs. Elizabeth MILLER - November 22, 1856, by H. M. SKYLES, J. P..
Willis M. TACKET to Mrs. Silpha BRIGS - February 9, 1856, by H. M. SKYLES, J. P..
John FLETCHER to Martha HAMILTON - December 25, 1856, by Daniel RITCHIE, J. P..
William AGEE to Cela PALMER - January 8, 1857, by Daniel A. RITCHIE, J. P..
George W. MAHANEY to Mary ESTES - February 8, 1857, by L. M. MAHANEY, M. G..
Thomas SHOCKLEY to Sarah DURBIN - January 29, 1857, by Joseph H. BARBARICK, J. P..
Henry C. SUNDAYMIRE to Mary Jane BRANSON - November 20, 1856, by Joseph H. BARBARICK, J. P..
William DOBESON to Mary Ann KINGCADE - January 8, 1857, by Joseph H. BARBARICK, J. P..
Henry LANGE to Dora HULLE - December 12, 1856, by Hermann RAHN, M. G..
Henry August WACKER to Catherine Charlotte ___ GEN - January 18, 1857, by Hermann RAHN, M. G..
Thomas JENKINS to Julia BRAUN - January 20, 1857, by John BURGESS, Elder.
John HARRIS to Sarah STOVEAK - January 29, 1857, by John BURGESS, Elder.
Rolly R. BRANSON to Louisa C. PARKHAM - December 4, 1856, by Alonza POTTER, J. P..
Eldridge A. PARKHAM to Elizabeth SHOCKLEY - December 18, 1856, by Alonzo POTTER, J. P..
Engel BAUMAN to Louise DANYEISEN (sic) - January 4, 1857, by Joel HUNDHAUSEN, J. P..
William HERMANN SCHLENDER to Mrs. Louise Caroline FRANKLIN, WEPELHORFT by birth - March 7, 1857, by Joel HUNDHAUSEN, J. P..
Jesse WATSON to Sarah I. JAMISON - February 5,

1857, by R. S. D. CALDWELL, M. G..
Thomas BRIMM of Franklin County, to Martha McKENNEY - January 22, 1857, by Kasten BUSCHMAN, J. P..
Jacob JAITE to Louise Amelia LORBUR - February 17, 1857, by A. RAUSCHENBUSCH, M. G..
Casper Dedrick HEUGSTENBERG to Elizabeth FISCHER, "heretofore married to Herman Dedrick HUELLE, dec'd" - March 5, 1857, by A. RAUSCHENBUSCH, M. G..
George LANG to Caroline HOFFMANN, widow, born FISCHER - February 12, 1857, by Charles NESTEL, M. G..
Gotfried BOHU (sic) to Mrs. Johanna NISCHE, widow born RICK - March 12, 1857, by Charles NESTEL, M. G..
Ignaz KOCH to Fanny FRANK - March 27, 1857, by Charles NESTEL, M. G..
Lewis F. HOLT to Elizabeth WILLIAMS - March 29, 1857, by Loyd M. MAHANEY, M. G..
William STEEN to Delila TOMPSON - March 31, 1857, by Benjamin LEACH, M. G..
Talton EASTUS to Maria SULLIVAN - April 12, 1857, by Benjamin LEACH, M. G..
Frederick August BEHREN to Louise SCHMIDT - March 6, 1857, by John C. HOECK, M. G..
Daniel M MAHANEY to Adalide DILLEN - April 15, 1857, by L. M MAHANEY, M. G..
John M. WHITE of Osage County, to Sarah BRANNUM - April 21, 1857, by L. M MAHANEY, M. G..
Matthias HAVERLE to Susanna LANIZ - April 30, 1857, by Francis W. BOING, J. P..
Peter WEINDLAND to Theresia Maria MILLER - May 10, 1857, by Francis W. BOING, M. G..
John KIRCHNER to Mary Anne STEAKE - January 7, 1857, by Fr. George TUERK.
John JAEGER to Elizabeth GRAIN - March 26, 1857, by Fr. George TUERK.
Daniel HOFFMAN to Mina HOLMER (sic) - May 22, 1857, by J. G. SCHAIBLE, M. G..
James H. COLLIER to Rebecca FANNON - June 7, 1857, by Joel HANDHAUSEN, J. P..
George Washington MILLER to Nancy Jane LANE - June 22, 1857, by Joel HANDHAUSEN, J. P..
Francis M. TUCKER to Julan PALMER - April 5, 1857, by Daniel A. RITCHIE, J. P..

Frederick PRIEP to Maria THURKON - April 19, 1857, by Hermann RAHN, M. G..
Johann HUMBURG to Catharina Maria BOTTERMANN - April 7, 1857, by Charles NESTEL, M. G..
Herman STOCK to Caroline DUKER - June 26, 1857, by J. G. SCHAIBLE, M. G., at the home of Henry NULLMEYER.
Silas CANTLY to Helen BUSCHARD - April 20, 1857, by H. E. SMITH, M. G..
Christian FLITSCH to Margarethe FELING - July 12, 1857, by Francis W. BOING, J. P..
Daniel MILLER to Diana LEACH - June 4, 1857, by John SULLINS, J. P..
William Tell PRYOR to Sary SHOCKLEY - April 30, 1857, by Kasten BUSCHMAN, J. P..
Dietrich SCHULTE to Christine REITEMEIER - August 7, 1857, by Herman RAHN, M. G..
Johannes HELMS to Marie SCHUNEMEIER - August 18, 1857, by Herman RAHN, M. G..
Johan HOMIER to Sina SIMERS - July 17, 1857, H. RAHN, M. G..
George MURPHY to Rachael ANDERTON - July 12, 1857, by Daniel A. RITCHIE, J. P..
Joseph KRATTLE to Maria BADER - August 29, 1857, by Francis W. BOING, J. P..
Joseph KIRCHNER to Katharina GREIN - June 3, 1857, by Fr. George TUERK.
Franz BIRK to Margareta NASKERMAN - July 13, 1857, by Fr. George TUERK.
George LEMMONS to Martha HAYNES - August 6, 1857, by Elder Charles RATLIFF, at the home of Luster Haynes.
Samuel E. LICKLIDER to Sarah E. CLYMER - July 30, 1857, by James R. BURK, M. G..
Rudolph Gottlieb BEHNKE to Otilie Auguste WOLTER - July 26, 1857, by Charles NESTEL, M. G..
Johann SULGER (sic), born at Richon, CANTON Basie, Switzerland, to Susanna BURIE, born at Kurtweil Amt Waldshut Guat, Duchy of Baden - October 15, 1855, by Charles BEHME, J. P..
Christian Bek (sic) to Rosine MUNZANMARIR - September 13, 1857, by Charles NESTEL, M. G..
Christopher LEWECKE to Amalia EHLERT - September 9, 1857, by C. HOCH, M. G..
Karl EHLERT to Augusta BICKER - October 18, 1857, by C. HOCH, M. G..

William O. JOHNSON to Jane K. FITZGERELD - September 3, 1857, by R. S. D. CALDWELL, M. G..
John SURGEY to Alsen HENSLEY - October 15, 1857, by Kasten BUSCHMAN, J. P..
A. N. MURPHY of Franklin County, to Eliza SMITH - November 15, 1857, John D. MURPHY.
Frederick BECK to Augusta RUDOLPH - November 27, 1857, by F. DREWEL, M. G..
Franz William STONER of Osage County, to Rosanna Regina Carolina MEYER - October 29, 1857, by H. Edward ROMANOWSKI.
Lewis N. MURPHY of Franklin County, to Mary A. STRAIN - October 1, 1857, Jas. B. BRALY.
Albert B. SORREL to Nancy P. EATON - December 10, 1857, by R. S. D. CALDWELL, M. G..
Henry HILKERBANMER to Louise GROTE - September 17, 1857, by J. G. SCHAIBLE, M. G..
Adalbert Alexander Oscar GOHRLICH to Johanna Maria Louise SCHULZE by birth, DAHLMEYER - December 12, 1857, by J. G. SCHAIBLE, M. G..
Louis LONGENOTTI to Maria BUTGANS - October 21, 1857, by Joel HUNDHAUSEN, J. P..
Henry SATTLER to Anna PUCHTA - October 22, 1857, by Joel HUNDHAUSEN, J. P..
Bernhard STEIN to Emilie STEIGER - November 23, 1857, by Joel HUNDHAUSEN, J. P..
Henry O. TIES to Caroline BRINKMAN - September 16, 1857, by Thomas L. POWELL, J. P..
Charles CUSCHEL to Albertine BOCK - December 14, 1857, by Thomas L. POWELL, J. P..
Phillip A. HULVEY to Aminda GRAHAM - November 26, 1857, by Daniel A. RITHIE, J. P..
Mark BULLARD to Sarah RITCHIE - December 27, 1857, by Daniel A. RITCHIE, J. P..
William VANLEY to Minerva Jane CRIDER - September 22, 1857, by Alonzo POTTER, J. P..
Martin MUELLER to Maria Ursula MUNDENGIR - December 7, 1857, by Fr. George TUERK.
Joseph Frederick GOTTHOF to Maria Berta HINEMANN - November 9, 1857, by Fr. George Tuerk.
Franz SPECKHALS to Genovera NOLDE - October 11, 1857, by Fr. George TUERK.
John Bernard NUHOFF (sic) to Katharina STRAUB - October 6, 1857, by Fr. George Tuerk.
Jacob BAER, born Canton Aragon, Community of Neider Wyl, Switzerland, to Elizabeth LEONARD,

widow of Jacob ZIMMERLEY, likewise born Canton Aragon, Community of Breteman, Switzerland - December 12, 1857, by Charles BEHNE, J. P..

Julius Albert SCHAEFER to Wilhelmine KULMAN - October 27, 1857, by Charles NESTEL, M. G..

Gustav BURCKHARDT to Emma KEHR - November 1, 1857, by Charles NESTEL, M. G..

John GRAFAUD (sic) to Adelheid CAPPELLE - January 17, 1858, by Charles NESTEL, M. G..

James A. ROBERTSON to Nancy HARRIS - December 6, 1857, by Kasten BUSCHMAN, J. P..

John D. MURPHY to Culperny ROGERS - February 18, 1858, by Benjamin LEACH, M. G..

Robert J. DAVIS of Johnson County, to Mary A. HILDEBRAN - March 7, 1858, by L. M. MAHANEY, M. G..

Linzey J. GREENSTREET to Malinda A. BRILS - March 17, 1858, by R. W. READ, M. G..

Frederick William DILTHEY, son of Matthias DELTHY and his wife, Catherine STOCK, formerly of Ueberdorff, Prussia to Barbara KUHN, born at Hambach, Germany, daughter of Francis George KUHN - January 10, 1858, by Charles BEHNE, J. P..

Bernhard HAGEDORN to Wilhelmina WEIPAL, widow of ECKHARDT, dec'd. - March 1, 1858, by Charles BEHNE, J. P..

Christian MEYER to Caroline HAUP - January 28, 1858, by Julius HUNDHAUSEN, J. P..

Anton MARX to Eva SCHWEIGHAUSER - January 31, 1858, Julius HUNDHAUSEN, J. P..

Frederick GABLER to Wilholmina RONNEBERGER - March 7, 1858, by Joel HUNDHAUSEN, J. P..

WEsley TIPPET to Elizabeth Jane RAY - June 25, 1857, by Thomas F. CLARY, J. P..

Hughey HUGHS to Matilda EBBERT - July 12, 1857, by Thomas F. CLARY, J. P..

Robert A. HEATH to Martha Jane LEVI - August 12, 1857, by Thomas F. CLARY, J. P..

Christian BECKMAN to S_____ EBERLIN - February 7, 1858, by Charles NESTEL, M. G..

Charles Frederic REIFSTECK to Joan Wilhelmine Amalia HECKELBOLDT - March 28, 1858, by Charles NESTEL, M. G..

Frederick August OBERMEIER to Lina KUHLEMANN - April 7, 1858, by Charles NESTEL, M. G..

Henry SCHMIDT to Rosina SCHIMPF - April 18, 1858, by Charles NESTEL, M. G..
Valantine ROGERS to Elizabeth GIBSON - March 24, 1858, by Joseph H. BARBARICK, J. P..
William ZAHL to Angelica ISDOUP (sic) - May 2, 1858, by Jonathan ROOK, J. P..
William NOGDT (sic) to Amelia POMMER - May 31, 1858, by Joseph LEPEL, J. P..
John L. HUFFMAN to Catherine REED - May 9, 1857, by John SULLINS, J. P..
John Adam ENGLERT to Mary Eva ZIGLER - May 27, 1858, by Fr. George TUERK.
Adam BICKEL to Mary KUCK - May 27, 1858, by Fr. George TUERK.
Drury LEE to Susan BAXTER - June 27, 1857, by Joseph PERRYMAN, M. G..
Robert M. RICHARDSON to Mary M. HALVEY - June 2, 1858, by R. W. READ, M. G..
Simon STORK to Florintine NOLLTING - February 10, 1858, by J. H. SCHAIBLE, M. G..
Frederick PRIP to Wilhelmina REHMI - May 5, 1858, by J. H. SCHAIBLE, M. G..
August THOPERN to Louisa ROLLFING - filed July 8, 1858, by J. H. SCHAIBLE, M. G., at the home of Frederick PRIP.
Jackson SMITH to Mary MATHEWS - June 27, 1858, by Benjamin LEACH, M. G..
Morgan ALLEN to Laura M. STAFFORD - March 28, 1858, by James GRISWELL, M. G..
L. W. L. WYATT to Amanda M. DOUGLAS - July 28, 1858, S. G. TREIVER, J. P..
Peter MUELLER to Rosalia NIEDERMEIER - July 5, 1858, by Fr. George TUERK.
John SHORNIWAUD (sic) to Fransciska SCHYGUDIA - July 15, 1858, by Fr. George TUERK.
Julius MAHAN to Susana JNO (sic) - September 8, 1858, by Fr. George TUERK.
Jacob MAEAR to Natalina SCHIEDECKER - June 28, 1858, by Jonathan ROOK, J. P..
Daniel A. KEFER to Amanda STUMP - March 25, 1858, by Lewis W. MURPHY, teaching elder, Christian Church.
Jacob KECH to Mrs. Rebekka MANN - August 30, 1858, by C. BEK, M. G..
William TAYLOR to Catherine HOLT - October 21, 1858, by Francis SULLIVAN, J. P..

John PRUIT to Phebe WATSON - August 5, 1858, by John T. DAVIS, M. G..
Benjamin F. JOHNSON to Maria GIBSON - September 1, 1858, by Joseph N. AROUTT, M. G..
William R. BRANSON to Martha COLEMMAN - September 23, 1858, by John R. DAVID, M. G..
George APRIL to Francesca ERNST - October 5, 1858, by Fr. George TUERK.
Adam POTTER to Dorothea MAKEL (sic) - October 11, 1858, by Alexander H. DEPP, J. P..
George MILLER to Jane WARDEN - November 8, 1858, Alexander H. DEPP, J. P., in the presence of Wiley WARDEN and James FRENCH.
Frederick WEIDEMAN to Amanda LINDEMAN - November 19, 1858, by Edward ROMANENSKI, M. G..
Henry William WEIDEMAN to Mary RUPRECHT - October 29, 1858, by Edward ROMANENSKI, M. G..
Franz Wilhelm DORMAN to Henriette BRANDENBURGER - August 26, 1858, by Edward ROMANENSKI, M. G..
William D. BALEY to Zerilda HUFFMAN - November 4, 1858, by J. W. ROOK, J. P..
William FOURT to Esther HOPTEN - November 8, 1858, by Benjamin LEACH, M. G..
Friedrick Wilhelm HEIDEBRINK to Anna Friedericka MEIER - December 10, 1858, by Edward ROMANEMSKI, M. G..
David E. KETCHUM to Margaret A. CHAPMAN - December 1, 1858, by John SULLINS, J. P..
John R. SHIVERS (sic) to Cyntha Elizabeth SULLENS November 9, 1858.
Frederick DRUVEL (sic) to Catherine HORSTMAN - October 6, 1858, by C. NESTEL, M. G..
Ethridge SCHMIDT to Elizabeth MICHEL - November 7, 1858, by C. NESTEL, M. G..
John SMITH to Catherine NEARM (sic) - January 15, 1859, by Thos. E. POWELL, J. P..
Charles RUTS to Mary Ann REED (sic) - November 26, 1858, by Henry SMITH, J. P..
Joseph SMITH to Arabella CARVER - December 5, 1858 at the house of Eben PUTMAN, by H. BENNER, J. P..
William JENNINGS to Nancy REAVES - January 2, 1859, by Alexander H. DEPP, J. P..
Laban K. FORD to Amelia SMITH - October 6, 1858, by Joel HUNDHAUSEN, J. P..
John Henry HOEHN (sic) to Mrs. Wilhelmina

Charlotte KRASK - December 19, 1858, by Joel HUNDHAUSEN, J. P..
William ADAM to Catherine GREULICK - December 26, 1858, by Joel HUNDHAUSEN, J. P..
John BRANNER to Helena NAAS - February 22, 1859, by Joel HUNDHAUSEN, J. P..
Melchier SCHINDLER to Mrs. Christina KOPP - March 2, 1859, by Joel HUNDHAUSEN, J. P..
John BECKER to Minnie TOBBE (sic) - August 9, 1857, by Joel HUNDHAUSEN, J. P..
Jacob LUTHY to Mrs. Anna NOLTE - May 6?, 1858, by Joel HUNDHAUSEN, J. P..
Jacob COLLING to Elizabeth EHRLING, EMMONS by birth - May 24, 1858, by Joel HUNDHAUSEN, J. P..
Melchier PORSCHEL to Mrs. Johanna HEINICKE - June 6, 1858, by Joel HUNDHAUSEN, J. P..
Adam SCHARFENBERGER to Mrs. Maria KREUTJER - June 6, 1858, by Joel HUNDHAUSEN, J. P..
Lorenz STRAUB to Amalie FRANKE - October 3, 1858, by Joel HUNDHAUSEN, J. P..
Comad (sic) LUHRING to Dorthea Louise KAHLE - February 25, 1859, by Edw. ROMANENSKI, M. G..
Frederic GAITZNER to Maria E. BESNER - March 9, 1859, by Joseph LEPEL, J. P..
Ferdinand ZEITZ to Kemigard STRAUB - December 24, 1858.
Prestly H. JOHNSON of Franklin County, to Cynthia MAUPIN - February 3, 1859, by L. M. MAHANEY, M. G..
Frederic W. SLINKMAN to Nancy LINCOLN - January 20, 1859, by John SULLINS, J. P..
Albert BOCK to Henrietta BOCK - January 18, 1859, by F. DREWEL, M. G..
Louis TAMUSCH to Auguste KUSCHER - March 10, 1859, F. DREWEL, M. G..
Karl RUEGGER to Caroline BINKMAN - March 8, 1859, by F. DREWEL, M. G..
Frederick STEEN to Martha THOMPSON - February 22, M 1859, by Benjamin LEACH, M. G..
Thomas ALPTON (sic) to Mrs. Lucinda THOMAS - March 14, 1859, by Benjamin LEACH, M. G..
James HAMMOCK to Lydia Jane BRAY, both of Franklin County - April 8, 1859, by Charles BEHME, J. P..
William SAWYERS to Mary Ann CARTER - March 15,

1859, by Andrew P. COWAN, J. P..
Henry METTENDORF to Louisa COLYER, born SKYLES - February 27, 1859, by Kasten BUSCHMAN, J. P..
Joh Hermann TEGGE to Elizabeth LINNEMANN - April 19, 1859, by F. DREWEL, M. G..
Simon MARSCHNER (sic) to Mary C. RASCHE - April 11, 1859, by Charles BEHME, J. P..
Alonzo B. COOPER to Betty STORY of Woodford County, Illinois - April 29, 1859, by Charles BEHME, J. P..
George M. FARRIS to Amanda RICHARDSON - April 24, 1859, by William P. DOUGLASS, J. P..
James SMITH to Eliza Ann REYNOLDS - April 24, 1859, by Wesley MASIE, J. P..
Alois BICKY to Caroline NOLTE - May 14, 1859, by W. SCHRECK, M. G..
Wilhelm HOBERIN to Mine LANGENBORY - September 8, 1859, by J. G. SCHAIBLE, M. G..
August REMART to Wilhelmina SCHAFERKETTER - December 22, 1858, by J. G. SCHAIBLE, M. G..
Henry Henrich STORK to Amalia Sophie Justine BUHLEMEYER - February 2, 1859, by J. G. SCHAIBLE, M. G., at the house of Herman STORK in Osage County.
Conrad RUGGER to Henriette BELLINGHAUSE - March 15, 1859, by J. G. SCHAIBLE, M. G..
Christoph BINKER to Hanna Frederika BEYER - April 19, 1859, by J. G. SCHAIBLE, M. G..
Franz KEHR to Henriette WESEMAN - May ?, 1859, by J. G. SCHAIBLE, M. G..
Jacob ROST to Eva Margaretha SCHRAM - March 12, 1859, by Joel HUNDHAUSEN, J. P..
John Michael HEINNEBERGER to Louise RICK - April 24, 1859, by Joel HUNDHAUSEN, M. G..
Joseph SIEDLER to Anna BIERS - June 13, 1859, by Joel HUNDHAUSEN, J. P..
James A. BLEVINS to Sarah E. SCANTLIN (sic) - April 28, 1859, by Samuel DUVAULT, J. P..
John B. HINTON to Sultana COLWELL - April 14, 1859, by Joseph PERRYMAN, M. G..
John W. JENNINGS to Elizabeth EDDELMAN - April 17, 1859, by Joseph PERRYMAN, M. G..
Martin SCHAMNBURGER to Bertha HOFER - April 17, 1859, by Charles NESTEL, M. G..
John MUTSCHENBACH to Eva Mary SIEFERT - June 9, 1859, by Charles NESTEL, M. G..

Henry FRITZEMEIER to Lisette HOFER - July 2, 1859, by Charles NESTEL, M. G..

John RILEY to Martha Ann EDMANSON - June 15, 1859, by Wm. SPURGIN, J. P..

John George BRENNER to Mary NAUPER (sic) - May 20, 1859, by B. MUNDEWEILLER, J. P..

John Henry DANHAUSER to Caroline REIFSTOECK - June 26, 1859, by Joel HUNDHAUSEN, J. P..

Freiderich BACKER to Anna STEINER - August 23, 1859, by Freid. HUNDHAUSEN, M. G..

William C. MONGUMERY to Nancy E. WHEAT - July 10, 1859, by William R. DOUGLASS, J. P..

Samuel BURCHARD to Marann JARVIS - July 19, 1859, by William R. DOUGLAS, J. P..

Herman MYER to Amy Mary BITTER - July 8, 1859, by J. W. ROOK, J. P..

Philipe POPE to Rachael B. HALVEY - August 3, 1859, by Robert READ, M. G..

James KERLY to Jane HENSLEY - August 28, 1859, by Kasten BUSCHMAN, J. P..

Gabriel FAN to Marian HARTMAN - July 9, 1859, by John P. DAVIS.

Freiderich Wilhelm FRISCHE to Caroline RODER - July 14, 1859.

Henry LANGENBERG to Louise HOLBEIN - August 14, 1859, by J. G. SCHAIBLE, M. G..

Heinrich NOLTE to Anna Martha HORMBURG - July 22, 1859, by J. G. SCHAIBLE, M. G..

Jas. Wilhelm KEHLENBRINK to Johanna Augusta KLICK - July 8, 1859, by Freid. DRUWELL, M. G..

Solomon KEFFLER to Ruby Jane HEADDRICH - September 15, 1859, by Lewis W. MURPHY, Elder.

Charles SPECKALS to Katharine NORDMANN - August 23, 1859, by Fr. George TUERK.

George SOUDERS to Caroline GARNER - August 4, 1859, by Henry BUNNER, J. P..

Jasper N. HENKEL to Louisa RIDENHOUR - August 8, 1859, by Henry SOUDERS, J. P., at the house of Susanna RIDENHOUR.

Patrick McCARTY of Osage County, to Anna DUNNSMORE - September 14, by Charles BEHNE, J. P..

John Charles WOERT, born at Buckore, Mecklenburg Schwirin, Germany, to Emily LEPEL, daughter of Joseph LEPEL, dec'd. - September 21, 1859, by Charles BEHNE, J. P..

William PRYER to Martha JACKSON - September 22, 1859, by Benjamin LEECH, M. G..
Christian ENNDER to Sarah WISEMAN - October 9, 1859, by Benjamin LEECH, M. G..
August RICK to Anna WEBER - November 11, 1859, by Joel HUNDHAUSEN, J. P..
Charles Willilam HETTICH to Carolina ROMMEL - October 25, 1859, by Joel HUNDHAUSEN, J. P..
Stephen W. LACY to Caroline LUSTER - September 11, 1859, by William R. DOUGLASS, J. P..
Louis TAMSCH to Auguste KUSCHEL - March 10, 1859, by Fred DREWELL, M. G..
John Christian BOHL (sic) to Ernestine KAMP - September 9, 1859, by Fred. DREWEL, M. G..
Herman EDMENSTEIN to Betta KANSCHELBACH - November 23, 1859, by Freid. HUNDHAUSEN, M. G..
Wilhelm DORMANN to Louise TOPPE - November 20, 1859, by Fred. DREWELL, M. G..
Thomas B. LUSTER to Sarah Jane TOPPE - November 20, 1859, by Fried DREWEL, M. G..
Thomas H. E. ROBERTSON to Sarah A. FINDALL - December 8, 1859.
Joseph BIEBER to Magdalena MEYER - November 11, 1859, by B. MUNDWELLER, J. P..
James SPURGIN to Maria C. BLEVIN - September 8, 1821, by John T. DAVIS, M. G..
John M. MITCHEL to Louisa J. HINTIN - November 9, 1859, by John T. DAVIS, M. G..
William M. CAAR to Louisa J. TAYLOR - November 9. 1859, by John T. DAVIS, M. G..
Joseph LICKLIDER to Sarah E. JACKSON - November 24, 1859, by John T. DAVIS, M. G..
Granville REYNOLDS to Ruthy Jane COOPER - October 20, 1859, by Jos. H. BARBARICK, J. P..
Henry ROUPET to Ruthy ROUPET - December 15, 1859, by Wesley MASIE, J. P..
Burton ROBERSON to Nelly HENSLEY - December 25, 1859, by W. A. COOPER, J. P..
Riley ROBERSON to Martha ADAMS - November 11, 1859, by W. A. COOPER, J. P..
Anton BROTT to Charlotte SCHAFERKETTER - October 28, 1859, by John G. SCHAIBLE, M. G..
John J. CAULT to Susan Jane GIBSON - October 20, 1859, by Elder Lewis W. MURPHY.
Carl FISCHER to Elizabeth WEBER - January 17, 1860, by Fried HUNDHAUSEN, M. G..

Casper SCHUBERT to Louise LINK - October 30, 1859, by Fr. George TUERK.

Jack WEIDMANN to Margaretha ENGEL - January 27, 1860, by Freid. HUNDHAUSEN, M. G..

Franz August KELLER to Louis SCHULTZ - November 4, 1859, by Charles NESTEL, M. G..

Johann George SEIFERT to Rosine Christine HOFFMANN - January 12, 1860, by Charles NESTEL, M. G..

George C. ROBINSON to Mary MASON - January 26, 1860, by Samuel G. TROWER, J. P..

Elija J. ROGERS to Rhoda SULLIVAN - November 20, 1859, by Wm. R. DOUGLASS, J. P..

Nicolaus KUHN to Hannah GAUS - January 15, 1860, by Andreas HOFFMANN, J. P..

August BUDDE (sic) to Parley BROWN - January 10, 1860, by Kasten BUSCHMANN, J. P..

Joseph REYNOLDS to Melvina ROOK - December 25, 1859, by John SULLINS, J. P..

Joseph COLTER (sic) to Emily E. ADAMS - November 23, 1859, by John SULLINS, J. P..

John H. WHITE to Jane TALON - December 8, 1859, by Henry SONDERS (sic), J. P..

John MUSKRAT to Welberga HAZLER - December 29, 1859, by J. PERRYMAN, M. G..

Nicolas MARTIN to Louisa LIETHER - February 11, 1860, by Freid. HUNDHAUSEN, M. G..

Joel REED to Lydia BRANSON - February 21, 1860, by Joshua W. ROOK, J. P..

Edmon C. GIBONS to Martha Ann McMILLIN - February 21, 1859, by Elder L. M. MAHANEY.

Birnhard MULLER to Berta Adelheid HASENRITTER - March 15, 1860, by Freid. HUNDHAUSEN, M. G..

Phillip STAPLETON to Orpha E. COLEMAN - December 11, 1859, by Samuel DUVAULT, J. P..

Samuel P. HUNTER of Osage County, to the widow Catherina M. MENAPANA (sic) - March 12, 1860, by George KLINGER, J. P..

William GARNER to Susan HIMES - January 6, 1860, by Henry SOUDERS, J. P..

George KREAMER to Caroline HINCHE - March 21, 1860, by Freid. HUNDHAUSEN, M. G..

Phillip KELLER to Louise MAIER - January 18, 1860, by Chr. BECK, M. G..

William M. SCOTT of Morgan County, to Sarah SHERMAN - April 11, 1860, by George KLINGE,

J. P..
John BANER to Elizabeth SCHMIDT - April 22, 1840, by George KLINGE, J. P..
David TURNER to Mary VAUGHAN - April 12, 1860, by B. LEACH, M. G..
William BOWEN to Martha T. EATON - April 15, 1860, by B. LEACH, M. G..
Isaiah HAYS to Mary E. SNYDER - April 16, 1860, by H. BENNER, J. P..
Victor SCHEIDECKER to Magdalena BODEN - April 7, 1860, by B. MUNDWELLER, J. P..
Enoch MAUPIN to Charity MATTOCKS - March 22, 1860, by Joshua W. ROOK, J. P..
Jacob D. SCHIEFER to Ellemine SCHIEFER - December 1, 1857, by W. V. SCHUACH. This certificate was issued by the circuit court of Scott County, Iowa.
Wilhelm BUKER to Sophia Cattrine RETEMEYER (sic) - May 3, 1860, by John G. GRANNEMAN, M. G..
Frank Anton WATTRON to Maria REBSAMEN (sic) - May 31, 1860, by Charles LANDBERG, J. P..
Freiderick Ludwig MULLER to Mrs. Johanne CORDSMEIER, born NEISMEGE - March 4, 1860 by Charles NESTEL, M. G..
Michael WELTING to widow Catharine GRAF — June 11, 1860, by George KING, J. P..
Lewis G. WRIGHT to Rebecca Jane STEPENSON - June 6, 1860, by Robert J. HEATH, J. P..
Archie CARROLL to Nancy Jane GIBSON - April 17, 1860, by John DUNBAR, J. P..
John P. NELSON to Elizabeth STERLING - May 2, 1860, by John DUNBAR, J. P..
August DEPPE to Maria EIKELSMANN - May 15, 1860, by Freid. DREWEL, M. G..
Wilhelm WEHMUELTOS (sic) to Wilhelmina GASTMANN - June 9, 1860, by Freid. DREWELL, M. G..
Jacob HAMELTON to Margaret REED - September 26, 1860, by John DURBIN, J. P..
Frederich NOLTE to Louise SCHLOEMER - September 22, 1860, by Gerhard TIMKEN, M. G..
Joseph NAUGH of Crawford County, to Nancy E. SOUDERS - October 25, 1860, by Elder Lewis W. MURPHY.
James M. HIATTE to Lucy A. COULTER - October 18, 1860, by Wesley MASIE, J. P..
John MEYER to Wilhelmina BEUERMAN - October 29,

1860, by Wesley MASIE, J. P..
Zacharia BELT to Evaline JOHNSTON - November 9, 1860, by Thos. F. CLARY, J. P..
William LUTON to Mary MILLIGAN - January 8, 1860, by Thos. F. CLARY, J. P..
John MUNSEL to Sophia BOCK - September 16, 1860, by Thos. F. CLARY, J. P..
Ausley SATTERFIELD to Lura Ordela PIDRERK (sic) - September 9, 1860, by William SPURGIN, J. P..
George STECK to Caroline BAIER - September 25, 1860, by Charles NESTEL, M. G..
Franz ONEKEN to Amanda DOZON - October 15, 1860, by Charles NESTEL, M. G..
Henry WALDECKER to Maria Chatharina PETERS - October 20, 1860, by J. G. SCHAIBLE, M. G..
Jacob KUHN to Barbara SCHAFER - December 6, 1860, by Fried. HUNDHAUSEN, M. G..
Franz KUHN to Maria Joppha TARBER - December 6, 1860, by Fried. HUNDHAUSEN, M. G..
William J. FARIS to Martha Ann LUSTER - December 5, 1860, by Lewis W. MURPHY.
Franz KLAUS to Therese KERMANN (sic) - October 22, 1860, by Fr. George TUERK.
John DOULAN (sic) to Regina WINDOLPH _ December 4, 1860, by Fr. George TUERK.
Eligha OWENS to Eliza J. SHOCKLEY - October 20, 1860, by Jos. H. BARBARICK, J. P..
Isaiah SHOCKLEY to Rachel CRIDER - December 27, 1860, by Jos. H. BARBARICK, J. P..
Wilhelm JOACHEM to Elizabeth REEFO (sic) of Osage County - November 11, 1860, by John GRANNEMAN, M. G..
Francis EVARED to Miss Sylvester D. MATHAEWS - November 19, 1860, by Benjamin LEACH, M. G..
Theron E. WILKERSON to Sarah E. WALTON - NOvember 23, 1860, by Benjamin LEACH, M. G..
Franklin COOPER to Prissilly MATTOCK - December 9, 1860, by Benjamin LEACH, M. G..
Jacob RIDENHOUR to Martha HOLT - December 30, 1860, by Lewis M. MURPHY.
Johnlow RICHARDSON to Elizabeth COOPER - November 1, 1860, by J. PERRYMAN, M. G..
John LAURIE to Margaret ALLENE - January 24, 1861, by Benjamin LEACH, M. G..
William M. SPALLDING to Elizabeth A. LUCAS - February 4, 1861, by R. W. REED, M. G..

Charles RIEK to Wilhelmina TULK - June 24, 1860, by Julious HUNDHAUSEN, J. P..

Clinton CATWELL to Nancy ADAMS - April 12, 1860, by Wesley MASIE, J. P..

August SCHEIDIGGER to Mrs. Anna Maria ERNY (sic) - July 12, 1860, by Julious HUNDHAUSEN, J. P..

Benjamin KERLEY to Jane PRYOR - July 14, 1860, Kasten BUSCHMAN, J. P..

Francis M. OLIVER to Mary GLENN - April 22, 1860, by Samuel DAVAULT, J. P..

John Frederick WEIGEMAN to Dorothea BREDEHORST - January 22, 1860, by John SCHIBLE, M. G..

William NUMWALD to Wilhelmina SCHREYMAN (sic) - February 18, 1860, by John SCHIBLER, at the home of Christopher SCHREYMAN.

Christop STRASS to Dorothea KOHLAGE - April 12, 1860, by John SCHIBLER, M. G., at the home of Freiderick BLANKE.

Christian BECKER of Callaway County, to Veronica TULYER - June 21, 1860, by John SCHIBLER, M. G., at the home of Henry TULYER.

Carl WEHKING to Amelia HELD - July 9, 1860, by John SHIBLER, M. G, at the home of Bernhard HELD.

Isaac C. MATHEWS to Lucinda E. SMITH - July 12, 1860, by Benjamin LEACH, M. G..

W. F. HAMBY to Elizabeth NAUGHS - June 3, 1860, by H. BENNE, J. P..

James M. ADAMS to Charlotty NEAL - June 7, 1860, by Elder L. M. MAHANEY.

M. C. WILKINSON to Mary I. WALTON - September 4, 1860, by Benjamin LEACH, M. G..

John NUGLE to Malinda J. HEDRICK - September 2, 1860, by Henry SOUDERS, J. P., at the home of Samuel KEPPER.

Asbury SHOCKLEY to Emanda MATHEWS _ September 6, 1860, by Jos. H. BARBARICK, J. P..

William F. MENNAHOUSE to Emeline KINNAMEN - August 19, 1860, by Samuel G. TROVER, J. P..

Louis BETHEMEYER to Sophie FREDERICKS of Franklin County - August 9, 1860, by Gerhard TIMKER, M. G..

Simon RUGGE to Wilhelmine BRINKMANS - June 26, 1860, by Fried. DREWEL, M. G..

Richard LUCY to Phebe I. (no surname) - September 6, 1860, by Sam'l DAVAULT, J. P..

Araen (sic) CHAICKE to Mary RICHARDSON - recorded September 12, 1860, by F. RABERTTSON, M. G..

Paul SCHMITT to Anna Mariea STRAHENER - September 15, 1860, by George KLINGE, J. P..

Heinrich Wilhelme POTTIY to Anna Coneadina Hermina WONNEL - April 29, 1860, by Johann P. WELSCHE, M. G..

Heinrich MEIER to Wilhelmina BITTER, widow of Frederick Wilhelm MEIER - March 11, 1860, by Johann P. WELSCH, M. G..

Herman ECKERMAN to Gitte DEPPE - September 28, 1860, by Henry AMELING, J. P..

John W. LUSTER to Sirina E. McWILLIAMS - August 23, 1860.

William McKINSIE to Eliza POWELL July 25, 1860, by John DURBIN, J. P..

John T. LEACH to Harriet E. MATTOCKS - December 20, 1860, by John SULLINS, J. P..

Fritz HINE to Rebecca HOLANDSWORTH - January 14, 1861, by Elder L. M. MAHANEY.

Henry J. STEVENS of Franklin County, to Lucindy SULLIVAN - February 7, 1861, by Elder L. M. MAHANEY.

John Alexander GEABER to Maryan FORREST - November 13, 1860, by William SPURGIN, J. P..

P. H. DICKASON to Virginia JACKSON - December 23, 1860, by John T. DAVIS, M. G..

M. Livingston WILLIAMSON to Christina BIERLY - February 2, 1861, by Robert S. HEEDT (sic), J. P..

R. W. ROMANOWSKE to Rebecca ROBISON - February 7, 1861, by Elder Lewis M. MURPHY.

H. A. GROF to Elizabeth Luscinde LEE - January 21, 1861, by A. VANDER LIPPE, M. G..

Robert F. PRYOR to Mahele SCHOCKLEY - December 2, 1860, by Henry ARUELING, J. P..

Benjamin R. MATHEWS to Belinda CRIDER - January 15, 1861, by Jos. H. BARBARICK, J. P..

Henry H. BENNECKE to Elizabeth JARVIS - February 24, 1861, by Benjamin LEACH, M. G..

Carafree (sic) HASEFELE to Emily Ann McMILLIAN - February 27, 1861, by Henry F. ROBERTSON, M. G..

Charles RITTER to Wilhelmine BIELMEYER - March 5, 1861, by A. VANDER LIPPE, M. G..

Frederick BIELMEYER to Caroline BUNTE - March 5,

1861, by A. VANDER LIPPE, M. G..
Samuel FISCHER to Johanne BECK - December 30, 1861, by Charles NESTEL, M. G..
Julius Henrich LYRUNA (sic) to Sarah Adelhaed GODIER, born VOLD - January 2, 1861, by Charles NESTEL, M. G..
Christian FLEISCH to Maria CHRISTEO, born GOTZ - February 7, 1861, by Charles NESTEL, M. G..
Bernhard STRALLNER to Franziska CHRISTMAN - April 1, 1861, by Fried HUNDHAUSEN, M. G..
Johann BUBER to Pauline VOGT - April 10, 1861, by Fried HUNDHAUSEN, M. G..
F. T. BRAND to Maria NEHMEIER - February 15, 1861, by Freid DREWEL, M. G..
Carl WALKE (sic) to Wilhelmina STONNER - March 26, 1861, by Freid DREWEL, M. G..
James HALL to Susanna BLOOK - April 14, 1861, by Freid HUNDHAUSEN, M. G..
Frederich Wilhelm ROHLFING to Christine MARIE - February 7, 1861, by Chr. BEK, M. G..
Henry WALDECKER to Maria Charlotte Catharina PETERS - October 26, 1860, by John SCHAIBLE, M. G..
Carl SAPHNEANSHAUSEN (sic) to Caroline BRANDHOLT - February 10, 1861, by John SCHAIBLE, M. G..
Frederick RUTHIP to Louise RITTERBUSH - March, 1861, by John SCHAIBLE, at the house of Frederick FISCHER.
Henry PETERS to Catherina Henriette ____well - April 1, 1861, by John G. SCHAIBLE, M. G..
Andreas HOFFMAN to Mina BOGE - April 3, 1861, by J. G. SCHAIBLE, M. G..
Friedrich WITTE to Caroline LANDWEHR - April 16, 1861, by J. G. SCHAIBLE, M. G..
Samuel LEE to Elise Welhelmina HOBISN - May 2, 1861, by J. G. SCHAIBLE, M. G..
Ernest HECK to Katharine MUTGEN - June 7, 1861, by Thomas F. CLARY, J. P..
James M. PULLAM (sic) to Mary J. DEWITT - May 25, 1861, by Elder Lewis M. MURPHY.
John M. RITCHEY to Emily A. JONES - April 2, 1861, by J. C. RITCHEY, M. G..
Michael TEULLINGSR to Elizabeth BOCE - May 25, 1861, by Joseph KESSLER, J. P..
Ludwig KLEE to Christina HENNEBERG - June 23, 1861, by Fried HUNDHAUSEN, M. G..

Friederich BINDE to Pauline MICHE - April 7, 1861, by John B. MICHE, J. P..
John METGLER to Mary ANDREE - May 25, 1861, by John B. MICHE, J. P..
Nicholus ELZOLD to Louise KROBER - April 15, 1861, by Charles NESTEL, M. G..
Louis HAAN to Katharina MEIER - May 19, 1861, by Fr. George TUERK.
Gottfried KOPPE to Elizabeth HAIREL - May 27, 1861, by Fr. George TUERK.
Peter NEUMAN to Caroline FRATTE - July 16, 1861, by Fr. George TUERK.
John NEIDHART to Elizabeth KLANS - August 13, 1861.
Louis RLAUS to Charlott ALBERT - August 13, 1861.
Joseph FINGLANG to Mina VOGLSANG - August 20, 1861, by George KLUNKE.
Henry KEHR to Auguste PLASKE - September 29, 1861, by Fried HUNDHAUSEN, M. G..
Henry FLEHE to Johanna B_____ (illegible) - September 13, 1861, by Chr. BEK, M. G..
Christopher DREWEL to Louise STOPPLEMAN - October 8, 1861, by Chr. BEK, M. G..
Wilhelm LANGENBERG to Louise MAYER - May 16, 1861, by J. G. SCHAIBLE, M. G..
Friederick LINKE to Henriette MELISS - August 1, 1861, by J. G. SCHAIBLE.
Simon NOLLING of Osage County, to Caroline SCHNEIDEWING - August 1, 1861, by J. SCHAILBE.
William COLIN to Louisa Jane EAGLIN - October 25, 1861, by Elder Lewis M. MURPHY.
Thomas H. ROBISON to Louisa ATKINS - July 18, 1861, by J. McKNIGHT, M. G..
Friederick ROTHKEN to Wilhelmine SILBERMAN - July 17, 1861.
Henry NEHEMEIER to Anna M. E. WINTER - November 4, 1861, by Henry HERMAN, M. G..
James MASON to Caroline MORGAN - December 3, 1861, by Frances SULLIVAN, J. P.. Witnesses were Jesse MELTON, Charles AUGEL, and Jesse LEEPER.
Briednich HENRICHS to Caroline W. TAPPE, widow - December 9, 1861, by Kasten BUSHMAN, J. P..
George SORRELL to Jane BRICE - December 5, 1861, by W. S. FERGUSON, M. G..
David SATTERFIELD to Martha PITCOCK - December 5,

1861, by W. S. FERGUSON.
George W. JACKSON to Nancy J. MARNER - November 18, 1861, by Robert W. REED, M. G..
Lorenzo CARROL to Nancy Ann GLANDEN - December 24, 1861, by Robert W. REED, M. G..
Carl RUSCHEL to Louise BRANDENHORST - October 12, 1861, by Fried DREWEL, M. G..
John SERVING to Emily REMERT - December 24, 1861, by Fried DREWEL, M. G..
August FEMMER to Anna STOCKER - January 9, 1862, by John GRANNEMANN, M. G..
Ames H. ROWLEY to Nancy J. COWEN - December 29, 1861, by Thomas F. CLARY, J. P..
Edward H. KEHR to uniganda STEINMITZ - January 20, 1862, by Charles SANDBERG, J. P..
Anton LAUER to Elizabeth STEINMITZ - January 20, 1862, by Charles SANDBERG, J. P..
Xavier DUFFNER to Caroline MILLER - January 20, 1862, by Charles SANDBERG, J. P..
John LOCKHART to Catharine KOZAK - January 30, 1862, by Fr. Martin SEIST.
Weyzel ROSLIK to Mary KOZAK - January 30, 1862, by Fr. Martin SEIST.
John PRUIT to Hedwig AMDEON (sic) - June 5, 1861, by Samuel DAVAULT, J. P..
John BECK to Christina BUEL - January 17, 1862, by Thos. L. POWELL, J. P..
Richard HAYNES to Elizabeth SCHOCKLY - March 6, 1862, by Wm. R. DOUGLASS, J. P..
Simon BOGE of St. Louis, to Mrs. Charlotte PETERS, widow of J. H. PETERS - J. G. SCHAIBLE, M. G..
David SILLYMAN to Susan BROWN - February 18, 1862, by Benjamin LEACH, M. G..
Henry B. ANGLE to Malissa J. STEVENS - February 20, 1862, by Benjamin LEACH, M. G..
Joseph P. BROWN to Nancy E. THOMPSON - March 4, 1862, by Benjamin LEACH, M. G..
Heinrich MEPTEMAKER to Maria SCHULTE - January 29, 1862, by J. G. SCHAIBLE, M. G..
Charles SCHREIMANN to Louise LIEMKUHLER - March 6, 1862, Andrea HOFFMAN, M. G..
Christian GILLIG to Maria STEPHAN - April 8, 1862, by Kasten BUSCHMAN, J. P..
William Johnes SMITH to Elizabeth Jane COUN - May 1, 1862, by George KLINGE, J. P..

Charles Campbell MANNARING to Amalia KEILMAN - December 5, 1861, by Charles NESTEL, M. G..
August GRAIBE to Susanna IPLER - December 5, 1861, by Charles NESTEL, M. G..
Louis BURKERT to Louise Maria Catharina DETERLE (sic) - July 30, 1862, by Chr. BECK, M. G..
Carl KAPELL to Maria LUSTER - April 28, 1862, by Fried HUNDHAUSEN, M. G..
Albert JOHNS to Sarah Anne JARVIS - May 1, 1862, by John SULLINS, J. P..
Francis SIRE to Frances SMITH - April 14, 1862.
Albert NUTTY to Mary E. MILLER - recorded May 13, 1862, by William FERGUSON, M. G..
William D. C. RICHARDSON to Josephine W. RICHARDSON - April 28, 1862.
Jonathan RICHARDS to Martha Ann FRIZER - April 28, 1862, by R. W. READ, M. G..
John T. WALLACE to Eliza J. EDGAR - April 20, 1862, by Samuel DUVEULT, J. P..
Benjamin L. OLIVER to Elizabeth C. AGEE - September 4, 1861, by Samuel DUVEULT, J. P..
William C. MARGAIN to Celia MASON - March 6, 1862, by William McDANIEL, J. P..
Jonathan HOLLINGSWORTH to Sarrah Ann REED - April 20, 1862, by William McDANIEL, J. P..
William DAVIS to Malinda THOMAS - recorded May 15, 1862, by William McDANIEL, J. P..
Michael NICKERMAN to Maria VAGEL - recorded May 16, 1862, by T. TRUPE, M. G..
Abednego TAYLOR to Sarah Ann CONNNIR - April 6, 1862, by Elder Lewis MURPHY.
George TAYLOR to Amanda E. HINKLE - May 22, 1862, Elder Lewis MURPHY.
Lynard MANTZIS to Mari TEGE - March 12, 1862, by Fried HUNDHAUSEN, M. G..
Carl BRACHES to Bertha DORNER - June 21, 1862, by Fried HUNDHAUSEN, M. G..
Louis WACHTER to Mary WAUSEHUND - November 21, 1861, by John B. MICHE, J. P..
Christopher SIMENS to Dina KIRCHOFF - November 20, 1861, by John B. MICHE, J. P..
Jacob CARL to Franceska BUMMER - January 28, 1862, by John B. MICHE, J. P..
Heinrich KOENIG to Gesche Adelheid BOTTCHEL - June 23, 1862, by A. PICKER, M. G..
Heinrich REIDIGER to Theudere (sic) OETERER -

June 2, 1862, by Charles SANDBERG, J. P..
Aaron WILLIAMS to Hellena ESTU___ - September 4, 1862, by Benjamin LEACH, M. G..
Gustav BOCK to Augusta KUSCHEL - April 4, 1862, by F. DRAVEL, M. G..
John Diederich SRINK to Marie Fredericka MARER - May 8, 1862, by F. DRAVEL, M. G..
F. LINDEMANN to Louise WIEDEMANN - May 22, 1862, by F. DRAVEL, M. G..
Wilhelme WOLLEMADE toElizabeth WEDEKING - May 4, 1862, by Charles NESTEL, M. G..
Johann _IFFELMAN to Barbara SCHULER, born BRANSWORTH - May 13, 1862, by Charles NESTEL, M. G..
Emil KLEIN to Emelia HEINKE - June 12, 1862, by Charles NESTEL, M. G..
Herman KLAUS to Rosalia STEIGER - August 11, 1862, by F. RUPE, M. G..
Johanne HANS to Maria FISCHER - September 9, 1862, by F. RUPE, M. G..
George W. STEEN to Louisa Jane RILES - September 16, 1862.
Jacob BAUMGARTNER to Louisa ZIMMERLE - October 21, 1862, by Freid HUNHAUSEN, M. G..
Jeremiah CRAVENS to Martha E. McCOURTNEY - August 24, 1862.
Christopher DRICKER to Louisa STOCK, both of Osage County - September 28, 1862, by J. G. SCHAIBLE, M. G., at the house of Herman STOCK.
Hiram P. MEYERS to Sarah HIATTE - July 10, 1862, by John SULLINS, J. P..
Isaac W. ROOK to Sarah REYNOLDS - September 7, 1862, by John SULLINS, J. P..
Heinrich Johpst (sic) WEHMEIER to Anna Maria Hebrin WINTER - November 12, 1862, by Fred DREWELL, M. G..
Franz DORMAN to Anna Margaretha STADTHORDER - November 28, 1862, by Fred DREWEL, M. G..
John FOSTER of Franklin County, to Sarah Jane HUFFMAN - January 1, 1863, by John SULLINS, J. P..
George MULLER to Carolina VOGLER - February 17, 1863, by F. RUBE, M. G..
Heinrich LEMMER to Anna Marie SCHINDEL - March 8, 1863, by Fred HUNDHAUSEN, M. G..
Samuel D. CRIDER to Minerva HAINS - March 19, 1863, by Wanville REYNOLDS, J. P..

Anthony LATCAR to Rebecca MIDGATE - March 12, 1863, by Robert W. REED, M. G..
Henry GROTE to Mina GROTE - April 23, 1863, by A. VANDER LIPPE, M. G..
Herman BOUSING to Doris VOLIZEN - February 19, 1863, by Charles NESTEL, M. G..
Henreich ETHER to Catherina BENDER - March 26, 1863, Charles NESTEL, M. G..
August BECKMAN to Elizabetha DANUSER - June 2, 1862, by Charles NESTEL, M. G..
Ludwig KOESTER to Heinrietta BOHL - April 15, 1863, Fred DREWEL, M. G..
William W. BRANSON to Nancy E. GIVENS (sic) - June 4, 1863, by Granville REYNOLDS, J. P..
Joseph WILSON to Marthy J. THOMPSON - September 3, 1863, by Frederich B. CRIDER, J. P..
Galba E. BRANSON to Eliza B. COOPER - October 5, 1863, by Granville REYNOLDS, J. P..
Rudolf THIEPAN to Emma LENSING - October 6, 1863, by George KLINGE, J. P..
Johanne GLOTZ to Elizabeth APRIL - October 31, 1863, by F. KUPER, M. G..
Xaver HAVERSTOCK to Josephina SCHUK - October 26, 1863, by F. KUPER, M. G..
Godfried KOPPE to Mary Ursala VOGEL - October 26, 1863, by F. KUPER, M. G..
Bernard FINLAND to Regina SLEVE - October 27, 1863, by F. KUPER, M. G..
Adam FURBER to _lbina HESNER - October 25, 1863, by Charles SANDBERGER, J. P..
Anderson CHAPMAN to Amelia ADAMS - October 1, 1863, by Elder L. M. MAHANEY.
Isaiah BOWEN to Nancy AMBLER - October 11, 1863, by Robert W. REED, M. G..
Conrade HUMBURG to Mrs. Margaretha PFATENHAUR, born PHILLIPS - August 18, 1863, by Charles NESTEL, M. G..
Johann Heinrich DAMME to Louise Charlotte PANDE - August 19, 1863, by Charles NESTEL, M. G..
Heinrich Louis HOCKMAN to Wilhelmina Justine KOTTER - October 25, 1863.
Robert MICHEL to Maria PHILLIP - October 24, 1863, by C. BEK, M. G..
M. W. COLLIER to Susan FANNON, both of Franklin County - July 13, 1863, by John B. MICHE, J. P..

Peter RAY to Julia Ann LANE, both of Franklin County - August 5, 1863, by John B. MICHE, J. P..

Charles SCHROEDER to Bertha KELLER - September 13, 1863, by John B. MICHE, J. P..

Jacob HABLER to Katharina KAUFMAN of Cole County - November 4, 1863, by John B. MICHE, J. P..

Elisha HOLLANDSWORTH to Betty M. THOMAS - July 2, 1863, by Benjamin LEACH, M. G..

Albert PETERS to Mathilda Cecilia PUCHTA - December 13, 1863, by John B. MICHE, J. P..

Franklin B. MATTOCKS to Lucy KINKEAD - November 26, 1863, by Elder L. M. MAHANEY.

Franklin HODGES to Margaret M. DANIEL - December 20, 1863, by Jonathan W. ROOK, J. P..

Jacob RICHARD to Nelly PRYOR - October 8, 1863, by William MEYER, J. P..

Edward BUCHER to Martha WINN - December 12, 1863, by William MEYER, J. P..

Francis VOTAW to Maria VOTAW, widow - March 17, 1864, by George VILINGE, J. P..

William H. WARREN to Hannah DEWITT - March 17, 1863, by Elder Lewis W. MURPHY.

Michael WEDLING (sic) to Anna WERLI - January 26, 1861, by B. MUNDWILLER (sic), J. P..

Louis PASCHEL to Maria STRICKER - January 17, 1863, by Charles NESTEL, M. G..

Rev. Otto NIETHAMMER to Sophia HEISE - Janeuary 21, 1863, by Charles NESTEL, M. G..

Conrad SCHUCK to Anna EMI (sic) - February 3, 1863, by Charles NESTEL, M. G..

Carl BOING to Elizabeth LIMMULE - April 4, 1863, by Charles NESTEL, M. G..

John TAYLOR to Clara HORN - February 18, 1863, by William H. CONNA (sic), J. P..

Thomas C. HOLLINGSWORTH to Charlotte ROSE - February 1, 1863, by Jonathan W. ROOK, J. P..

Anton APRIL to Scharlotta KLAUS - December 8, 1863, by F. RUPE, M. G..

John HORSFELT to Ellen WHITE - July 12, 1863, by James COLLIER, J. P..

Baptist VOGEL to Catherine WEBER - December 28, 1863, by J. B. MICHE, J. P..

Carl VOGEL to June CRAIG, both of Montgomery County - January 12, 1864, by J. B. MICHE, J. P..

Christian DILTHEY to Waldburger PETER - February 9, 1863, by J. B. MICHE, J. P..
William K. HOLT to Hudah LEACH - March 24, 1863, by John SULLINS, J. P..
James ATKINS to Mary A. BENFROM - April 21, 1863, by John SULLINS, J. P..
James HENSON to Susan JARVIS - April 3, 1863, by John SULLINS, J. P..
William SHEA to Mary HINDRICKS - April 15, 1863, by Frederic B. CRIDER, J. P..
Henry LINDEMANN to Scharlotte MAUR - April 23, 1863, by Fred DREWEL, M. G..
Henry ERFMANN to Rebekka BUSCHMAN - April 28, 1863, by Fred DREWEL, M. G..
Martin SMALLWOOD to Elizabeth Ann McCAMMENT - April 17, 1863, by James H. VAUGHN.
Kilgmann BOTCHER to Margaretha KONIG - April 12, 1863, by A. PICKLER, M. G..
William B. McDANIEL to Narcissus C. MATHEWS - June 9, 1863, by Frederick B. CRIDER, J. P..
John B. BRUGLEB to Spicy F. TERRY - May 3, 1863, by Robert W. REED, M. G..
Eberhard SCHWER to August NOVAK - August 10, 1864.
George HOLT to Mary GERKING - July 30, 1863, by Benjamin LEACH, M. G..
Willis BRUMLEY to Sarah Jane SHOCKLEY - June 12, 1863, by WIlliam P. LAMBET, M. G..
Henriech HENZE to Caroline VOIGHT, late Mrs. BRANDENBURG - December 20, 1862, by Freid HUNDHAUSEN, M. G..
Wm. METLOCK to Caroline SMITH.- January 11, 1864, by B. A. MATHEWS, J. P..
Frederick BRITTHORST to Augusta TOBEL - November 20, 1863, by Wm. KLEINSCHMIDT, M. G..
Christoph WEHMEIER to Anna Mary STEFFEN - December 3, 1863, by Philipp KUHL, M. G..
Eli HAINES to Prucilla CHILDERS - December 24, 1864, by Frederick B. CRIDER, J. P..
Hiram H. HAINES to Mary CHILDERS - January 7, 1863, by Frederick B. CRIDER, J. P..
William SOUDERS to Hannah E. WARE - December 13, 1863, by Samuel LEMONS, J. P..
Geo. W. CARR to Nancy A. GIBSON - January 14, 1864, by Henry SOUDERS, J. P..
Chisley SOUDERS to Roseanna STRAIN - January 14,

Jacob STRAPNER to Emma RONNEBERGER - February 26, 1863, by Charles SANDBERGER, J. P..
Charles HOHN to Louise AMELING - January 27, 1864, by P. G. SCHAIBLE, M. G., at the house of Henry AMELING.
Frederic BOGE to Mina BUCKER - March 17, 1864, by P. G. SCHAIBLE, M. G., at the house of Conrad BUCKER.
William KIOKER (sic) to Mina BUNTE - March 27, 1864, by P. G. SCHAIBLE, M. G..
Henrich BRINKMANN to Louisa HESS - April 7, 1864, by Fried. HUNDHAUSEN, M. G..
Hiram Riley ROBERTSON to Elisabeth Susan TINDEL - February 25, 1864, by William MEYER, J. P..
Edward EPPLE to Mary NEUMANN - May 12, 1864, by F. RUPE, M. G..
William BORGMANN to Elise BENTE of Franklin County - March 7, 1864, by E. A. ELFELD. Witnesses were Ferdinand WOLKING and Louisa WOLKING.
P. D. Christian SCHULZ of De KALB County, Illinois, to Caroline BORGMANN of Franklin County - March 17, 1864, by E. A. ELFELD.
Envoch HADIRN of Sangamon County, Illinois, to R. A. BECK - April 3, 1864, by Henry L. ALLRICHT.
Jacob ROTHFUCHS to Maria NEIDHART - July 19, 1864, by Fried. HUNDHAUSEN, M. G..
Edward ERNY to Maria Anna SCHOERNT (sic) - June 21, 1864, by F. RUBE, M. G..
Henry HOMAN to Caroline BEBION, both of St. Louis County - May 26, 1864, by John B. MICHE, J. P..
Albert RIEBSAMEN to Christina HEINLEN - July 23, 1864, by Fried. HUNDHAUSEN, M. G..
Johann Jacob SEIFERT to Christine Mathelda DIERTERLE - May 10, 1864, by Charles DOEHRING, M. G..
Ferdinand CRESCHIEN to Albertine LOBEL - June 8, 1864, by A. PICKER, M. G..
Carl CRESCHIEN to Albertine STEPHAN - August 17, 1864, by A. PICKER, M. G..
Jacob RUPP to Levisee M. COLVIN - August 7, 1864, by Benjamin LEACH, M. G..
Moses R. REVE to Elen T. COOPER - August 8, 1864, by Benjamin LEACH, M. G..
Joseph McKINNEY to Manerva CARRELL - September 10, 1864, by Frederick B. CRIDER, J. P..

George KELMANN to Dorethea TAMMER - April 7, 1864, by John B. MICHE, J. P..
Frank BERKEL (sic) to Eliza BAUMGARTNER - May 7, 1864, by John B. MICHE, J. P..
Henry PETERS to Sophia DOERCH - September 4, 1864, by Charles SANDBERGER, J. P..
Jonathan CARDER to Selah AGEE - October 23, 1864, by Samuel DEVAULT, J. P..
Johann WILHELME to Babette WELTE - October 14, 1864, by Charles NESTEL, M. G..
Frederich HUBER to Catharine _LOPFER, born LANG - October 12, 1864, by Charles NESTEL, M. G..
Christian DANUSER to Verena Christine BOTTERMANN - May 27, 1860, by Charles NESTEL, M. G..
Johann Jacob SCHNIEDER to Maria LEIST - August 6, 1864, by Charles NESTEL, M. G..
Bernharde PETRUS to Freidericke NEUHAUFER - August 18, 1864.
Fritz DANENBERG to Henrietta NELSEE - September 8, 1864, by E. A. ELFELD, M. G..
Wm. MOSELY to Amanda J. BROWN - October 9, 1864, by Henry F. ALBROGHT.
Mr. MICHAEL to Mary LEVY - June 12, 1864, by W. H. CONN.
August ERDMAN to Johanna BREIDPOHT - October 21, 1864, by A. HOFFMANN, M. G..
Wilhelm HECKMANN to Anna BERTHE - December 7, 1864, by Freid. HUNDHAUSEN, M. G..
Anton Dietrich HELMES to Caroline STRUCKER - September 10, 1864, by Frederick SCHEICHAUM.
John PFANTECH to Catherine NEINERT - November 24, 1864, by F. A. SHOMMBERGER.
William H. ADAMS to Mary DETTWILLER - September 14, 1864, by Charles SANDBERGER, J. P..
August BEEDMAN to Flora BAER - November 29, 1864, by Freid. HUNDHAUSEN, M. G..
Frederick PETRUS to Sophia Wilhelmina WAGNER - January 1, 1865, by Freid. HUNDHAUSEN, M. G..
William T. SCANTH___ to Mary A. RILEY - December 29, 1864, by R. W. REED, M. G..
Nathan B. COLTER to Louiza CHILDERS - January 8, 1864, by John SULLINS, J. P..
Frederich LANGE to Dina BUCKHOLZ - December 18, 1864, by Fred. DREWEL, M. G..
Charles FISCHER to Franceska FINKLANG - September 25, 1864, by John B. MICHE, J. P..

James DOWLER to Sarah ALLELMANN - July 3, 1864, by John B. MICHE, J. P..
John COLLIER to Julia HUDSON, both of Franklin County - July 5, 1864, by John B. MICHE, J. P..
Bernharde SPALTE to Sophia Wilhelmina TULLEY - February 16, 1865, by Freid. HUNDHAUSEN, M. G..
August KRUGER to Anna BOTTCHER - February 7, 1865, by A. PICKER, M. G..
Christian P. ANDERSON to Anne E. FESSEN - March 10, 1865, by Robert W. REED, M. G..
Thomson M. RODGERS to Sarah BAYLESS - February 16, 1865, by Elder Lewis MURPHY.
Harland M. SMITH to Sarah B. SMITH - March 16, 1865, by Wm. R. DOUGLASS, J. P..
William QUINN to Susan VAUGHN - April 25, 1865, by F. RUBE, M. G..
Phillip DIEDERICK to Caroline SPECKHALS - April 27, 1865, by F. RUPE, M. G..
Francis STEIN to Elizabeth MULLER - February 27, 1865, by F. RUPE, M. G..
Peter STRACK to Carolina Charlotte GOBEL - December 2, 1864, by John H. BRUNE, M. G..
Herman BUNTE to Eliza MELIES - September 30, 1864, by John G. SCHAIBLE, M. G..
John COLEMAN to Rhoda EDDLEMAN - March 5, 1865, by John B. MICHE, J. P..
WIlhelm EHLERT to Catharine Louise BURGETT - February 16, 1865, by H. BRUNE.
M. M. V. LANE to Annis HENSLEY - November 9, 1864, by Wm. H. CONN, J. P..
Phillip WEIST to Rosena JAMISON - ? 31, 1865 (month was not included), recorded April 27, 1865, by Wm. H. CONN, J. P..
Thomas UNCHY (sic) to Lucy ULEY - April 29, 1865, by Wm. H. CONN, J. P..
Joseph H. WINN to Martha E. MURPHY - April 21, 1865, by John B. MICHE, J. P..
Conrad BLOCK to DOROTHEA HOMEIR - April, 1865 (no day included), by Fred DREWEL, M. G..
Johannes FLEUCKE to Dorothea STAEMMER - March 29, 1865, by Fred DREWELL, M. G..
David WALKER to Anna BLUME - January 15, 1865, by Charles NESTEL, M. G..
Herman Hendrich Lenge MEYER to Margaretha RASCHER - April 6, 1865, by Wm. KLEINSHMIDT.
Carl BOOKMAN to Emma Dorothea RASHER - March 16,

1865, by E. A. ELFIELD, M. G..
H. AUFDEZHEDE to Ottilie STOKENBLOKEN - May 2, 1865, by John H. BRUNE.
Christopher WEBER to Ida KAGELIEN - May 31, 1865, by Freid. HUNDHAUSEN, M. G..
Jacob VOGEL to Catherine VOGEL - June 5, 1865, by F. RUPE, M. G..
Nicholas NAUGLE to Poley SOUDERS - March 30, 1865, by Henry SOUDERS, J. P., at the house of John SOUDERS.
William B. HOLENSWORTH to S_____ BUTMIER - March 23, 1865, by Henry SOUDERS, M. G..
Heinrich JAGER to Maria STECKLIN - June 17, 1865, by Fr. F. RUPE.
Jephy BYRD to Harriet P. GRIPLET - June 15, 1865, by Benjamin LEACH, M. G..
John B. HUBER to Mena ULENSMAN - June 15, 1865, by John B. MICHE, J. P..
Bernard STRASNER to Mary SCHMIDT - June 22, 1865, by John B. MICHE, J. P..
Seth BURTON to Frances HENTON - March 30, 1865, by Andrew P. COWAN, J. P..
Landon BROWN to Frances G. NICKS - April 16, 1865, by Andrew P. COWAN, J. P..
William MINHORSE to Charlotte MASTENEM - April 11, 1865, by Andrew P. COWAN, J. P..
Peter ALBERTZ to Elizabeth HAID (sic) - July 18, 1865, by John B. MICHE, J. P..
Gottfred EHRLACH to Anna HOLT - July 14, 1865, by Benjamin LEACH, M. G..
Joshua SHOCKLEY to Mary Jane CRIDER - July 13, 1865, by W. R. DOUGLASS.
John GUIDER to Frederica SUTES - July 15, 1865, by W. R. DOUGLASS.
John WEENNLENGER to Leviza C_____ - August 10, 1865, by John B. MICHE, J. P..
W. WEHMEIER to Florintine STOCK - June 10, 1865, by E. A. ELFELD, M. G..
William P. W. LEE to Isadory MISNER - August 16, 1865, by W. F. HAMBY, J. P..
Jasper SMITH to Nancy Ann BUSCHART - August 13, 1865, by W. F. HAMBY, J. P..
George WOODS to Louisa J. CORDER - August 3, 1865, by Robert W. REED, M. G..
Conrad AMES to Auguste BOSCHE - August 21, 1865, by Freid HUNDHAUSEN, M. G..

Johanne SHERER to Maria Louisa SLEIGER - August 20, 1865, by Freid HUNDHAUSEN, M. G..
Henry AHEING to Sophia LANGE of Osage County - August 9, 1865.
Eptaheu (sic) RHADINE to H. Margaretha SCHRAMME - August 27, 1865, by John B. MICHE, J. P..
Robert F. LETCHER to Margaret McGUFFY, both of St. Louis - September 11, 1865, by John B. MICHE, J. P..
Jacob HAUCH to Christine KRESSEY, widow of Michael BURCHARDT - September 17, 1865, by Fred HUNDHAUSEN, M. G..
Daniel DAVIS to Emeline THOMAS - August 24, 1865, by Francis SULLIVAN, J. P..
Francis DAILEY to Sarah Ann SHENEY (sic) - October 9, 1865, by Robert REED, M. G..
Nicholas YOUNG to Mary BRANSON - October 5, 1865, by Herman OBERKROM, J. P..
Thomas JOHNSON to Sinderina CRADER - October 22, 1865, by Herman OBERKROM, J. P..
Carl HOLTSCHUK to Serilita (sic) JUCKINE - August 19, 1865, by Herman OBERKROM, J. P..
Henry REAVES to Eliza FANNEN - September 3, 1865, by Armsteadt MEYERS, J. P..
John CONNER to Sarah JANNETT - September 10, 1865, by Armsteadt MEYERS, J. P..
Claton R. HIATT to Mary Sirabeth ROBESON - October 9, 1865, by Armsteadt MEYERS, J. P..
Herman TOLLE to Amalia SCHRADER - November 11, 1865, by E. A. ELFELD, M. G..
Gottlieb MEYER to Caroline AHERENS - November 4, 1865, by E. A. ELFELD, M. G..
Casper SCHMIDT to Louise DEPPE - November 14, 1865, by Fred DREWEL, M. G..
Ludwig NEESE to Anya Katharina BOETCHER - November 11, 1865, by Fred DREWEL, M. G..
John MASON to Nancy J. BROWN - July 13, 1865, by Andrew P. COWAN, J. P..
Franz Xavier SCHNEIDER to Anna NORTMAN - December 5, 1865, by F. RUPE, M. G..
Christian KULEN to Emma BERGNER - November 13, 1865, by John B. MICHE, J. P..
George ALLEN (sic) to Anna Margarethe TANNER - December 2, 1865, by John B. MICHE, J. P..
Peter MUELLER to Agatha BECKER, widow of Christian BECKER, born HUBER - filed December

8, 1865, By George KLINGE, J. P..
William TOLDTMAN to Katharine MEYERS - November 20, 1865, by George KLINGE, J. P..
James KERLEY to July Ann HOW - September 14, 1865, by William M,EYER, J. P..
Hiram Riley ROBERTSON to Elizabeth PAREE - November 5, 1865, by William MEYER, J. P..
Isaac PERKINS to Emily POWELL - November 5, 1865, by William MEYER, J. P..
Heinrich HELMS to Pauline CHRISTEL - August 2, 1865, by Charles NESTEL, M. G..
Heinrich LUCHSEGER to Maria SCHINDLER - September 3, 1865, by Charles NESTEL, M. G..
Johann Henrich GRUBER to Martha ERNS, born PILANT - September 13, 1865, by Charles NESTEL, M. G..
Carl REIFSTECK to Paulina HEINKE - August 3, 1865, by Charles NESTEL, M. G..
Carl KLEINDIENST to Fredricka WILDE - December 3, 1865, by Fred HUNDHAUSEN, M. G..
Wilhelm HASINRITTER to Paulina RETZHOFF - December 23, by Fred HUNDHAUSEN, M. G..
August VOGT to Alalia HASENRITTER - December 23, 1865, by Fred HUNDHAUSEN, M. G..
Jacob ROMMEL to Catherina BUSHNLESS - December 25, 1865, by Fred HUNDHAUSEN, M. G..
Wolfgang THEUERLY (sic) to Mina SCHMIDT - January 5, 1865, by John B. MICHE, J. P..
Carl GIDENHAGEN to Elizabeth GIDENHAGEN - December 5, 1865, by A. HOFFMAN, M. G..
Francis M. LEA to Susan M. MERIDITH - December 28, 1865, by Robert REED, M. G..
James K. LACY to Margaret BRIDGES - December 31, 1865, by Sam'l DEVAULT, J. P..
Paul GAST to Emilie SENNOR - November 27, 1865, by Fred DREWEL, M. G..
Martin JERLI to Cacilie SCHNELLER, born GOLD - October 21, 1865, by Charles NESTEL, M. G..
Wilhelm ROTHEMEIER to Christine SUBER - October 20, 1865, by Charles NESTEL, M. G..
Johanne ZIMMERLI to Maria Elizabeth LANDEOCHER - October 5, 1865.
John McLAUGHLIN to Mary DUESSMONS - January 1, 1866, by F. RUPE, M. G..
Carl SCHWARR to Christina KAISER - January 2, 1866, by Fr. F. RUPE.
John W. SEXTON to Martha M. LANE, both of

Franklin County - January 25, 1866, by John B. MICHE, J. P..
John DAHL to Sophia Frederike Christena WILLTEN - January 29, 1866, by John B. MICHE, J. P..
Christian LENTY to Louisa ROLOFF - January 1, 1865, by John B. MICHE, J. P..
Martin V. HARRINGTON, age 33, to Sarah F. WHITLOW, age 20 - December 21, 1865, by John GOAD, M. G..
Adolph WITTENBACH to Julie APEL - January 31, 1866, by H. F. SCHURBAUM, M. G..
Freidrich BOCK to Maria WITTENBUCK - December 16, 1865, by H. F. SCHURBAUM, M. G..
John SCHEIDEGGER to Christine BADE of Franklin County - February 9, 1865, by John B. MICHE, J. P..
William CARROLL to Lisebet SMITH - February 4, 1866, by Herman OBERKROM, J. P..
Louis BRANSON to Nancy REYNOLDS - November 21, 1866, by Herman OBERKROM, J. P..
Phillip CRAISTER to Sally FAAKER - February 7, 1866, by Herman OBERKROM, J. P..
Henry DOMINICA to Nancy P. STONE - December 28, 1865, by John SULLINS, J. P..
Robert T. LEACH to Nancy L. HOLT - January 11, 1866, by John SULLINS, J. P..
Frederick GAILEMEYER to Anna Catherina SCHMIDT - January 23, 1866, by Herman TUELLE, M. G..
Henry VON BOAPEN (sic) to Theresia NORTMANN - February 6, 1866, by F. RUPE, M. G..
Archer THOMAS to Johanna WILBER - March 14, 1866, by Jas. W. OWENS, Judge of the 9th Judiciary.
John J. MERIDITH to Elizabeth HEDRIC - March 4, 1866, by Robert W. REED, M. G..
Allen PARHAM to Eliza M. DOUGLASS - February 8, 1866, by Green C. TERRY.
Charles F. KIRKLAND to Mary C. JAMES - February 1, 1866, by Henry SOUDE, J. P., at the house of John JAMES.
Henry C. GIBSON to Adaline GIBSON, both colored - March 18, 1866, by Henry SOUDER, J. P..
Azuael THOMPSON to L. B. REED - March 25, 1866, by Henry SOUDER, J. P..
Joseph KINKEAD to Mary LANE - February 15, 1866, by Sam'l DEAVULT, J. P..
Andrew ASTMUNN to Lavisa PRUITT - February 11,

1866, by Sam'l DEAVULT, J. P..
Peter A. B. SCENBYE to Maria J_____ - March 20, 1866, by Sam'l DEAVULT, J. P..
Adolph SCHULTMIER to Elizabeth HUGG - December 19, 1865, by Charles NESTEL, M. G..
Jacob SCHMIDT to Phillipbina SCHMIDT - January 1, 1866, by Charles NESTEL, M. G..
Heinrich BECKMAN to Fredericka GRUBER - March 19, 1866, by Charles NESTEL, M. G..
David ERNI to Sophia SCHIETZ - April 2, 1866, by Charles NESTEL, M. G..
Barney RIDENHOUR to J. K_____ AGLIN - April 12, 1866, by David TAYOR.
Conrad GEIBER to Clara STERN - March 1, 1866, by by F. RUPE, M. G..
John DOYLE to Elizabeth CARR - April 14, 1866, by F. RUPE, M. G..
George STEINMETZ to Maria Catharina LOHENUT - April 23, 1863, by F. RUPE, M. G..
Jacob KAMPER to Catharina FEBY - March 1, 1866, by F. RUPE, M. G..
William SCHAFFERCOLTER to Sophia HOFFORTH - February 1, 1866, by Armstead E. MEYERS, J. P..
Perry D. COOPER to Milinda LEACH - March 29, 1866, by John SULLINS, J. P..
James BAKER to Margaret JARVIS - April 9, 1866, by Green C. TERRY.
William OBERKROM to Christine KRUGER - April 12, 1866, by Herman RAHN.
Heinrich SHAFFERKOLTER to Maria HAGAMEIER - April 12, 1866, by Herman RAHN.
Herman ENKE to Christine HOSSFELD - April 15, 1866, by Herman RAHN.
Adolph BRANDERBURGER to Doris TUPPE - April 24, 1866, by Herman RAHN.
Christoph REITEMEZER to Julie NEIDAV - April 25, 1866, by Herman RAHN.
Henry MUSKAT to Elizabeth FARRIS - May 6, 1866, by Green C. TERRY.
Elisha HIBLER to Elizabeth SMITH - May 11, 1866, by Sam'l DEVALT, J. P..
D. C. CANTRELL to L. L. McINTIRE - April 17, 1866, by W. S. WOODWARD, M. G..
Francis M. GARNER to Mary E. LOCKHART - April 8, 1866, by Henry SOUDERS, J. P..
Herman MORLOCK to Lena Rofalia KEGFER - March 29,

1866, by Fred HUNDHAUSEN, M. G..
Christopher OETTERER to Auguste BOCK - June 19, 1866, by Fred HUNDHAUSEN, M. G..
Herman Frantz Wilhelm DUETZELED (sic) to Elise NASSE - June 21, 1866, by Fred HUNDHAUSEN, M. G..
Heinrich LUEDERS to Charlotte BUCKHOLZ - April 21, 1866, by F. DREWEL, M. G..
John C. SPANDING to Caroline FREY - June 8, 1866, Green C. TERRY.
Henrick SCHUCK to Wilhelmina HOFFMAN - July 24, 1866, by Fred HUNDHAUSEN, M. G..
Henry KONE to Christina CANNEL - June 8, 1866, by Benjamin LEACH, M. G..
Rudolph KEMICH to Bernhardine BECKMANN - April 9, 1866, by Charles NESTEL, M. G..
Friedrick BRUNSWICK to Antonette BROEMSER - July 19, 1866, by Charles NESTEL, M. G..
John SHOEMAKER to Susan H. LEE - June 27, 1866, by W. F. HAMBY.
Gottlieb BUTSCHE to Mrs. Maria DIETZ, born DIMLER - May 6, 1866, by Charles NESTEL, M. G..
Friedrich WILD to Louisa BUDDMEYER - April 19, 1866, by Charles NESTEL, M. G..
Johann HELMENDOCH to Maria BERKING - April 19, 1866, by Charles NESTEL, M. G..
Martin BROWN to Emley Catherine BLY - recorded July 5, 1866, by Francis SULLIVAN, J. P..
William R. YOUNG to Nancy J. REED - July 1, 1866, by Henry SOUDERS, J. P..
Mark EBELE to Auguste KLINK - August 31, 1866, by John B. MICHE, J. P..
Daniel STRANTON to Johanna WILLIAMS - September 13, 1866, by John B. MICHE, J. P..
John WIDMER to Anna FISHER, widow of Rudolph FISHER - September 30, 1866, by George KLINGE, J. P..
George WILBURN to Anna JACKSON - October 5, 1866, by John B. MICHE, J. P..
George C. SOUDER to Louisa HINKLE - recorded July 3, 1866, by David TAYLOE, J. P..
William ROGERS to Susan COLLIER - August 5, 1866, by Henry SOUDERS, J. P..
Simon Wilhelm PRISS to Bertha KEHR - September 19, J. F. SCHURBAUM, M. G..
William H. RUMSFORD to Frances J. MILLER - May 13, 1866, by Samuel DUVAULT, J. P..

13, 1866, by Samuel DUVAULT, J. P..
Jesse SCANLEN to Elizabeth Ann HAMILTON - October 21, 1866, by Samuel DEVAULT, J. P..
Fielding J. SMITH to Isabella R. LEMMON - October 4, 1866, by Benjamin LEACH, M. G..
Martin V. CRIDER to Lucinda CHILDERS - November 5, 1866, by Jas. H. BARBARICK, J. P..
Gustav SPARTE (sic) to Susanna Dorothea KIENTS - November 4, 1866, by John B. MICHE, J. P..
Henry BOTTCHEN to Elise CRENAN - September 28, 1866, by George BRIEGEMANN, M. G..
Ludwig SCHLOEMER to Caroline SCHAUNBURG - October 26, 1866, by William WILKENING, M. G..
Nathaniel GRAVES to Elise CRANDER - October 21, 1866, by Henry SOUDERS, J. P..
Alexander READ to Elizabeth RENFROW - August 28, 1866, by Benjamin LEACH, M. G..
George SCHNEIDER to Marie BERRON, widow of Joseph BERRON - November 10, 1866, by George KLINGE, J. P..
W. R. McMILLAN to Frances A. WILLARD - September 26, 1866, by Green C. TERRY, J. P..
John F. LEHNHOFF to Martielda Ann HASFELD - November 2, 1866, by Green C. TERRY, J. P..
George BLACKWELL to Elizabeth C. OLIVER - September 30, 1866, by Samuel DEVAULT, J. P..
Allen SPURGIN to Martha J. DAVIS - August 9, 1866, by Samuel DEVAULT, J. P..
Edward CHIDSEY to Mary A. BARNER - July 1, 1866, by Samuel DEVAULT, J. P..
John KAEDING to Scharlotte KEAAS - October 28, 1866, by John MEYER, M. G..
William Martin BADER to Sarah WHEAT - November 20, 1866.
John Henry KAHLE to Mary BLOCK - November 19, 1866, by George BERGMAN, M. G..
Heinrich GRANNAMAN to Karolina Christine BOHLFING, born BAHRON (sic) - November 6, 1866, by Charles Fried DOEHRING, M. G..
Jacob HUNNEBURGER to Louisa KUENSTER - October 9, 1866, by Wm. Fr. KLEONIGHAUS.
James H. ANDERSON to Mary E. HARRIS - December 3, 1866, by William PLAMPKE, J. P..
George MEIER to Josephine SCHAEFER - November 20, 1866, by William KLEONIGHAUS, M. G..
John M. CLYMER to Minerva B. COLLIER - December

23, 1866, by John M. HAMBY, M. G..
William POWELL to Malinda MOODY - November 4, 1866, by William MEYER, J. P..
Thomas MEYER to Margaret HIATT - December 20, 1866, by William MEYER, J. P..
Johann STOTARED to Elise MEYER - November 3, 1866, by Charles NESTEL, M. G..
Rudolph BAUMGARTNER to Louise FRETZMEIER - October 20, 1866, by Charles NESTEL, M. G..
Charles M. SERCE to Matilda BARBARICK - December 6, 1866, by Lewis TACKETT, J. P..
John W. INGRAM to Virginia ROLOFF - January 6, 1867, by John B. MICHE, J. P..
Nicolaus WEILNLAYED (sic) to Catharina MÜLLER - January 29, 1867, by Fr. Wm. KLEONIGHAUS.
Eustachuss PFANTSCH to Catharina CAMPER - January 12, 1867, by Fr. Wm. KLEONIGHAUS.
Carl TODTMAN to Elizabeth KLASENER - January 10, 1867, by J. F. SCHEIRBAUM, M. G..
Philipp MEYER to Catharine EICKHOLZ - January 21, 1867, by Fr. Wm. KLEONIGHAUS.
Henry TREASE to Mary J. IRMAN (sic) - January 15, 1867, by Henry SOUDERS, J. P..
John L. BELLINGTON to Sarah L. SOUDERS - November 21, 1866, by Henry SOUDERS, J. P..
Milton H. MURPHY TO Mattie H. SOUDERS - December, 1866 (no day included), by Henry SOUDERS, J. P..
John FILLA to Augustina FILLA - November 23, 1866, by Fr. Martin SURL in Franklin County.
Joseph ZENNON to Mary KOONAY, both of Crawford County - November 22, 1866, by Fr. Martin SURL in Franklin County.
Frederick Wilhelm FISKY to Christina Wilhelmina ENEMEYER - February 3, 1867, by ? BRUEGARMEYER, M. G..
William SCHAPPENHORST to Catharina Mary UBMEIER - March 4, 1867, by William WILKENING, M. G..
W. Young MARTIN to Martha C. ISAM - December 31, 1866.
August STEINBECK to Louise TAPPE - March, 1867 (no day included), by F. DREWEL, M. G..
Wilhelm TODTMAN to Wilhelmina Louise MEIER - February 6, 1867, by F. DREWEL, M. G..
Herman ENGELKING to Wilhelmina BRUNE - February 14, 1867, by F. DREWEL, M. G..

Marshall CLAY to Francesca PATTEN - October 10, 1866, by Albert HALLAND, M. H..
Lewis RHASDES to Edna PIERSON - February 20, 1867, by Albert HOLLAND, M. G..
Silvester STEIGER to Mavis Theresia PIFFER - March 14, 1867, by Fr. William KLENHAUS.
Anton FLUCHT to Johanna NIENHAUSEN - March 4, 1867, by Fr. William KLENHAUS.
Albert Theodore GREINICKE and Hermina Johanne PREUSS - April 5, 1867, by G. BRUGMAN, M. G..
Elisha HOLLINDSWORTH to Mary Ann McDANIEL - March 17, 1867, by Francis SULLIVAN, J. P..
Gottlieb Heinrich HELKERBEUNER to Louise Wilhelmina WOLLBRINK - March 14, 1867, by H. H. HALTGREVE, M. G.. Witnesses were Johst HELKERBEUNER and Friederich WOLLBRINK.
Casper Heinrich BERGER to Maria Elizabeth BOHEMEISTER - April 4, 1867, by H. H. HALTGREVE, M. G.. Witnesses were Fried C. BOHEMEISTER and Heinrich BERGER.
John G. Mahany to Mary Elizabeth ERICKSON - January 31, 1867, by L. M. MAHANY, M. G..
L. McKINNEY to Fanny FERREL - February 21, 1867, by B. A. MATHEWS, J. P..
James M. SKAGGS to Margaret A. BECK - March 3, 1867, by L. M. MAHANY, M. G..
William STONE to Rebecca SMITH - March 3, 1867, by L. M. MAHANY, M. G..
Irwin Hardin KERLEY to Sarah MERPHY - March 24, 1867, by Wm. MEYER, J. P..
Friederick SCHWEDER to Wilhelmina LANGE - April 1, 1867.
Albert SMITH to Caroline BLACKWELL - April 13, 1867, by Christian ANDERSON, J. P..
Morgan JACKSON to Easter JENNINGS - March 17, 1867, by Christian ANDERSON, J. P..
William HUTCHESON to Louisa CRESON - April 14, 1867, by Christian Peter ANDERSON, J. P..
Jesse Hamen MAILAND to Helena JESSEN - April 17, 1867, by Christian P. ANDERSON, J. P..
Fritz LANGENBERG to Emilie NIEWALD - April 12, 1867, by E. A. ELFELD, J. G..
Thomas CHAPMAN to Jemima S. AGEE - April 22, 1867, by Samuel DEVAULT, J. P..
Abraham SOUDERS to Helena MARIS - April 7, 1867, by Henry SOUDERS, J. P..

Simon WIEMAN to Wilhelmina WILLEMAN - April 24, 1867, by Herman TOELLE, M. G..
Henry BOEHM to Mollie RUDGER - April 27, 1867, by F. P. REICHERT, M. G..
James RUSH to Scharlotte MAHRIE - April 22, 1867, by Fried HUNDHAUSEN, M. G..
Joseph APRIL to Helena GERMEAN (sic) - April 30, 1867, by Fr. Wm. KLOENINGHAUS.
Karl LANGE to Wilhelmine VON BERN - May 6, 1867, by William WILKENING, M. G..
Henry KOCH to Marie SASMAHAUSER - May 16, 1867, by Herman RAHN, M. G..
Christian HAFFNER to Christina KLOTT - May 14, 1867, by Fried HUNDHAUSEN, M. G..
Jasper P. SOUDERS to Martha J. WEELY - April 14, 1867, by Green C. TERRY, J. P..
Peter Henry BAISTEN to Wilhelmina H. WEHMEIER - May 29, 1867, by L. S. KRIEB, M. G..
Joseph BAYER to Ursula PETECHE (sic) - May 28, 1867, by Fried HUNDHAUSEN, M. G..
Peter WEBER to Maria Magdelina PHILIPP - May 9, 1867, by Fr. Wm. KLEONINGHAUS.
Jolen HAMILTON to Ann Eliza FITZGEREL - May 3, 1867, by R. M. BURNS, M. G..
Charles M. MATTHEWS to Hellon HENTON - March 31, 1867, by B. A. MATTHEWS, J. P..
F. J. REICHERT to A. C. KERRELL - May 28, 1867, by E. A. ELFELD, M. G..
August IDEL to Louise EICKERMANN - May 25, 1867, by E. A. ELFELD, M. G..
B. SCHINDLER to Ursula JULL, alias BOESH - June 3, 1867, by F. J. REICHERT, M. G..
John Anton VALENDARN to Anna Mary ANEGER, born ADAMS - June 17, 1867, by Fr. Wm. KLEONINGHAUS.
John BUDDING to Elizabeth DALLER, born ENING - May 30, 1867, by Fr. Wm. KLEONINGHAUS.
William F. MITCHELL to Malcheny CARDER - May 12, 1867, by Christian ANDERSON, J. P..
Fred William SIEGMAN to Anna Maria HAKAMP - June 24, 1867, by L. E. KNIEF, M. G..
John Y. BRANER to Deliley EANOLL - May 4, 1867, by Lewis TACKETT, J. P..
Heinrich Wilhelm HARING to Fredericke WESTHOLZ - April 12, 1867, by F. DREWEL, M. G..
Heinrich EITMANN to Johanna MAIER - April 12, 1867, by F. DREWEL, M. G..

Friederich GEDEMEYER (sic) to Dorothea DOUISH (sic) - July 6, 1867, by George BRUGMANN.
Jacob MAECKLY to Sidaria ALLEMAN - July 11, 1867, by Fried HUNDHAUSEN, M. G..
Reinhold BIBER to Charlotte Caroline MILLER - July 18, 1867, by Geo. SAUL, M. G..
Riley OUTMANS to Esther M. CLYMER - July 21, 1867, by J. W. COWAN, M. G..
Oliver M. SHOCKLEY to Elizabeth Jane LEWIS - July 20, 1867, by William MEYER.
John W. TYREE to Joann PRAT - May 12, 1867, by Henry SOUDERS, J. P..
Henry A. OBENHAUS to Louise BRANDT - July 30, 1867, by A. VANDER LIPPE, M. G..
Franz RUBSAMAN to Catharina HOLDER - August 21, 1867, by Fried HUNDHAUSEN, M. G..
Houston L. TERRELL to Martha T. JARVIS - August 22, 1867, by William BRIDGES.
John Henry KONING to Henrietta EBBER - June 21, 1867, by Herman TOELLE, M. G..
Johan MATTHIAS HOFFMAN to Maria WETHE - May 17, 1867, by Chas. NESTEL, M. G..
Ferdinand Phillip FRAUTWEIN to Amelia Fredericke GENTNER - July 4, 1867, by Charles NESTEL, M. G..
Carl FENDEL to Margaretha HANE, born PETUCH (sic) - July 23, 1867, by Charles NESTEL, M. G..
Henry BRAUN to Mary Barbara STORCH - July 20, 1867, by J. F. SCHERBAUM, M. G..
Carl LASEN to Marie HOFFMAN - August 4, 1867, by Charles NESTEL, M. G..
John NEIDHART to Joanna KLAUS - September 10, 1867, by Fr. Wm. KLEONINGHAUS.
Carl SANDBERGER to Anna HERBSTREILER - September 12, 1867, by Fried HUNDHAUSEN, M. G..
Henry SCHAERMANN to Fredericka BRINKMAN - July 20, 1867, by J. F. SCHERBAUM, M. G..
Edmon J. SANDS to Mary M. SMITH - July 20, 1867, by L. M. MAHANY, M. G..
Friederich Wm. BRINKMAN to Henriete BLEUME - September 22, 1867, by John MEYER, M. G..
Johann Heinrich WOLLBRINK to Anna Catherine LANGENBERY - August 30, 1867, by H. H. HOLTGREVE, M. G..
Eli Mc J. LAMPBETH to Martha R. A. BURGESS - September 12, 1867, by F. M. COOPER, J. P..

Friederick LEIMBERGER to Elizabetha ROTHELE - September 12, 1867, by C. RUBENAU, J. P..
Gottfried MOCHEL to Anna Maria SEIFER - October 28, 1867, by Fred HUNDHAUSEN, M. G..
Isaiah DOBDSON to Mary Ann E. JAMES - August 25, 1867, by H. CHRISTIAN KOCHE, J. P..
David HARTMAN to Mary E. BARNES - September 1, 1867, by Henry SOUDERS, J. P..
William KINKEAD to Lucy Ann HIBLER - October 10, 1867, by John SULLINS, J. P..
Armstead E. MEYERS to Eliza BAILEY - October 8, 1867, by John SULLINS, J. P..
Wm. DOWLER to Matilda CUTHBERTSON - October 6, 1867, by Samuel DEVAULT, J. P..
George HAEFFMANN to Marie BEBE - November 1, 1867, by Fred HUNDHAUSEN, M. G..
William George HAEFFNER to Catherina HAEFFNER - November 12, 1867, by Fred HUNDHAUSEN, M. G..
Edward HAUPT to Ricke NOLTEUSMEIER - September 20, 1867, by John H. GRANNAMAN, M. G..
Louis WEISS to Wilhelmina BUER - September 20, 1867, by Charles SANDBERGER, J. P..
Julius HUNDHAUSEN to Charlotte LEIMER, born RAMSAHL - November 24, 1867, by Fred HUNDHAUSEN, M. G..
Casper Heinrich STONNER to Caroline KOCH, widow - August 9, 1867, by F. DREWEL, M. G..
Christoph HUMBURG to Matha Applonia HELLBERG - September 5, 1867, by Charles NESTEL, M. G..
Heinrich Friederich WEIDERMAN to Anna HAINKE - June 30, 1867, by F. DREWEL, M. G..
Johann Friederick HELMICH to Louise Friedericke Henriette BRINKMAN - August 15, 1867, by F. DREWEL, M. G..
Isaac M. LUCAS to Ann BRANSON - December 4, 1867, by F. McCuin COOPER, J. P..
Alvie M. KLING to Clarissa BROWN of Osage County - July 10, 1867, by John B. MICHE, J. P..
Bernhard NIEHOFF to Amalia REITH - October 22, 1867, by John B. MICHE, J. P..
Henry L. LEACH to Elizabeth HOLT - October 31, 1867, by W. R. VAUGHAN, M. G..
William FANNON to Anna Williamson of Franklin County - May 5, 1867, by John B. MICHE, J. P..
Jerry MEYERS to Susan COLEMAN - September 28, 1867, by John B. MICHE, J. P..

Adolph SELEE (sic) to Eliza MOECKLY - December 19, 1867, by Fried HUNDHAUSEN, M. G..
Joseph BAYER to Veronia STINEMAN - December 30, 1867, by Fried HUNDHAUSEN, M. G..
Joseph BENDER to Catharine MULLER - January 4, 1868, by Fred HUNDHAUSEN, M. G..
Herman AEFT to Elizabeth HASFELD - January 1, 1868, by H. Christian KEHR, J. P..
Francis WOVLSCHECK to Bernimia DEWITT - January 2, 1868, by H. Christian KEHR, J. P..
John N. ALLESON to Frances PRYOR - January 2, 1868, by Christian P. ANDERSON, J. P..
Christin JESSOM to Mettie Maria SAMSE - October 30, 1867, by Christian P. ANDERSON, J. P..
James HERSEY to Manerva PANKEY - November 14, 1867, by Christian P. ANDERSON, J. P..
Perry C. AGEE to Louisa D. SATTERFIELD - November 25, 1867, by Christian P. ANDERSON, J. P..
Joseph M. PELMER to Sarah SHOCKLEY - September 19, 1867, by Lewis TACKETT, J. P..
John W. HALEY to Meriah COTTON - September 9, 1867, by Lewis TACKETT, J. P..
Anton HUNEBERGER to Theresia EPPLE - January 23, 1868, by Fr. Wm. KLEONINGHAUS.
George W. STRAIN to Mary J. RIDENHOUR - December 3, 1867, by Henry SOUDERS, J. P..
Daniel H. CLYMER to Emma ELDRIDGE - December 25, 1867, by William M. BRIGGS, M. G..
Thomas ELDRIDGE to Nelly COOPER - December 24, 1867, by Sam'l SMITH, J. P..
John SKILES to Bewian (sic) COLLIER - February 2, 1868, by H. Christian KEHR, J. P..
Wm. Henry TAYLOR to Martha RUNNOLLS - January 9, 1868, by H. Christian KEHR, J. P..
August Fred BUTTESMEIER to Albertine KUBITZ - January 5, 1868, by Hermann RAHN, M. G..
Fred. William BARLESCH to Johanna Henriette Wilh. BUTRICK - February 2, 1868, by Herman RAHN, M. G..
John C. YOUSE to Nancy SMITH - January 30, 1868, by Benjamin LEACH, M. G..
Claton ADAMS to Martha RUTT - January 30, 1868, by E. B. HENSLEY, J. P..
Carl WEBER to Christina KUHLENCAMP - February 14, 1868, by Fried HUNDHAUSEN, M. G..
Alfred REBSAMEN to Louisa BRINKMANN, born HESSE -

February 15, 1868, by Fred HUNDHAUSEN, M. G..
Peter EMO to Regina JORDAN - February 13, 1868, by Fr. Wm. KLOENINGHAUS.
Herman FEES to Catherine STEIN - February 18, 1868, by Fr. Wm. KLOENINGHAUS.
Thomas M. COOPER to Elizabeth MATTHEWS - November 29, 1867, by G. F. HILBER, J. P..
George HOKEL to Flori EIKERMANN - December 3, 1867, by William MEYER, J. P..
William JARVIS to Emilie AMELING - November 3, 1867, by William MEYER, J. P..
Steven Ach GLANDIN to Alwine PENKINS - February 18, 1868, by G. BRUGEMAN, M. G..
Wendelin D. HOWARD to Anna J. MURPHY - February 13, 1868, by Benjamin LEACH, M. G..
Joseph E. CAHILL to Malinda E. SMITH - February 18, 1868, by L. M. MAHANY, M. G..
Richard WHITE to Henrietta NOONAN - February 4, 1868, by Fr. Martin SEISL. The bride was married with the consent of her parents.
Robert WHITE to Margaret TAYLOE - February 4, 1868, by Fr. Martin SEISL.
Jackson WHITE to Sarah BROWN - January 29, 1868, by C. RABENAU, J. P..
Joseph HERZOG to Dorothea WERTHMEIN - January 14, 1868, by C. RABENAU, J. P..
Christian Frederich W. HAGEMEISTER to Christine Gshe (sic) Adelheld KNIEF - February 16, 1868, by L. E. KNIEF, M. G..
Elija William ROARK to Margarete KRUTTLY - November 21, 1867, by William MEYER, J. P..
Loui LAUER to Fredericka KLAGES - March 13, 1868, Fred HUNDHAUSEN, M. G..
Herman SCHAEPERKOTTER to Karolina RETHEMEIER - January 5, 1868, by A. HOFFMAN.
Thomas B. OUSLEY to Mary A. OWEN - March 7, 1868, by T. McCuin COOPER.
William D. BUMPASS to Isabella C. PERKINS - January 26, 1868, by T. McCuin COOPER.
William R. VAUGHAN to Semantha W. MATTHEWS - March 8, 1868, by Benjamin LEACH, M. G..
Heinrich SOLINS to Caroline SOHNS - December 19, 1867, C. NESTEL, M. G..
Heinnrich SEIMS to Louise FIEG - January 20, 1868, by C. NESTEL, M. G..
Johann Wilhelm SONDERWORTH to Maria MEIER - March

6, 1868, by F. DREWELL, M. G..
Heinrich HEESELMAN to Louise SCHWEPPE - February 12, 1868, by F. DREWEL, M. G..
Heinrich WEIDERMANN to Maria Catharina HAPERMEHL - February 29, 1868, by F. DREWEL, M. G..
Friederick KAHL to Dorothea REMMERT - December 26, 1867, by F. DREWELL, M. G..
Johann Fischer to Anna HEINKE - February 4, 1868, by C. NESTEL, M. G..
Johann Jacob BLATTNER to Justine HOFFMAN - March 17, 1868, by C. NESTEL, M. G..
Frederick KLASSNER to Pauline HOFFMAN - March 19, 1868, by C. NESTEL, M. G..
Frederick KLASSNER to Pauline HOFFMAN - March 17, 1868, by C. NESTEL, M. G..
Frederich KELLER to Emma LANGENDORFER - March 19, 1868, by C. NESTEL, M. G..
William SIMONS to Margaretha CRIDER - January 3, 1868, by G. F. HILBERT, J. P..
George STOBEALL to Davidea L. JENKINS - January 9, 1868, by G. F. HILBERT, M. G..
Will P. STAFFORD to Anna McCONNEL - April 7, 1868, by Chas. SANDBERGER, J. P..
Henry DASE to Elizabeth HEMINGER - February 19, 1868, by Chas. SANDBERGER, J. P..
Joh. Wilhelm TILTY to Johannete HEBERLEN - April 14, 1868, by Fred HUNDHAUSEN, M. G..
George MITTENDORF to Caroline GRANNAMAN - April 16, 1868, by John GRANNAMAN, M. G..
Henry STUDDY to Magdalenia AUFDERHEIDE - March 13, 1868, by E. A. ELFELD, M. G..
John SCHMEIDER to Magdalenia HORNER - August 24, 1868, by Chr. BECK, M. G..
John W. SOUDERS to Nancy RIDENHOUR - March 13, 1868, by Henry SOUDERS, J. P..
James W. BULLINGTON to Rachel SOUDERS - January 16, 1868, by Henry SOUDERS, J. P..
James M. DUNCAN to Nancy J. McKENNY - April 16, 1868, by T. McCuin COOPER, J. P..
George SYFERT to Catherine HAMLER - May 4, 1868, by John B. MICHE, J. P..
Johann HEINLEIN to Anna Maria PILOT - May 4, 1868, by Fried. HUNDHAUSEN, M. G..
Heinrich DREWELL to Maria DIEBOLD - April 1, 1868, by Herman RAHN, M. G..
Friederick RITTERBUSCH to Anna Gesine (sic)

HOMEYER, widow - March 16, 1868, by Herman RAHN, M. G..
Ferdinand Wilhelm BORLESCH to Johanna Harriette BUTRICK - February 2, 1868, by Herman RAHN, M. G..
Carl LAUER to Louise WITTMAN - May 12, 1868, by Fried. HUNDHAUSEN, M. G..
Berr BROWN to Mrs. Sarah GANISON - April 7, 1868, by H. Christian KEHR, J. P..
John F. HARTMASTER to Caroline BROWN - May 7, 1868, by B. M. MATTHEW, J. P..
Gerle CHILDERS to Malessa A. BROWN - May 2, 1868, by B. M. MATTHEWS, J. P..
Christian Ludwig UPHOFF to Henriette Maria HAMMEL - May 11, 1868, by John B. MICHE, J. P..
John Carl Heinrich NIERMANN to Louise KLINGER - June 2, 1868, by Fred. DOEHRING, M. G..
Wilhelm BECKER to Auguste SENGENBERGER - April 25, 1868, by C. NESTEL, M. G..
Daniel KRAMPE to Auguste MILLER - April 5, 1868, by C. NESTEL, M. G..
Chrispimus (sic) BERNHARD to Anna KIAKLI - May 17, 1868, by Charles NESTEL, M. G..
Heinrich STRUMPT to Johanne SADERWERTH - April 29, 1868, by F. DREWEL, M. G..
Wilhelm Heinrich HOFFMAN to Anna Christine Louise BRINKMAN - April 13, 1868, by F. DREWEL, M. G..
Frank FRECKMANN to Pauline KLIEDUNST - March 16, 1868, by C. RABENAU, J. P..
Charles BUSHMEYER to Fredericka RUEGGER - June 14, 1868, by F. J. REICKERT, M. G..
Adolph WILLENBACH to Friedericke TOEDEMANN - May 14, 1868, by J. F. SCHIERBAUM, M. G..
Martin FILLA to Agnes PITOWEZYK - May 13, 1868, by Fr. Alexander MATHEW.
Nicholas YOUNG to Mahaley E. CARTER - November 5, 1867, by Lewis TACKETT, J. P..
James CARR to Mary E. NEELY - June 2, 1868, by Lewis TACKETT, J. P..
John KILEAN to Mary A. CARDER - December 28, 1867, by Lewis TACKETT, J. P..
Benjamin F. COLTER to Mary A. BRANSON - November 7, 1867, by Lewis TACKETT, J. P..
John M. TACKETT to Malinda Ann STRATFORD - December 5, 1867, by Lewis TACKETT, J. P..
William M. SMITH to Susan F. TERRELL - March 1,

1868, by Lewis TACKETT, J. P..
James SULLIVAN to Nancy E. BRANSON - August 4, 1868, by B. A. MATTHEWS, J. P..
Christin HEMME to Adelheid ESSING - August 26, 1868, by Fr. Wm. KLOENINGHAUS.
Dominick DUFNER to Josephine FEES - August 11, 1868, by Fr. Wm. KLOENINGHAUS.
Hermann NURRE to Eva MEIN - August 9, 1868, by Fr. Wm. KLOENINGHAUS.
Wilhelm Heinrich REITEMEYER to Anna Cathatina LANDENDORFER - June 25, 1868, by F. DREWEL, M. G..
Johann Frederick SEBO to Dorothea Maria EHEMANN - August 27, 1868, by F. DREWEL, M. G..
Friederick OZESCHIEN to Henriette SCHLOTTOCH - September 18, 1868, by G. BRUGEMANN, M. G..
JOseph DIEBOLD to Anna Margaretha CLARY - July 9, 1868, by G. F. HILBERT, J. P..
Henry SCHMITZ to Caroline LINZ - September 24, 1868, by C. RABENAU, J. P..
John GROBEN to Theckla (sic) VOIGHT - October 5, 1868, by Chas. SANDBERGER, J. P..
Joseph BAUMAN to Anna Maria LICHTENSTEIN - May 30, 1868, by John B. MICHE, J. P..
Valentine FAERBER to Magdalena GLEINNER - May 30, 1868, by John B. MICHE, J. P..
William PHELPS to Virginia C. TRAIL - October 1, 1868, by William BRIDGES, M. G..
Squire W. H. FITZGERALD to Mary Jane MELTEN - October 15, 1868, by William BRIDGES, M. G..

Frank ROTHETE to Veronica BERUD - September 10, 1868, by Fr. Will HINSEN.
Frank LUTNER to Catherine GREEN - October 8, 1868, by Fr. Will HINSEN.
Martin BRAUMOARTH to Berta NAEGELIN - October 27, 1868, by Fred HUNDHAUSEN, M. G..
Christian HOFFMAN to Eva Margrethe HOECHSTENBUCH - October 25, 1868, by Fried. HUNDHAUSEN, M. G..
James A. HOLT to Elizabeth J. WARDEN - October 8, 1868, by E. B. HENSLEY, J. P..
Nathan RICHARDSON to Lucinda RICHARDSON - November 5, 1868, by Henry C. KEHR, J. P..
Albert GARNER to Albertine MAIDE - November 9, 1868, by Henry C. KEHR, J. P..

Fred. RANTER to Phillippine Henritte SCHMIDT - October 7, 1868, by E. A. ELFELD, M. G..
Edward BRINSDON to Eva DOEHLER - November 28, 1868, by Fried. HUNDHAUSEN, M. G..
Franz GREBLER to Emilie RONNENBURGER - September 17, 1868, by Charles NESTEL, M. G..
Louis IRLE to Anna SANDBERGER - September 29, 1868, by Charles NESTEL, M. G..
Johann GLEENY to Bertra CHUILET - October 6, 1868, by Charles NESTEL, M. G..
Rev. Heinrich Conrad ZIMMER to __ina DILG - October 22, 1868, by Charles NESTEL, M. G..
Edward TRAUTWEIN TO Jacobine KRUNMP, born LANGENDOERFER - November 1, 1868, by Charles NESTEL, M. G..
Hermann BOHL to Johanne TOMAECHKE - December 16, 1868, by Charles NESTEL, M. G..
Matthias ENDULS to Barbara HELBER, born REICHERT - November 8, 1868, by Charles NESTEL, M. G..
Heinrich WICKS to Marie RIETER - November 30, 1868, by Charles NESTEL, M. G..
Samuel BAUMGARTNER to Bertha STRECKER - December 4, 1868, by Charles NESTEL, M. G..
William J. CANTLY to Sarah E. ROBERTS - October 29, 1868, by William BRIDGES, M. G..
Hermann MADE to Anne WITTCOCK - December 22, 1868, by G. BURGGEMAN, M. G..
Albert FILLA to Francesca FILLA - October 8, 1868, by Fr. Martin SAIL.
Friedrick BAECKOR to Elisabeth STORCK - November 25, 1868, by C. RABENAU, J. P..
Daniel HAEFFNER to Adelheid SCHUH - December 10, 1868, by C. RABENAU, J. P..
Richard STEVENS to July Ann WASHINGTON - October 29, 1868, by C. RABENAU, J. P.. Named as the children of Richard STEVENS: J. A. WASHINGTON, beget while co-habitating; Mary Catherine LANE, and RIchard.
Joseph JOHNSON to Michele GRAHAM - October 29, 1868, by C. BATEMAN, J. P..
Henry B. WARDER to Pheba A. CARR - December 31, 1868, by Henry SOUDERS, J. P..
F. H. BULLE to Barbary A. BARNES - January 14, 1868, by HEnry SOUDERS, J. P..
Thomas J. BRANSON to Martha A. BARBARICK - January 25, 1868, by WM. V. NARYHAM.

Charles FISCHER to Wilhelmina STRUESEL - January 29, 1868, by Earnest KEOH, J. P..
George NAYLEN to Barbara STROBEL - December 1, 1868, by Earnest STRECH, J. P..
August BILES to Margaret E. RICHARDSON - January 21, 1869, by HEnry C. STEKE, J. P..
Jacob RICHARD to Maria PRYOR - April 9, 1868, by William MEYER, J. P..
Jacob WICK to Barbara BIZLER - April 20, 1868, by William MEYER, J. P..
Thomas H. B. HENELEY to Missourim ROBINSON - April 30, 1868, by Wm. MEYER, J. P..
McCern MEYER to Elvira ROBINSON - January 28, 1868, by William MEYER, J. P..
Thedor VOLMANN to Elisabeth KUCK - August 4, 1868, by Wm. MEYER, J. P..
Philipp VOGEL to Martha GESCHWIND - February 25, 1868, by Fried HUNDHAUSEN, M. G..
Wm. BRAND of Warren County, to Henriette Wehmise (sic) - January 1, 1869, by H. C. ZIMMER, M. G..
Fred EIKERMANN to Helene HAEFNER - January 7, 1869, by H. C. ZIMMER, M. G..
Gottleib ENGELAGE to Emilie VAZELPOHL (sic) - both of Warren County - February 7, 1869, by H. C. ZIMMER, M. G..
Nicolaus REIF to Elisabeth SCHARFENBERGER - January 7, 1869, by Fr. Will. HINFSEN (sic).
Andres BERND to Susanna SPECKHOLS - January 26, 1869, by Fr. W. HINFSEN.
Lorenz WEIFSER to Veronica STOLLER - January 22, 1869, by Fr. W. HINFSEN.
John NOLTE to Mary WEBER - January 19, 1869, by Fr. W. HINFSEN.
Willis PENNINGTON to Sarah LEMMONS - December 22, 1854 (or 1864), by Jos. H. BARBARICK, J. P.. Marriage was not recorded until 1869.
Dudley A. JENKENS to Sarah PENNINGTON - November 16, 1863, by Henry C. KEHR, J. P..
Henry YOUNGEBLUT to Hanna BLANKE - March 4, 1869, by Henry BLANKE, M. G..
J. C. DAILY to Mrs. Mary L. A. STITES- February 28, 1869, by William BRIDGES, M. G..
John DAILY to Mary STITES - February 28, 1869, by William BRIDGES, M. G..

Phillip DOLL, son of Jacob DOLL to Christine Margaretha DIETERLIE, daughter of Gott. Fr. DIETERLIE - March 29, 1869, by Wilhelm F. BECK, M. G..

Joseph H. BAIBERRICK to Marie M. SCHOCKLEY - March 22, 1869, by Lewis TACKETT, J. P..

Herod WILSON to Sintha ROGERS - April 18, 1869, by Lewis TACKETT, J. P..

William NOLTENMEYER to Cornelia HAUPT - March 29, 1869, by JOhn M. GIWEAN (sic), M. G..

Wilhelm SIEDMEIER to Marie SCHNEIDER - March 28, 1869, by C. NESTEL, M. G..

Carl SCHWARTZEL to Anna Catharine BALTZ, born KUHN - March 2, 1869, by C. NESTEL, M. G..

David REMBOLD to Mrs. Anna Maria FRANK, born WUNZ - January 17, 1869, by C. NESTEL, M. G..

Friedrich KLINGER to Elisabetha STRAUB - December 27, 18686, by C. NESTEL, M. G..

Thomas J. McCONNEL to Missouri E. BOSTON - April 1, 1869, by L. M. MAHANEY, M. G..

Perry A. RICHARDSON to Susan S. JOHNSTON - March 21, 1869, by Henry C. KEHR, J. P..

Ferdinand August Fredk. BOHL to Louise Catharine SPOHRER - December 22, 1868, by Fredrick von der LIPPE, M. G..

Louis SPORER to Marie Caroline Ernestrine BOHL - February 25, 1869, by Frederick von der LIPPE - M. G..

Christian JESSEN to Lisabeth A. SANDS - May 23, 1869, by Christian P. ANDERSON, J. P..

Robert J. NORIMMER to Sary Lisabeth BARTER - May 28, 1869, by Christian P. ANDERSON, J. P..

William B. SORRELS to Elizabeth J. KLASNER - May 30, 1869, by Henry C. KEHR, J. P..

Carl KLICK to Caroline HELD - June 11, 1869, by H. C. ZIMMER, M. G..

Medford A. L. TRAVESTER to Martha E. HONESTEY - April 1, 1869, by Willaim WESTLOCK, J. P..

Frederich HENIG to Henrietta LANGE - April 20, 1869, by F. DREWELL, M. G..

Wilhelm LAUBERT to Johanna NIERMANN - May 5, 1869, by F. DREWELL, M. G..

Frederick BEHRMANN to Anna BERGER - June 8, 1869, by F. DREWELL, M. G..

Jacob BARIES (sic) to Fredericke Sophia FLAKE - April 20, 1869, by C. NESTEL, M. G..

Wilhelm ROTHERMEYER to Annie WILD - April 7, 1869, by C. NESTEL, M. G..
Christopher SEEMS to Barbara SCHEIFFER - May 21, 1869, by E. KRECH, J. P..
Adolph BRANDENBURGER to Maria Christine STOHLMANN - May 18, 1869, by E. KRECH, J. P..
Newton Jasper REYNOLDS to Phoebe J. MILLER - January 20, 1869, by William MILLER.
Gottleib SIEGER to Marie BRAEVILLE - April 4, 1869, by C. NESTEL, M. G..
Johann Jacob HOFER to Catherine BUMMER - July 29, 1869, by Fred HUNDHAUSEN, M. G..
Heinrich RONNEBURGER to Henrietta TOMASCHKE - August 8, 1869, by Fred HUNDHAUSEN, M. G..
Gottfried AUKEY to Minnie DURSH (sic) - August 2, 1869, by Francis SULLIVAN, J. P..
William J. SHEIREL to Eliza M. CARROLL - May 6, 1869, by Lewis TACKETT, J. P..
James CARROLL to Mahaley J. SHOCKLEY - May 9, 1869, by Lewis TACKETT, J. P..
Robert J. SHOCKLEY to Lucy Jane PALMER - May 13, 1869, by Lewis TACKETT, J. P..
John DOMANN to Mrs. Wilhelmina SHEIDECK - August 4, 1869, by F. J. RUCHERT, M. G..
Ferdinand SOHLOTTOCH to Albertine KOTTWITZ - August 11, 1869, by G. BURGMANN, M. G..
George RICHARDSON to Lilly Ann BILES - August 16, 1869, by Henry C. KEHR, J. P..
Friederich HEINLEIN to Lize J. PIERPOINT - May 23, 1869, by C. RABENAU, J. P..
William T. McKINNEY to TAbitha LEWIS - September 5, 1869, by William P. LAMBETH, M. G..
Benjamin P. RICHARDSON to Martha J. JOHNSTON - August 29, 1869, by Henry C. KEHR, J. P..
Benjamine SPALDING to Mary ELizabeth FARRIS - September 1, 1869, by Henry C. KEHR, J. P..
Charles WEISER to Richarda HATT - August 23, 1869, by Wm. HINSON, M. G..
Anton NEBEL to Rosa HATT - August 30, 1869, by Wm. HINSON, M. G..
Henry SCHWARZ to Rosina NEIDHARDT - June 15, 1869, by Wm. HINSON, M. G..
Theodore VOLLMER to Louise LOSTER - September 24, 1869, by Fred HUNDHAUSEN, M. G..
Carl SONNTAG to Auguste SCHUTT - July 9, 1869, by H. C. DIMMER, M. G..

Christian Frederick William KRIEGER to Christian Anna Ilesbein KIESHL - August 26, 1869, by L. E. KNIEF.
Ulrich PEPE to Kearoline RAUSTHER - June 17, 1869, by Henry BRINKMANN, M. G..
Fritz NESE to Caterina GEERKE - March 12, 1869, by Henry BRINKMANN, M. G..
Herman GEVILE to Karoline GICK - April 22, 1869, by HEnry BRINKMANN, M. G..
George W. YARNIER to Elizabeth HAMBY - September 9, 1869, by Henry C. KEHR, J. P..
Max Louis WELHELMI to Mary JACOB - October 1, 1869, by E. B. HENSLEY, J. P..
Samuel MORGAN to Sarah MICKS - September 13, 1869, by Benjamin LEACH, M. G..
Thomas MERIDETH to Juramyra E. GRAHAM - November 11, 1869, by Henry C. HEHR, J. P..
Thomas LILLMAN to Mrs. Charlotta TUNING - November 2, 1869, by Henry C. KEHR, J. P..
William H. WRIGHT to Mrs. Mary Ann BURCHARD - October 30, 1869, by Henry C. KEHR, J. P..
Ferdinand WOLKING to Caroline BUNTE - September 3, 1869, by Frederick V. D. LIPPE, M. G..
William WATERMANN to Dorothea KRAMANS - October 29, 1869, by J. BRUGEMANN, M. G..
David L. KINKLE to Elizabeth MAHANEY - October 7, 1869, by William BRIDGES, M. G..
Carl VOGT to Bertha SCHMIDT - August 28, 1869, by C. NESTEL, M. G..
Diedrich LOMPE to Johanna SCHNETH (sic) - November 24, 1869, by Fred HUNDHAUSEN, M. G..
Chas. August WERNER to Mrs. Anna Margaretha AUNECKE - December 8, 1869, by E. KRECH, J. P..
Rev. Carl KANTZ to Louise HORSTMANN - October 7, 1869, by C. NESTEL, J. P..
Henry TOLLE to Heinriette KUGGE (sic) - September 10, 1869, by E. A. ELFELD, M. G..
Christian WERNER to Caroline POCHE, born SCHOLLAND - December 16, 1869, by Fried. HUNDHAUSEN, M. G..
Christian KLOPPER to Mary ROHLFING - October 8, 1869, by Y. J. RIVCHERT, M. G..
Louis Franz Carl KLENKE to Louise Friederica MULLER - November 26, 1869, by F. HUNDHAUSEN, M. G..
Francis C. KLOGGES to Sintha M. MATTHEWS -

September 25, 1869, by lewis TACKETT, J. P..
William CARR to Mary E. SHIRRELL - October 2, 1869, by Lewis TACKETT, J. P..
Silis CANTLEY to Amenda NELSON - November 25, 1869, by Lewis TACKETT, J. P..
Heinrich Frederich LUENBURG to Marie Caroline STPEHEN - November 26, 1869, by C. RABENAU, J. P..
Fritz LAMS to Sarah Elizabeth LAURA - November 28, 1869, by C. RABENAU, J. P..
Henry TINNERMEIER to Mary BOHM - November 17, 1869, by C. KANTZ, M. G..
Wiley Ed LUSTER to Hannah S. WOODRUFF - January 2, 1869, by Francis SULLIVAN, J. P..
Simon FRITZEMEIER to Maria KEINKULLER - November 20, 1869, by A. HOFFMAN, M. G..
Freiderich STAUDE (sic) to Emma GREINER - January 13, 1870, by Fried. HUNDHAUSEN, M. G..
Lindsay MAUPIN to Malinda HOLT - December 12, 1869, by E. B. HENSLEY, J. P..
Christian KLOSSNER to Theresa GNADT - December 23, 1869, by Johann BLANTGEN, M. G..
John Henry BORGMANN to Marie Katherina HESTERMASER - December 9, 1869, by Fred ROEDEL, M. G..
Wilhelm BIMMERT to Josephine BRINKMANN - December 10, 1869, by F. DREWELL, M. G..
Frederich Wilhelm BIRGER to Anna Fr. HEIDBRINK - December 21, 1869, by F. ROEDERL, M. G..
F. Heinrich MAIER to Sophie BIERWIRTH - December 23, 1869, by F. DREWEL, M. G..
Benjamin PIBBONS to Margaret N. BURCHARD - June 9, 1870, by Henry C. KEHR, J. P..
Henry J. McKINEY to Sarah J. HOWARD - December 7, 1869, by Benjamin LEACH, M. G..
Drut (sic) Clinton HOLLINDSWORTH to Nancy C. BAYLESS - February 10, 1870, by Benjamin LEACH, M. G..
John BURGER to Maria BRUNIWAST - March 5, 1870, by C. RUBENAU, J. P..
Henry STENE to Anna SCHUMUCKER - February 24, 1870, by C. RABENAU, J. P..
Christian SCHMIDT to Louise RUEDIGER - March 1, 1870, by C. RABENAU, J. P..
Friederick HILBER Sr., to Mrs. Margaretha MARSH, born KERN - December 17, 1869, by C. NESTEL, M. G..

Theodore WICKELL to Charlotte SEMKEN - December 21, 1869, by C. NESTEL, M. G..
Hermann LESSEL to Julia NEITZER - January 21, 1870, by C. NESTEL, M. G..
Carl SCHMIDT to Auguste HOFFMAN - February 6, 1870, by C. NESTEL, M. G..
Adam HEINEDH to Anna BREUMLING - February 25, 1870, by C. NESTEL, M. G..
Ferdinand LOEB to Louisa EBERLING - March 3, 1870, by C. NESTEL, M. G..
George NISCHE to Julie HOFFMAN - March 3, 1870, by C. NESTEL, M. G..
Stephen LAUER to Pauline WILLMANN - March 31, 1870, F. HUNDHAUSEN, M. G..
Frank KLICK to Lina OLPEL - December 28, 1869, by H. C. ZIMMER, M. G..
Henry WILLEMANN to Marie AUSTERMANN - March 13, 1870, by Fred ROEDERL, M. G..
Heinrich GASTNER to Henrietta DRIER - April 9, 1870, by F. HUNDHAUSEN, M. G..
James WHEEL to Mrs. Elizabeth ALLCORN - April 7, 1870, by Benjamin LEACH, M. G..
Otto STREHLY to Marie ROBENAU - April 21, 1870, by F. HUNDHAUSEN, M. G..
James McQUIEN to Molessa ROGERS - January 27, 1870, by Lewis TACKETT, J. P..
Friedrich MITTENDORF to Bertha KOTTWITZ - March 28, 1870, by Adolph PICKER, M. G..
Peter HICKS to Mary E. J. SMITH - January 13, 1870, Lewis TACKETT, J. P..
Andrew McKINNEY to Hanner P. YAK - February 3, 1870, by Lewis TACKETT, J. P..
William SCHLOMANN to Elizabeth STRAUB - April 20, 1870, by John M. DERWIN, M. G..
Frederick KOENIG to Caroline BRANDT - April 26, 1870, by Henrich BRINKMEYER, M. G..
Henry TRACHT to Maria WESTHOLD - March 13, 1870, by Henrich BRINKMEYER, M. G..
Henry GROTTER to Susan MAUPIN - May 12, 1870, by Benjamin LEACH, M. G..
Nicolaus HEINIES to Cathrine NICHOLI - March 10, 1870, by W. WETTLOCK, J. P..
William ZIMMER to Minna ROHL - April 20, 1870, by C. C. ZIMMER, M. G..
Clemens MAMATH to Katharine KERN - June 8, 1870, by C. C. ZIMMER, M. G..

Julius BEIRMANN to Caroline BARRIER - April 7, 1870, by C. KAUTZ, M. G..
Adolph Josep PRUDOT to Anna Sara STEIGER - June 16, 1870, by Fred HUNDHAUSEN, M. G..
Ferdinand NOWACK to Bertha Johanna PETRUSCHKE - July 1, 1870, by Adolphus PICKER, M. G..
Chr. Turner EREKSON to Mary Jane DOUGLASS, both colored - April 10, 1870, by G. F. HILBERT, J. P..
Johannes SCHNEIDER to Mrs. Louisa GLOVE - June 8, 1870, by F. ROEDEL, M. G..
Wilhelm BICKER to Henriette GELLER - July 10, 1870, by F. ROEDEL, M. G..
Hermann Heinrich WINTER to Johanne WITTE - May 26, 1870, by F. ROEDEL, M. G..
J. D. PARKER to Mary Cath CHATHAM - August 4, 1870, by H. DIETZEL, J. P..
Friederick SCHMATSLE (sic) to Mrs. Mina KOBUSH, born ZOFENER - June 6, 1870, by C. NESTEL, M. G..
Johann HAID to Sophia HEINRICH - April 26, 1870, by C. NESTEL, M. G..
Heinrich LANGHORST to Elizabeth HUBERMEHL - June 4, 1870, by C. NESTEL, M. G..
Joseph REBSUENER to Lina HENZE - August 18, 1870, by Fried. HUNDHAUSEN, M. G..
C. F. KARSTEDT to Catharine MILLER - June 16, 1870, by E. B. HENSLEY, J. P..
Albert JONES to Mrs. John BUNER - May 13, 1870, by Ernst KRECH, J. P..
Ferdinand KAUFMAN to Katharine FEIL - May 18, 1870, by Ernst KRECH, J. P..
George KOSENBERGER to Lisbeth McQUALITY - August 25, 1870, by Ernst KRECH, J. P..
John Henry ELSENRADD to Johanna VON BECK - August 23, 1870, by Fr. Meinrad BURGLER.
Heinrich Wilhelm BRACHT to Louise Wilhelmine GISHNER - July 19, 1870, by P. WASELOH.
John HOMFELDT to Margaretha BOTTCHER - August 19, 1870, by George BRUGMANN, M. G..
Richard WITZEL to Magdalen KUEBLER - September 13, 1870, by Fr. Meinrad BURGLER.
Henry BREMER to Theodora May VARHOLT - September 14, 1870, by Fr. Meinrad BURGLER.
Henry THEE to Diena UPHOFF - September 27, 1870, by Fr. Meinrad BURGLER.

Henry ROHLFING, son of Frederic ROHLFING to Louise BERGER, daughter of Peter BERGER - September 1, 1870, by William Frederic BEK, M. G..
Michael KRATTLE to Caroline MUELLER - October 27, 1870, by Fred FRANKENFELD.
Friederich LOLK to Maria SUNKEL - November 17, 1870, by Heinrich BRINKMEYER, M. G..
Melchior HOFFERTH to Ernestina ROEMER - November 18, 1870, by Fred HUNDHAUSEN, M. G..
Carl BOCK to Johanna HOPP - October 4, 1870, by H. C. TIMMER, M. G..
Friedrich BURGER to Ellen BROMLY - August 27, 1870, by C. RABENAU, J. P..
Thomas S. BREMELL to Pauly GERNER - September 1, 1870, by C. RABENAU, J. P..
E. W. QUICK to Dulcinia ZUMWOOD (ZUMWALT) - November 1, 1870, by C. RABENAU, J. P..
Vincent MULLER to Paulina GUENERT - September 28, 1870, by Fr. Alexander MOTHAUSHER.
Michael JORDAN to Friedericka STONNER - October 5, 1870, by August SCHELLING, M. G..
Nicolaus KUEBLER to Maria Magdelina BLIELE - October 18, 1870, by August SCHELLING, M. G..
Hermann NELSON to Margaretha KRUSE - October 19, 1870, August SCHELLING, M. G..
Christian HOFFMANN to Johanna POLMANN - November 4, 1870, by August SCHELLING, M. G..
Gustav Adolph MERTENS to Amanda KAEMPF - August 28, 1870, by C. NESTEL, M. G..
Friederich EBERHARDT to Rosalie KEPLER - October 4, 1870, by C. NESTEL, M. G..
Gustav ETTMULLER, Dr., to Emma MONIG - December 1, 1870, by C. NESTEL, M. G..
Gottfried BAY to Jacobine BEHLHEM - October 9, 1870, by C. NESTEL, M. G..
John A. BARRETT to Anna Augusta Magaretha KRECH - September 11, 1870, by Ernest KRECH, J. P..
Edward LEIMBERGER to Henrietta HAMMELMANN - October 1, 1870, by F. DREWEL, M. G..
Fre. William BRUEGGENMANN to Auguste BACKER - December 1, 1870, by F. DREWEL, M. G..
Heinrich Ernst GRUEN to Malinda Josephine BRINKMANN - December 2, 1870, by F. DREWEL, M. G..
Henry BRINKHOLTER to Mrs. Louise KELLER - September 22, 1870, by F. ROEDEL, M. G..

John R. WEST to Margaret ELMING STRATFORD - December 3, 1870, by Heinrich KOENIG, J. P..
Wilhelm PRISZ to Carolina SPRENGER - December 26, 1870, by F. ROEDEL, M. G..
Thomas POLSTON to Nancy DILLERING RATTLIF - January 12, 1871, by Herrich KOENIG, J. P..
A. AUFDERHEIDE (sic) to Henriette NIEWALD - November 10, 1870, by E. A. ELFELD, M. G..
Friedrich BOCK to Henriette PODJADKE - January 5, 1871, by Adolphus PICKER, M. G..
Christ GRAH to Louise MEYER - February 25, 1871, by Peter HOHNER, M. G..
Simon ELSENRAT to Gertrude EPING - February 20, 1871, by Fr. A. SCHELLING.
Hermann EPING to Catharine DALLER - February 9, 1871, by Fr. Aug. SCHELLING.
Hermann FEES to Maria Magdelina WATZ - December 13, 1870, by Fr. August SCHELLING.
Jan VONHARD to Margaretha GERMAN - February 16, 1871, by Fr. August SCHELLING.
R. J. LANE to Mary DOWLER - January 15, 1871, by John GRANNEMANN, M. G..
Wilhelm SCHULTE to Charlotte Henriette DOERMANN - January 21, 1871, by F. DREWEL, M. G..
Andrew HOFFMANN to Auguste SOUDER - December 22, 1870, by And. HOFFMANN, M. G..
Andrew Peter FEDDERSEN to Maria Doette WORTHMANN - February 16, 1871, by P. WESELOH, M. G..
Andrew POLSTON to Mary J. DAVAS - March 2, 1871, by Heinrich KOENIG, J. P..
Jacob ANDERSON to Elisabeth JOHNSON - February 23, 1870, by Heinrich KONIG, J. P..
Friedrich W. PETTERSON to Bertha STEPHAN - February 2, 1871, by C. RABENAU, J. P..
Conrad SOHUCK to Pauline HASENRITTER - March 25, 1871, by F. H. HILKER, J. P..
Marion HAYNES to Berbera BARBERICK - March 23, 1871, by F. McCuin COOPER, J. P..
Julius Friedrich SILBER to Caroline HECKMANN - December 31, 1870, by C. NESTEL, M. G..
Andreas MUSTER to Mathilda DIECKER, born FORSTER - February 22, 1871, by C. NESTEL, M. G..
Henry PFIEFER to Martha WERREN - May 16, 1871, by Henry C. KEHR, J. P..
Friederich GIDINGHAGEN to Hanna LUMKUELER - April 27, 1871, by A. HOFFMANN, M. G..

Heinrich HOENER to Wilhelmina BRINKMANN - March 31, 1871, by A. HOFFMANN, M. G..
Friederich LEIMKUELER to Anna Maier - May 12, 1871, by A. HOFFMANN, M. G..
Friedrick SHOENNER to Sophia DOERMANN - March 29, 1871, by F. DREWEL, M. G..
Jacob BOESCH to Dorothea DREWEL - March 14, 1871, by F. FRANKENFELD, M. G..
Jesley ENGE to Sarah C. KLOPNER - May 21, 1871, by Henry C. KEHR, J. P..
Frederick RINGEISEN to Nancy L. LEACH - May 31, 1871, by Henry C. KEHR, J. P..
Refuse E. FRASHER to Mary Ann GRAHAM - June 29, 1871, by Henry C. KEHR, J. P..
Leander BAKER to Annie M. BOND - June 27, 1871, by Benjamin LEACH, M. G..
John UFFELMANN to Friedricka SONTAG - June 6, 1871, by C. RABENAU, J. P..
John WEILSEL to Katharina HELLEGEN - June 25, 1871, by C. RABENAU, J. P..
Benjamin F. SMITH to Mandy P. ERKSON - July 16, 1871, by C. L. DURBIN, J. P..
H. Jackson HAINES to Adeline REED - August 6, 1871, by Henry C. KEHR, J. P..
Charles SCHROEDER to Emilie SCHUTH - September 7, 1871, by Fried HUNDHAUSEN, M. G..
Welhelm FRICKE to Agathe DUFNER - September 7, 1871, by Fried. HUNDHAUSEN, M. G..
Heinrich SCHAUMBURG to Theresia MULLER - May 4, 1871, by C. NESTEL, M. G..
Weldman Ferdinand MERTENS to Clementine BAIR - June 6, 1871, by C. NESTEL, M. G..
Conrad UTHE to Henriette WILMS - June 22, 1871, by F. DREWEL, M. G..
Ferdinand RETKE to Henriette HARTKE, widow - July 30, 1871, by H. C. TIMMER, M. G..
Franz BAER to Auguste OTTEMEIER - August 18, 1871, by C. NESTEL, M. G..
Christian GRABENSTEIN to Catherina GROP - August 21, 1871, by C. NESTEL, M. G..
Henry NUEHMANN to Mary RAHLE - September 7, 1871, by F. DREWEL, M. G..
J. Wieley BILES to Mandy RICHARDSON - October 26, 1871, by Henry C. KEHR, J. P..
Henry AHRENS to Margareth PHILIP - September 23, 1871, by F. J REICHERT, M. G..

Adolph BIEKER to Verenah PLUMER - September 26, 1871, by F. DREWEL, M. G..
Rudolph MUELLER to Anna SUTTER - July 27, 1871, by F. FRANKENFELD, M. G..
Robert BAUMGARTNER to Carolina FISCHER - November 16, 1871, by Friederich HUNDHAUSEN, M. G..
J. J. RICHARDSON to E. A. BAKER - November 19, 1871, by Henry C. KEHR, J. P..
Heinrich NAHNER to Pauline PLUST - November 28, 1871, by Fried HUNDHAUSEN, M. G..
Carl Heinrich WOLKING to Dina Anna SCHULTE - November 2, 1871, by H. BLANKE, M. G..
Friedrich Johan SCHULTE to Maria Dorothea WOLKING - November 2, 1871, by H. BLANKE, M. G..
Henry Alexander STAUFFER to Anna MEYER - November 3, 1871, by H. BLANKE, M. G..
Heinrich LIESMEIER to Sophie STRANK - November 9, 1871, by H. BLANKE, M. G..
Friedrich W. NULLMEIER to Charoline FLACHMANN - November 23, 1871, by H. BLANKE, M. G..
Daniel W. LEMONS to Lilly Ann JENKINS - November 8, 1871, by Wm. R. VAUGHAN, M. G..
Friederich BRINKMANN to Anna LUETTHAUS - November 10, 1871, by A. HOFFMANN, M. G..
Friedrich ENKE to Ernestine Maria VALENTIN - September 3, 1871, by Adolphus PICKER, M. G..
Jacob WEBER to Louise ROTHFUCHS - October 3, 1871, by C. NESTEL, M. G..
Henry W. KRAMME to Sarah A. THOMAS - February 20, 1872, by Wm. R. VAUGHAN, M. G..
Friederick Wil KLICK to Anna BEUL - March 8, 1872, by F. M. HAFELE, M. G..
Wilhelm WEHMEIER to Karoline Auguste KLICK - March 8, 1872, by F. M. HASFELE, M. G..
Nahman REED to Margaret BRUER - February 4, 1872, by Henry C. KEHR, J. P..
Charles DIEBOLL to Wilhamine G. C. DRUSH - March 22, 1872, by H. E. MICHELS, M. G..
George STARK to Laura FELDMANN - April 2, 1872, by F. H. HILKER, J. P..
Thesphil SCHAFFNER to Louise HOFFMANN - May 26, 1872, by Fried HUNDHAUSEN, M. G..
Wesley MASEY to Elisabeth A. BIRD - April 4, 1872, by C. F. KARSTEDT, J. P..
Wilhelm KUHLMANN to Heurina HOEFELS - February 6, 1872, by Fr. August SCHELLING.

Modest EPPLE to Elisabeth CHAMUTH - April 23, 1872, by Fr. August SCHELLING.
Gustav HAHUKE to Henrietta GEST - April 27, 1872, by Friederich HUNDHAUSEN, M. G..
Wilhelm MUELLER to Wilhelmine HOFFMANN - February 2, 1872, by A. HOFFMANN, M. G..
Fr. Aug. ACHERHAUSEN to Elisa LIELE - ? 27, 1872, recorded May 4th, by Peter HEHUER, M. G..
Herman MEYER to Caroline STRACK - May 15, 1872, by Charles STEINMEYER, M. G..
Peter TILTY to Betta HORN - May 15, 1872, by Fried HUNDHAUSEN, M. G..
John LIPERIN to Lizzie ROBINSON - May 16, 1872, by Fr. Aug. SCHELLING.
John MISLLER to Elizabeth FREY - May 6, 1872, by Fr. August SCHELLING.
Heinrich CORVEY to Magdelina ANDRY - May 27, 1872, by H. BLANKE, M. G..
Hermann BERGMEN to Emilie EBERLIN - June 23, 1872, by F. H. HILKER, J. P..
Daniel BOCHUR to Wilhelmina HUNOLD (sic) - June 19, 1872, by P. HEHNER, M. G..
Peter NOLTING to MIna LANGENDORFER - June 14, 1872, by Peter HEHNER, M. G..
Martin PASCH to Friederice LENICKE - June 26, 1872, by Fried HUNDHAUSEN, M. G..
Carl FACH to Cornelia EITZEN - May 14, 1872, by C. NESTEL, M. G..
Bernhard HEUMANN to Dorothea WEIDEMANN - April 7, 1872, by F. DREWEL, M. G..
Wilhelm HOCHSTENBACH to Wilhelmina WEINDMEIER - April 10, 1872, by C. NESTEL, M. G..
Wilhelm KLEE to Mathilda KETTELMANN - March 19, 1872, by C. NESTEL, M. G..
John HOLT to Mary A. BALEY - June 30, 1872, by Henry C. KEHR, J. P..
Henderson WATSON to Mary C. HOLT - July 21, 1872, by Benjamin LEACH, M. G..
Joseph COULTER to Lucinda F. CHUMLEY - May 28, 1872, by Wm. BRIDGES, M. G..
Samuel WALKER to LIddie MASON - July 26, 1872, by F. H. HILKER, J. P..
George W. LEMONS to Elvira J. JENKINS - July 7, 1872, by Wm. R. VAUGHAN, M. G..
F. A. ACKENHAUSEN to Louise MARTIN - December 27, 1871, by P. HEHNER, M. G..

John Henry ROEDEL to Louise BAHMEISTER - May 21, 1872, by Friedrich ROEDEL, M. G..
Christine LANGENDORFER to Magdalena CUNE - June 20, 1872, by Henri ROUPOT (sic), J. P..
Samuel ALLEMANN to Margareth ALLEMANN - August 17, 1872, by F. H. HILKER, J. P..
Heinrich BUSCHMEIER to Wilhelmine Caroline GAERTNER - August 22, 1872, by Fried HUNDHAUSEN, M. G..
William P. COOPER to Elizabeth HIBLER - August 25, 1872, by Benjamin LEACH, M. G..
Severin NUTHARD to Catharina KAMPER, born FREY - May 3, 1872, by Fr. A. SCHELLING.
Charles KUMMEL to Annette OPNER - August 8, 1872, by Fr. A. SCHELLING.
Bernard SCHILDMACHER to Maria SELKER - August 20, 1872, by Fr. A. SCHELLING.
Bernard STEIN to Louisa SOHIVARY (sic) - September 17, 1872, by Fr. A. SCHELLING.
Hiram N. STETS to Sarah MAUPIN - September 15, 1872, by Benjamin LEACH, M. G..
Jacob BAER to Louise Wilhelmine OTTERMAEIER - October 12, 1872, by Fried HUNDHAUSEN, M. G..
Johann Heinrich STRUBE to Pauline MULHAUS - October 14, 1872, by Fried HUNDHAUSEN, M. G..
Julius HUNDHAUSEN to Clara Wilhelmine HOLSHAUS - October 22, 1872, by Fried HUNDHAUSEN, M. G..
Ludwig BAECKER to Carolina HOLMER - November 13, 1872, by Fried HUNDHAUSEN, M. G..
Heinrich ERFMANN TO Louise BUSCHMANN - August 22, 1872, by Fred HUNDHAUSEN, M. G..
Hermann MICHELS to Emilie Maria BOHRENPOHE - October 16, 1872, by F. DREWEL, M. G..
John H. WITTROCK to Anna Margaretha Bielfeldt - October 27, 1872, by H. E. MICHELS, M. G..
John BOOS (sic) to Mathilda PETRUS - December 5, 1872, by F. H. HILKER, M. G..
James W. RAMEY to Lidia A. MISKER - December 14, 1872, by Peter TOON, J. P..
George JANST to Anna Margaretha ALLEMANN - September 12, 1872, by C. RABENAU, J. P..
Robert L. BIELS to Martha MATTHEWES - December 5, 1872, Heinrich KONIG, J. P..
Conrad HUMBURG to Pauline SHUTZ - August 27, 1872, by C. NESTEL, M. G..
Rev. Friedrich WERNER to Bertha BERLICH -

September 5, 1872, by C. NESTEL, M. G..
Carl RIEGER to Louise PFOTEUHAUSEN - September 12, 1872, by C. NESTEL, M. G..
Johann SCHMIDT to Bertha REHMERT - September 19, 1872, by C. NESTEL, M. G..
William WEHMUELLER to Auguste SEGER - October 3, 1872, by F. M. HARFELE, M. G..
Theodor Philipp STORK to Emma FEISCHEL - December 21, 1872, by C. NESTEL, M. G..
Charles HOUNEMAN to Virginia PRICE - December 12, 1872, by Henry C. KEHR, J. P..
Joseph BEREND to Theresia SPECKHALS - November 19, 1872, by Fr. August SCHELLING.
Andreas MUELLER to Elisa FRICKER - January 14, 1873, by Fr. August SCHELLING.
Friederich PRISZ to Louisa FRITZEMIEIR - December 19, 1872, A. HOFFMANN, M. G..
Scott MASON to Martha HENNAWAY - January 26, 1873, Benjamin LEACH, M. G..
John George ALLEMANN to Magdalena HUG - February 25, 1873, by Remit JANSEN, M. G..
Rynold RAPP to Clara MICHAELS - March 21, 1873, by Peter ZORN, Jr., J. P..
Carl Mathias KEFSTER to Justine Clara FEITZEL - March 24, 1873, by Fried HUNDHAUSEN, M. G..
Fredrich RUTHEMEIER to Mrs. Dorothea EPTON - February 14, 1873, by F. DREWEL, M. G..
Ferdinand August KLICK to Johanne Adeline GABER - March 22, 1873, by F. M. HESFELS, (sic) M. G..
Edward LOELLER to Emilie EBERLEU - March 13, 1873, by C. NESTEL, M. G..
Charles MASEY to Mary Ann HOOD - April 6, 1873, by F. McCuin COOPER, J. P..
Henry VOLK to Maria BRANDHORST - April 23, 1873, by F. M. HASFELE, M. G..
Christian HASFNER to Emilie EIGELMANN - April 24, 1873, by F. M. HASFELE, M. G..
Bernhard HESEMANN to Hanna HORSTMANN - March 21, 1873, by P. WESELSH, M. G..
Joseph CANTLEY to Virginia JOHNSON - March 16, 1873, by Henry C. KEHR, J. P..
Heinrich GISDINGHAGEN to Louise LIEMKUELER - April 3, 1873, by And. HOFFMANN, M. G..
Jackson NIEBRUEGE (sic) to Maria KUHLHOELTER - April 17, 1873, by And. HOFFMANN, M. G..
Friedrich WILD to Johanna BRAENOLLE - May 5,

1873, by C. RABENAU, J. P..
Rudolph HIRZEL to Mathilda NAPE - April 19, 1873, by C. NESTEL, M. G..
Thomas F. HANES to Lucy E. ADKINS - July 2, 1871.
Maria Margaretha PUCHTA and Adam PUCHTA gave gave their statements as witnesses to the wedding of Louis MESSMEYER and Margaretha Barbara PUCHTA, a daughter of John PUCHTA, who was now deceased. This marriage occurred February 5, 1852, and was performed by Joseph LEPEL, J. P., who had also died. Recorded August 31, 1871.
John F. HARTWIG to Mina Matta HIMPELMANN - October 17, 1871, by H. E. NICHOLS, M. G..
Gustave HIMPELMANN to Margarete HARTWIG - November 3, 1871, by H. E. NICHOLS, M. G..
Asa PINNELL to Catharine E. McALLISTER - December 24, 1871, by N. M. BUCK, M. G..
William L. BRANSON to Martha A. PERKINS - December 14, 1871, by Wm. P. LAMBETH, M. G..
Christian GRACHER to Amalia BAUMBACH - November 24, 1871, by H. E. NICHOLS, M. G..
Henry NIEWALD to Louise ROTHSCHAEFER - November 22, 1871, by W. POHREN.
Hiram COLLIER to Emaline ROGERS - February 7, 1872, by James H. ALLEN, M. G.. Witnesses were Elwing HANES and Isic ROGERS.
William R. HIP to Malisa M. MURPHY - April 4, 1872, by Milton F. MURPHY, J. P..
Joseph LANGE to Ida RADKIN - March 12, 1872, by Fred V. D. LIPPE, M. G..
Friederich SCHMIDT to Jane ROBERTSON - November 3, 1871, by H. HANKEMEYER, M. G..
Thuisko (sic) MAHL to Louise BREPER of Montgomery County - May 8, 1872, by F. N. HILKER, J. P..
Albert W. EATHERTON of St. Louis, to Nancy Jane SORRELL - March 28, 1872, by Wm. BRIGS.
Tollerman F. GROOS to Margaret E. JARVIS - February 15, 1872, by L. M. MAHANEY, M. G..
Tenon DOOLER to Sarah F. THOMPSON - March 24, 1872, by Elder Daniel J. FERGUSON.
Thomas ARMSTRONG to Agnes C. POHLMANN - April 15, 1872, by C. P. KORSTEDT, J. P..
Hiram F. COLTER to SArah C. HOUSLEY - June 20, 1872, by C. P. KORSTEDT, J. P..
Conrad RUGGE to Henriette MOELLING - July 11,

1872, by W. POHREN.
Mayo KEHR to Anna WITTRICK - August 28, 1872, by H. E. MICHEL, M. G..
Lorenzo D. VIEMAN to Mary M. McMILLEN - September 19, 1872, by M. F. MURPHY, J. P..
John P. SMITH to Frances J. HUFFMAN - December 19, 1872, by N. H. BUCK, M. G..
B. Henry NUBRUEGGE to E. M. BRANDENBURGER - November 15, 1872, by W. SCHORER.
Edward E. DENNIS to Mary J. LEWIS - January 12, 1873, by William P. LAMBETH, M. G..
George MITTENDORF to Elizabeth GRANNAMANN - January 25, 1873, by George W. REITZ, M. G..
Peter ROISTE to Mrs. Johanne FISCHER - December 29, 1872, by William SCHRECK, M. G..
William H. H. POINTER to Lizzie WERNER of West Point, Iowa - January 9, 1873, by William SCHRECK, M. G..
William KINGKADE to Liza HIBLER - January 27, 1873, by L. M. MAHANY, M. G..
Irvin THOMAS to Leriny STEPHENS - February 27, 1873, by Benjamin LEACH, M. G..

INDEX

---GEN, 55
-LOPFER, 80
ACHERHAUSEN, 111
ACKENHAUSEN, 111
ADAM, 62
ADAMS, 9 26 44 65 66
  69 76 80 91 94
ADKINS, 114
AEFT, 94
AGEE, 6 8 11 13 14 43
  55 74 80 90 94
AHEING, 83
AHERENS, 83
AHRENS, 109
AIKEN, 13 48
AITKEN, 51
AKERS, 18
ALBER, 41
ALBERT, 72 82
ALBROGHT, 80
ALDERS, 40
ALEMANN, 26
ALKIRE, 1 3 7
ALLCORN, 105
ALLELMANN, 81
ALLEMAN, 92
ALLEMANN, 112 113
ALLEN, 60 83 114
ALLENE, 68
ALLESON, 94
ALLRICHT, 79
ALPTON, 62
AMBLER, 76
AMDEON, 73
AMELING, 21 70 79 95

AMES, 82
AMMERMAN, 14
ANDERSON, 8 10 12 49
  81 88 90 91 94 101
  108
ANDERTON, 57
ANDREE, 72
ANDRY, 111
ANEGER, 91
ANGLE, 73
APEL, 28 85
APRIL, 61 76 77 91
AREND, 30
ARMSTRONG, 114
ARNOTT, 26 27 36
AROUTT, 61
ARTHUR, 38
ARUELING, 70
ASHLEY, 13
ATKINS, 51 53 72 78
ATMUNN, 85
AUD, 2
AUFDERHEIDE, 96 108
AUFDERHEIDEN, 45
AUFDEZHEDE, 82
AUGEL, 72
AUKEY, 102
AUNECKE, 103
AUSTERMAN, 50
AUSTERMANN, 27 105
AVERY, 10-12 20
AWBERRY, 14
AYERS, 24
B----, 72
BACHER, 36

BACK, 16
BACKER, 64 107
BACKUS, 4 9 13 15 16
BADE, 85
BADER, 57 88
BAECKER, 112
BAECKOR, 99
BAER, 27 35 52 58 80 109 112
BAHMEISTER, 112
BAHRON, 88
BAIBERRICK, 101
BAIER, 68
BAILEY, 93
BAISTEN, 91
BAJER, 51
BAKCUS, 16
BAKER, 3 12-15 17 86 109 110
BALDRIDGE, 2
BALDUS, 9
BALEY, 55 61 111
BALL, 3
BALLARD, 18 47
BALLBACK, 22
BALLEW, 3
BALTZ, 101
BALTZER, 53
BANAM, 45
BANER, 67
BANTO, 16
BARBARICK, 2 6 12 17 27 30 51 54 55 60 65 68-70 88 89 99 100
BARBERICK, 108
BARBRAKE, 5
BARBRICK, 25
BARCLAY, 4 5 7 8
BARHOLT, 106
BARIES, 101
BARIS, 31
BARLESCH, 94
BARNER, 88
BARNES, 93 99
BARNS, 41
BARRARICK, 40 47 48

BARREIA, 51
BARRETT, 107
BARRIER, 106
BARTER, 101
BARTIGAM, 22
BARTLETT, 35
BARTMAN, 17
BARTZ, 21
BATEMAN, 99
BATES, 47
BATTAGER, 43
BAUER, 17 18 21 37
BAUL, 15
BAUMAN, 55 98
BAUMBACH, 114
BAUMGARTNER, 75 80 89 99 110
BAXTER, 18-20 24 52 60
BAY, 107
BAYER, 19 20 48 91 94
BAYLES, 6
BAYLESS, 81 104
BEBE, 93
BEBION, 79
BECK, 6 29 31 51 53 58 66 71 73 74 79 90 96 101
BECKER, 29 62 69 83 97
BECKMAN, 59 76 86
BECKMANN, 87
BECKMEISTER, 51
BEDE, 51
BEEDMAN, 80
BEHLHEM, 107
BEHME, 57 62 63
BEHNE, 25 35 42 45 47 49 59 64
BEHNEY, 36
BEHNKE, 57
BEHR, 26
BEHREN, 56
BEHRMANN, 101
BEIBER, 37
BEIERMANN, 29
BEIRMANN, 106
BEK, 60 71 72 76 107

BELK, 12
BELL, 11
BELLINGHAUSE, 63
BELLINGTON, 89
BELT, 68
BENDER, 76 94
BENFROM, 78
BENKER, 25
BENNE, 69
BENNECKE, 70
BENNER, 61 67
BENTE, 79
BENTON, 3 9
BEREND, 113
BERGER, 50 90 101 107
BERGMAN, 88
BERGMANN, 35
BERGMEN, 111
BERGNER, 83
BERKEL, 80
BERKHARD, 30
BERKING, 87
BERKLING, 47
BERLICH, 112
BERNARD, 21 33 37
BERND, 100
BERNHARD, 97
BERNICKE, 52
BERRON, 88
BERRY, 1
BERTHE, 80
BERTINKAMP, 26
BERUD, 98
BESCHOFF, 52
BESE, 50
BESNER, 62
BEST, 20
BETHE, 51
BETHEMEYER, 69
BETHMAN, 20
BETZHOLD, 33
BETZOLD, 18
BEUERMAN, 50 67
BEUL, 110
BEYER, 63
BEYERSDORFF, 18

BIBER, 92
BICKEL, 60
BICKER, 57 106
BICKY, 63
BIDICKS, 24
BIEBER, 65
BIEBUSCH, 53
BIEKER, 50 110
BIELMEYER, 70
BIELS, 112
BIERLY, 70
BIERS, 63
BIERWIRTH, 104
BIGALOW, 21
BILES, 26 100 102 109
BIMMERT, 104
BINDE, 72
BINEYARD, 7
BINKER, 63
BINKMAN, 62
BIRD, 110
BIRGER, 104
BIRK, 57
BIRKEMEIER, 50
BIRKNER, 37-39 42 44
BISCH, 39
BISCHOFF, 34
BITTER, 64 70
BITTICK, 7 13
BIZLER, 100
BLAARER, 29 30
BLACK, 33
BLACKWELL, 23 39 88 90
BLANKE, 53 69 100 111
BLANTGEN, 104
BLATTNER, iii 96
BLEILE, 26
BLEUME, 92
BLEVENS, 24 42
BLEVIN, 53 65
BLEVINS, 63
BLIELE, 107
BLISH, 13
BLOCK, 81 88
BLOOK, 71
BLUME, 81

BLY, 87
BOCE, 71
BOCHUR, 111
BOCK, 18 37-40 43 44
  52 58 62 68 75 85 87
  107 108
BOCKSTIC, 39
BODEN, 67
BOEHM, 91
BOEING, 23
BOESCH, 30 109
BOESH, 91
BOETCHER, 83
BOGE, 71 73 79
BOHEMEISTER, 90
BOHL, 38 65 76 99 101
BOHLFING, 88
BOHLKEN, 21
BOHM, 47 104
BOHRENPOHE, 112
BOHU, 56
BOILS, 27 53
BOING, 36-41 44-57 77
BOLES, 18
BOLTON, 9 10
BOLWARE, 5
BOMET, 48
BOND, 109
BOOKMAN, 81
BOON, 11 13
BOONE, 48
BORCHARDT, 38
BORGMANN, 79 104
BORLESCH, 97
BORSCH, 49
BOSCH, 37
BOSCHE, 82
BOSSEN, 17
BOSTON, 101
BOTCHER, 78
BOTTCHEL, 74
BOTTCHEN, 88
BOTTCHER, 81 106
BOTTERMANN, 57 80
BOTTLER, 22
BOUGHAN, 43

BOUNDS, 13 14 18
BOUSING, 76
BOWEN, 24 52 67 76
BOWER, 6
BOWIN, 17 31
BOWLWARE, 25
BRACHT, 106
BRADFORD, 3-6 8 11
BRADSHAW, 23
BRAENOLLE, 113
BRAEVILLE, 102
BRAKEHOFF, 13
BRALY, 41 42 58
BRAMBLE, 38
BRAND, 37 71 100
BRANDENBURG, 78
BRANDENBURGER, 61 102
  115
BRANDENHORST, 73
BRANDERBURGER, 86
BRANDHOLT, 71
BRANDHORST, 22 54 113
BRANDIGAM, 25
BRANDT, 44 92 105
BRANER, 91
BRANNAM, 41
BRANNER, 62
BRANNUM, 56
BRANSOM, 22
BRANSON, 6-12 14-18 22
  24 26 27 32 36 43 44
  49 53 55 61 66 76 83
  85 93 97-99 114
BRANSWORTH, 75
BRASHEAR, 5 7-9
BRASHER, 6 7
BRASILL, 6
BRAUMOARTH, 98
BRAUN, 55 92
BRAUNNORTH, 51
BRAY, 13 62
BREDEHORST, 69
BREHE, 29
BREIDPOHT, 80
BREMER, 106
BRENNER, 64

BREPER, 114
BREUMLING, 105
BREWER, 40
BRICE, 72
BRIDGES, 84 92 98-100 103 111
BRIEGEMANN, 88
BRIGES, 5
BRIGGS, 94
BRIGS, 11 55 114
BRILS, 59
BRIMM, 56
BRINGMANN, 30
BRINKHOLTER, 107
BRINKMAN, 28 37 58 92 93 97
BRINKMANN, 79 94 103 104 107 109 110
BRINKMANS, 69
BRINKMEYER, 105 107
BRINKOTTER, 39
BRINSDON, 99
BRISCH, 38
BRISTO, 3
BRITTHORST, 78
BROCK, 18
BROEMSER, 87
BROMLY, 107
BROTT, 65
BROWN, 2-5 7 11 18 20 23 30 40 47 66 73 80 82 83 87 93 95 97
BRUEGARMEYER, 89
BRUEGGENMANN, 107
BRUER, 110
bBRUGEMAN, 95
BRUGEMANN, 98 103
BRUGLEB, 78
BRUGMAN, 90
BRUGMANN, 92 106
BRUMLEY, 6 21 26 78
BRUMLY, 25
BRUNE, 81 82 89
BRUNGRABER, 52
BRUNIWAST, 104
BRUNS, 31

BRUNSWICK, 87
BUBER, 71
BUCHER, 77
BUCK, 114 115
BUCKER, 29 54 79
BUCKHOLZ, 80 87
BUDDE, 39 66
BUDDMEIR, 37
BUEL, 73
BUER, 93
BUESH, 48
BUHLEMEYER, 63
BUKER, 67
BULLARD, 58
BULLE, 99
BULLINGTON, 96
BUMMER, 74 102
BUMPASS, 1-6 8-12 15 17 18 95
BUNER, 106
BUNKER, 53
BUNKHARDT, 52
BUNNER, 64
BUNTAE, 39
BUNTE, 46 70 79 81 103
BURCHARD, 2 4 8 11 14 17-21 27 30 32 35 37 45 64 103 104
BURCHARDT, 83
BURCKHARDT, 55 59
BURGER, 15 104 107
BURGES, 23 25
BURGESS, 5 6 11 12 15 16 18-21 24 25 30-33 36 46 47 54 55 92
BURGETT, 81
BURGGEMAN, 99
BURGLER, 106
BURGMANN, 102
BURGOYNE, 2
BURHLE, 35
BURIE, 57
BURK, 24 57
BURKERT, 74
BURKS, 25 35
BURLE, 37

BURLEY, 46
BURNE, 43
BURNS, 25 91
BURRITT, 48
BURTE, 34
BURTON, 82
BURTZ, 30
BUSCH, 21 35
BUSCHARD, 57
BUSCHART, 82
BUSCHMAN, 53 56-59 63 64 69 73 78
BUSCHMANN, 66 112
BUSCHMEIER, 112
BUSHMAN, 50-52 72
BUSHMANN, 23 37
BUSHMEYER, 97
BUTCHER, 16 17 44
BUTGANS, 58
BUTLER, 2 4 7
BUTLESS, 12
BUTMIER, 82
BUTRICK, 94 97
BUTSCHE, 87
BUTTESMEIER, 94
BYONSIDES, 2
BYRD, 82
CAAR, 65
CAHILL, 95
CAIN, 1
CALDWELL, 3 7 8 27 38 39 41 42 46 47 49 51 52 54 56 58
CALLAWAY, 5
CAMPBELL, 4 11 12 15 23 24
CAMPER, 89
CANNEL, 87
CANON, 45
CANTLEY, 104 113
CANTLY, 57 99
CANTRELL, 86
CAPEHART, 2 5 12
CAPELLA, 52
CAPHART, 5
CAPHARTE, 3

CAPPELLE, 59
CAPTAIN, 5
CARDER, 80 91 97
CARL, 30 74
CARLSON, 13
CARR, 78 86 97 99 104
CARRELL, 79
CARROL, 73
CARROLL, 9 21 40 41 47 48 67 85 102
CARTER, 1 31 32 62 97
CARTRIGHT, 8
CARVER, 61
CASEBOLT, 4
CASON, 8 16
CATWELL, 69
CAULT, 65
CERLEY, 31
CHAICKE, 70
CHAMUTH, 111
CHAPMAN, 61 76 90
CHAPPEL, 16
CHAPPLE, 12
CHAREL, 24
CHARESINBERRY, 25
CHASE, 10
CHATHAM, 106
CHIDSEY, 88
CHILDERS, 8 40 46 78 80 88 97
CHRISEMANN, 39
CHRISMAN, 7 8
CHRISMON, 1
CHRISTEL, 25 84
CHRISTEO, 71
CHRISTMAN, 71
CHUILET, 99
CHUMLEY, 111
CLAREY, 36 41
CLARK, 7 26 38
CLARY, 59 68 71 73 98
CLAUS, 23 36
CLAUSS, 31
CLAY, 90
CLEMENS, 15
CLINTON, 1 2 3

CLUBB, 12
CLYMER, 57 88 92 94
COALTER, 44
COFFEE, 17
COFFELT, 27
COFFETT, 11 12 15
COIL, 8
COLE, 38
COLEMAN, 66 81 93
COLEMMAN, 61
COLIN, 72
COLLENS, 8
COLLIER, 50 52 54 56
  76 77 81 87 88 94
  114
COLLING, 62
COLTER, 50 66 80 97
  114
COLTON, 8
COLVAN, 9 10
COLVIN, 51 79
COLWELL, 63
COLYER, 63
COMBS, 22
CONEL, 31
CONN, 80 81
CONNA, 77
CONNER, 83
CONNNIR, 74
CONNORS, 46
COOPER, 6 18 21 22 25-
  27 35 36 45 47 48 51
  63 65 68 76 79 86
  92-96 108 112 113
COPELAND, 7 13
COPPEDGE, 2 3 4
CORDER, 82
CORDRAY, 39
CORDSMEIER, 67
CORNELIUS, 2
CORRIGAN, 16
CORTES, 41
CORVEY, 111
COTTON, 94
COULTER, 67 111
COUN, 73

COURTRIGHT, 8
COWAN, 13 82 83 92
COWEN, 5 8 73
COWIN, 10
COWINS, 7
COX, 5 6 9-11 14-20 23
  25 27 31 40
COYLE, 2
CRADER, 83
CRAIG, 5 77
CRAISTER, 85
CRANDER, 88
CRAVEN, 37
CRAVENS, 75
CRAWFORD, 17
CREEK, 41
CRENAN, 88
CRESCHIEN, 79
CRIDER, 1 2 4 19 23 34
  37 40 43 44 46 51 54
  58 68 70 75 76 78 79
  82 88 96
CRISMAN, 5 23
CROUCH, 11
CROW, 4 21
CULBERSON, 31
CUNE, 112
CURTIS, 5 9
CUSCHEL, 58
CUTBIRTH, 7
CUTHBERTSON, 49 52 93
DAHL, 85
DAHLMEYER, 58
DAILEY, 83
DAILY, 100
DALTER, 32
DAMME, 76
DANENBERG, 80
DANFORTH, 9
DANHAUSER, 64
DANIEL, 7 9 77
DANUSER, 43 76 80
DANYEISEN, 55
DASE, 96
DAUBE, 35
DAVAS, 108

DAVAULT, 69 73
DAVENPORT, 10
DAVID, 5 6 10 11 16 20 23 34 61
DAVIDSON, 9
DAVIS, 3 10 13 15 17 24 59 61 64 65 70 74 83 88
DAY, 1
DEARBIN, 27
DEAVULT, 85 86
DECKHANER, 39
DEIBOLD, 30 37
DEITS, 46
DELTHY, 59
DEMWOLF, 39
DENNIS, 115
DENOE, 4
DEPP, 61
DEPPE, 67 70 83
DERBIN, 47
DERWIN, 105
DETERLE, 74
DETHARDING, 35
DETTWILLER, 80
DEVALT, 86
DEVAULT, 80 84 88 90 93
DEWITT, 71 77 94
DICKASON, 70
DICTRICK, 50
DIEBOLD, 19 96 98
DIEBOLL, 110
DIECKER, 108
DIEDERICK, 81
DIEDRICK, 50
DIERTERLE, 79
DIETERLIE, 101
DIETZ, 87
DIETZEL, 106
DILG, 99
DILLEN, 56
DILLERD, 37
DILLERING, 108
DILTHEY, 53 59 78
DIMLER, 87

DIMMER, 102
DOBDSON, 93
DOBESON, 55
DOCEMANN, 51
DODDS, 8 25
DODSON, 32
DOEHLER, 99
DOEHRING, 79 88 97
DOERCH, 80
DOERMANN, 108 109
DOESS, 22
DOGETT, 16
DOLL, 101
DOMANN, 102
DOMINICA, 85
DOOLER, 114
DOPPE, 44
DORMAN, 61 75
DORMANN, 65
DORNE, 25
DOTSON, 24 51
DOUGLAS, 45 49 51 60 64
DOUGLASS, 18 19 63-66 73 81 82 85 106
DOUISH, 92
DOULAN, 68
DOWLER, 49 81 93 108
DOWLING, 31
DOWNS, 5
DOYLE, 2 86
DOZON, 68
DRAVEL, 75
DRAWE, 49
DREKES, 32
DRESON, 90
DRESWELL, 50
DREWEL, 58 62 63 67 69 71-73 76 78 80 81 83 84 87 89 91 93 96-98 104 107-113
DREWELL, 65 67 75 81 96 101 104
DRICKER, 75
DRIER, 105
DRUSH, 110

DRUVEL, 61
DRUWELL, 64
DUCKWORTH, 12 16
DUESSMONS, 84
DUETZELED, 87
DUFFNER, 73
DUFNER, 98 109
DUKER, 57
DUNBAR, 67
DUNCAN, 1 3 4 32 39 96
DUNICA, 9
DUNN, 46
DUNNSMORE, 64
DURBIN, 15 17 27 34 35
  40 42 55 67 70 109
DURBORN, 19
DURSH, 102
DUTSCHES, 37
DUVALLS, 39
DUVAULT, 63 66 87 88
DUVEULT, 74
DYKMAN, 40
EADDS, 1
EADS, 18
EAGLIN, 72
EANOLL, 91
EASTUS, 51 56
EATHERTON, 114
EATON, 58 67
EBBER, 92
EBBERT, 59
EBELE, 87
EBELER, 22
EBERHARDT, 107
EBERLEU, 113
EBERLIN, 59 111
EBERLING, 105
EBERS, 25
EBERSTEIN, 44
ECKBLATT, 25
ECKELHAFT, 34
ECKERMAN, 70
ECKHARDT, 59
ECKYMEYER, 16
EDDELMAN, 63
EDDLEMAN, 81

EDDS, 3
EDES, 5
EDGAR, 74
EDMANSON, 64
EDMENSTEIN, 65
EDMISTON, 14
EDMONDSON, 1
EDSELL, 29
EHEMANN, 98
EHLERT, 57 81
EHRLACH, 82
EHRLING, 62
EICKERMAN, 44
EICKERMANN, 91
EICKHOLZ, 89
EIGELMANN, 113
EIKELSMANN, 67
EIKERMANN, 95 100
EITEL, 28
EITMANN, 91
EITZEN, 21 39 111
ELDREDGE, 26 32 45 47
ELDRIDGE, 27 94
ELFELD, 79 80 82 83 90
  91 96 99 103 108
ELFIELD, 82
ELLER, 19
ELLIS, 20 38
ELMING, 108
ELSENRADD, 106
ELZOLD, 72
EMERSON, 45
EMI, 77
EMMONS, 62
EMO, 95
ENDECOTT, 18
ENDULS, 99
ENEMEYER, 89
ENFIELD, 14
ENGE, 109
ENGEL, 66
ENGELKING, 89
ENGLERT, 60
ENKE, 110
ENNDER, 65
EPING, 108

EPKER, 36
EPPLE, 79 94 111
EPTON, 113
ERBSCHLOE, 30
ERDMAN, 80
EREKSON, 106
ERFMANN, 78 112
ERICKSON, 90
ERKSON, 109
ERNI, 43 86
ERNS, 84
ERNST, 61
ERNY, 69 79
ESSING, 98
ESTES, 1 8 45 55
ESTU----, 75
ETHER, 76
ETTMULLER, 107
EVANS, 4 5 9 11
EVARED, 68
EVINS, 10
EYSVOGEL, 25 33-36 38
FAAKER, 85
FACH, 111
FADDERSEN, 108
FAERBER, 98
FAIRBANK, 26
FALLENS, 50
FALTEY, 45
FAN, 64
FANCE, 53
FANNEN, 83
FANNON, 56 76 93
FARIS, 25 68
FARRIS, 19 63 86 102
FAZER, 26
FEDDERSEN, 108
FEES, 95 98
FEHNER, 36
FEIL, 106
FEISCHEL, 113
FEITZEL, 54 113
FELDMANN, 36 110
FELING, 57
FELY, 26
FEMMER, 73

FENDEL, 92
FERGUSON, 72-74 114
FERREL, 90
FERRELL, 49
FESSEN, 81
FIEG, 95
FIELDMANN, 50
FILLA, 89 97 99
FILLINS, 43
FINDALL, 65
FINDLY, 16
FINGLANG, 72
FINKLANG, 80
FINLAND, 76
FINLEY, 15
FINN, 19
FIRN, 33
FISCHER, 41 56 65 71
    75 80 96 100 110 115
FISHER, 17 18 20 22 33
    40 87
FISKY, 89
FITZGERALD, 25 49 51
    98
FITZGEREL, 91
FITZGERELD, 58
FIX, 29
FLACHMANN, 110
FLACK, 12
FLAKE, 101
FLATT, 4 9
FLEHE, 72
FLEISCH, 71
FLETCHER, 55
FLETT, 4
FLEUCKE, 81
FLITSCH, 57
FLUCHT, 90
FOELLING, 46
FOLEY, 46
FOLLEY, 42
FORD, 61
FORREST, 70
FORSTER, 108
FORSYTH, 51 52
FOSTER, 29 36 75

FOULK, 1
FOURT, 61
FOWLER, 20
FRAKER, 36
FRANK, 45 56 101
FRANKE, 44 53 62
FRANKENFELD, 107 109 110
FRANKLIN, 55
FRASHER, 109
FRATTE, 72
FRAUTWEIN, 92
FRECKMANN, 21 23 97
FREDERICKS, 69
FREEMAN, 1
FREIDAG, 45
FRENCH, 61
FRETZMEIER, 89
FREUKBIP, 53
FREY, 87 111 112
FRICK, 30
FRICKE, 35 39 109
FRICKER, 26 113
FRISCHE, 64
FRITZ, 21 33 37
FRITZEMEIER, 38 64 104
FRITZMIEIR, 113
FRIZER, 74
FRUBER, 48
FUGGER, 36
FULKS, 40 45 50
FULLMAN, 52
FUNCH, 44
FURBER, 76
FURGISEN, 18
GABER, 113
GABLER, 22 46 49 59
GADDEN, 18
GAERTNER, 112
GAILEMEYER, 85
GAITER, 47
GAITZNER, 62
GALLAWAY, 6 8
GALLIWAY, 6
GAMBLING, 41
GANISON, 97

GARNER, 32 50 64 66 86 98
GARTMANN, 35
GAST, 84
GASTMANN, 67
GASTNER, 105
GATTS, 51
GATZAMEIER, 36
GAU, 51
GAUS, 66
GAXLICKS, 14
GEABER, 70
GEAR, 54
GEDEMEYER, 92
GEERKE, 103
GEERLER, 14
GEIBER, 86
GEILMANN, 34
GELLER, 106
GENTNER, 92
GEPPE, 50
GERKING, 78
GERMAN, 108
GERMEAN, 91
GERREYDH, 4
GESCHWIND, 100
GEST, 111
GEVILE, 103
GHBERT, 20
GIBONS, 66
GIBSON, 3 14 20 37 39 60 61 65 67 78 85
GICK, 103
GIDENHAGEN, 84
GIDINGHAGEN, 108
GIELMAN, 44
GILES, 31 32 34 39
GILLESPY, 3
GILLIG, 73
GILMORE, 13 18
GISDINGHAGEN, 113
GISHNER, 106
GIVENS, 76
GIWEAN, 101
GLANDEN, 73
GLANDIN, 95

GLEENY, 99
GLEINNER, 98
GLENN, 69
GLOTZ, 76
GLOVE, 106
GLOVER, 20
GNADT, 104
GOAD, 85
GOBEL, 81
GODIER, 71
GOETTE, 31
GOETZ, 22 25
GOHRLICH, 58
GOLD, 84
GOOCH, 15
GOODALL, 13
GOTTHOF, 58
GOTZ, 18 71
GRABENSTEIN, 109
GRABOR, 41
GRACHER, 114
GRAF, 46 67
GRAFAUD, 59
GRAFF, 15
GRAH, 108
GRAHAM, 58 99 103 109
GRAHARD, 4
GRAIBE, 74
GRAIN, 56
GRAINERMAN, 20
GRANNAMAN, 88 93 96
GRANNAMANN, 115
GRANNEMAN, 67 68
GRANNEMANN, 73 108
GRASMAN, 17
GRAVES, 88
GRAZIER, 14
GREBLER, 99
GREEN, 98
GREENSTREET, 16 22-25
    27 28 36 59
GREIN, 57
GREINER, 104
GREINICKE, 90
GREULICK, 62
GREVY, 46
GRIFFEY, 11
GRIFFITH, 21
GRIFFY, 11
GRIPLET, 82
GRISWELL, 60
GROBEN, 98
GROF, 70
GROFF, 9 19 34
GROH, 20 35
GROOS, 114
GROP, 109
GROSS, 25 30 34 41
GROSSMAN, 21
GROSSMANN, 23
GROTE, 58 76
GROTTER, 105
GRUBER, 23 26 42 84 86
GUEDEN, 52
GUENERT, 107
GUETNER, 46
GUIDER, 82
GUMPER, 27
GUNTHER, 36
GUNTNER, 33
GUTTMAN, 45
GUYLER, 17
HAAK, 31
HAAN, 72
HABLER, 77
HADIRN, 79
HAEFFMANN, 93
HAEFFNER, 93 99
HAEFNER, 100
HAFELE, 110
HAFER, 53
HAFFNER, 91
HAGAMEIER, 86
HAGEDORN, 59
HAGEMEISTER, 95
HAGEN, 52
HAHN, 40
HAHUKE, 111
HAID, 82 106
HAIN, 41
HAINES, 53 55 78 109
HAINKE, 93

HAINS, 8 10-12 15 47 75
HAIREL, 72
HAKAMP, 91
HALE, 32
HALEY, 94
HALL, 8 19 23 29 41 71
HALLAND, 90
HALLAWAY, 15
HALTER, 37
HALTGREVE, 90
HALVEY, 60 64
HAMBURG, 29
HAMBY, 33 40 45 69 82 87 89 103
HAMELTON, 67
HAMIER, 33
HAMILL, 34
HAMILTON, 55 88 91
HAMLER, 96
HAMMEL, 48 97
HAMMELMANN, 107
HAMMOCK, 62
HANDHAUSEN, 28-30 33-35 43-45 56
HANDON, 14
HANE, 92
HANES, 114
HANKE, 40
HANKEMEYER, 114
HANNEGAN, 44
HANS, 53 75
HAPERMEHL, 96
HAPTON, 29
HARDISTER, 2
HARFELE, 113
HARING, 91
HARLIN, 33
HARNER, 41
HARNESH, 29
HARRINGTON, 85
HARRIS, 10 11 55 59 88
HARRISON, 1-3 6-8 11 13-15 17 35 37 45 46
HARTKE, 109
HARTMAN, 64 93

HARTMASTER, 97
HARTUNG, 44
HARTWIG, 114
HASEFELE, 70
HASENHOLZ, 47
HASENRITTER, 66 84 108
HASFELD, 88 94
HASFELE, 110 113
HASFNER, 113
HASINRITTER, 84
HATT, 102
HAUCH, 83
HAUP, 59
HAUPT, 93 101
HAVERLE, 56
HAVERSTOCK, 76
HAWKINS, 8 11 12 17 24
HAYEMEYER, 36
HAYNES, 22 48 57 73 108
HAYS, 67
HAZLER, 66
HUBERMEHL, 106
HEADDRICH, 64
HEARST, 34
HEART, 47
HEATH, 17 18 20 21 25 29 59 67
HEBBER, 26
HEBERLIN, 96
HECK, 33 34 41 71
HECKELBOLDT, 59
HECKMAN, 40
HECKMANN, 80 108
HEDRIC, 85
HEDRICK, 69
HEEDT, 70
HEESELMAN, 96
HEHER, 103
HEHNER, 111
HEHR, 103
HEHUER, 111
HEID, 43
HEIDBRINK, 55 104
HEIDEBRINK, 61
HEILERT, 53

HEIMSER, 50
HEINEDH, 105
HEINICKE, 62
HEINIES, 105
HEINKE, 75 84 96
HEINLEIN, 96 102
HEINLEN, 79
HEINNEBERGER, 63
HEINRESHS, 21
HEINRICH, 106
HEISE, 77
HELBER, 99
HELD, 32 35 44 69 101
HELKERBEUNER, 90
HELLBERG, 93
HELLEGEN, 109
HELLER, 53
HELMENDOCH, 87
HELMES, 80
HELMICH, 93
HELMS, 2 57 84
HELTON, 2 3 5 7 8 11
  12 16
HEMINGER, 96
HEMME, 98
HENCHY, 7
HENDERSON, 10 14
HENELEY, 100
HENGE, 41
HENIG, 101
HENKEL, 64
HENNAWAY, 113
HENNEBERG, 71
HENNEBERGER, 29
HENRICHS, 72
HENRICKS, 37
HENSLEY, 4 16 17 21 27
  31 40 58 64 65 81 94
  98 103 104 106
HENSLY, 31
HENSON, 23 39 42 43 78
HENTON, 82 91
HENZE, 78 106
HERBSTREILER, 92
HERMAN, 72
HERMANNSCHLENDER, 55

HERSCH, 33
HERSEY, 94
HERZOG, 95
HESEMANN, 113
HESFELS, 113
HESNER, 76
HESS, 46 79
HESSE, 94
HESTERMASER, 104
HETHERLY, 5
HETTICH, 65
HEUGSTENBERG, 56
HEUMANN, 111
HEWS, 3
HEYER, 29 34
HIATT, 34 83 89
HIATTE, 67 75
HIBLER, 16 20-22 24 27
  28 37 40 43 45-47 50
  51 86 93 112 115
HICKE, 52
HICKMAN, 39
HICKS, 105
HILBER, 95 104
HILBERT, 96 98 106
HILDEBRAN, 59
HILDEBRANDT, 44
HILKER, 108 110-112
  114
HILKERBANMER, 58
HILL, 3 5 14
HILSMAN, 24
HIMES, 66
HIMPELMANN, 114
HINCHE, 66
HINCHY, 3
HINCKE, 19
HINDRICKS, 78
HINE, 70
HINEMANN, 58
HINFSEN, 100
HINKLE, 21 27 30 42 74
  87
HINSEN, 98
HINSON, 1 102
HINTIN, 65

HINTON, 63
HIP, 114
HIRSH, 45
HIRZEL, 114
HOBACK, 1
HOBERIN, 63
HOBISN, 71
HOBOUGH, 5
HOBSON, 22
HOCH, 57
HOCHEN, 50
HOCHSTENBACH, 111
HOCKMAN, 76
HODGES, 77
HOECHSTENBUCH, 98
HOECK, 54 56
HOEFELS, 110
HOEHN, 61
HOENER, 109
HOFER, 63 64 102
HOFFERTH, 107
HOFFMAN, 28 34 38 49
 54 56 71 73 84 87 92
 95-98 104 105
HOFFMANN, 33 56 66 80
 108-111 113
HOFFNER, 45
HOFFORTH, 86
HOGAN, 3
HOHN, 79
HOHNER, 108
HOKEL, 95
HOLANDSWORTH, 70
HOLBEIN, 64
HOLBERT, 2
HOLDEN, 11
HOLDER, 3 92
HOLENSWORTH, 82
HOLLAND, 20 90
HOLLANDSWORTH, 19 38
 40 77
HOLLINDSWORTH, 90 104
HOLLINGSWORTH, 74 77
HOLLIWAY, 1 6
HOLLMAN, 39
HOLMER, 50 56 112

HOLSHAUS, 112
HOLT, 17 19 23 27 56
 60 68 78 82 85 93 98
 104 111
HOLTGREVE, 92
HOLTSCHUK, 83
HOLTWICK, 40
HOMAN, 45 79
HOMEIER, 46
HOMEIR, 81
HOMEYER, 97
HOMGELDT, 106
HOMIER, 35 57
HONESTEY, 101
HONIG, 32
HONSFIELD, 54
HOOD, 113
HOODENPYL, 5
HOOPS, 1 5-7 10 11 16
HOPP, 107
HOPSON, 21 24-26
HOPTEN, 61
HOPTON, 12
HORMBURG, 64
HORN, 12 77 111
HORNER, 41 96
HORSFELT, 77
HORSTMAN, 61
HORSTMANN, 103 113
HOSINGER, 3
HOTTINGER, 48
HOUNEMAN, 113
HOUSINGER, 1
HOUSLEY, 114
HOW, 84
HOWARD, 3 6 18 42 50
 95 104
HUBER, 23 24 34 80 82
 83
HUDSON, 81
HUELLE, 56
HUFFMAN, 5 8 15 23 27
 60 61 75 115
HUG, 40 113
HUGG, 86
HUGH, 1

HUGHES, 3 16
HUGHS, 5 7 9 10 59
HULL, 2 3
HULLE, 55
HULLION, 19 20
HULVEY, 58
HUMBURG, 57 76 93 112
HUMPHREY, 1
HUMPHRIES, 1 2
HUNDHASEN, 32
HUNDHAUSEN, 22-26 28-
  33 38 41 46-49 51 52
  54 55 58 59 61-66 68
  69 71 72 74 75 78-84
  87 91-100 102-107
  109-113
HUNEBERGER, 94
HUNHAUSEN, 75
HUNNBURGER, 88
HUNOLD, 111
HUNTER, 66
HUSMAN, 29
HUSMANN, 24 28 44
HUSVALDEN, 32
HUTCHESON, 90
HUTTENRAUCH, 19
HUTTON, 8
HYATT, 9 37
IDEL, 91
IFFELMAN, 75
IHRE, 52
ILSENRAT, 108
INGRAM, 89
IPLER, 74
IRLE, 99
IRMAN, 89
ISAM, 89
ISBEEL, 10
ISBELL, 6
ISDOUP, 60
ISLER, 40
ISLY, 44
ISREAL, 54
IVERS, 20
J----, 86
JACKSON, 2 13-15 17 65

JACKSON (Continued)
  70 73 87 90
JACOB, 24 44 103
JAEGER, 45 56
JAGER, 82
JAITE, 56
JAMES, 22 30 85 93
JAMESON, 30
JAMISON, 47 55 81
JANNETT, 83
JANSEN, 113
JANST, 112
JARVIS, 8 21 29 64 70
  74 78 86 92 95 114
JEAGER, 34 36
JENKENS, 100
JENKINS, 21 36 41 48
  55 110 111
JENNINGS, 55 61 63 90
JERLI, 84
JESSEN, 90 101
JESSOM, 94
JETT, 14
JEWEL, 6 14
JINKINS, 15
JNO, 60
JOACHEM, 68
JOHNS, 9 16 21 24 37
  38 41 42 50 74
JOHNSON, 11 35 43 44
  58 61 62 83 99 108
  113
JOHNSTON, 68 101 102
JONES, 1 41 44 71 106
JONSTON, 10
JOOD, 27
JORDAN, 95 107
JUCKINE, 83
JULL, 91
JUMP, 14
JUST, 29 44 49
JUTTHOUSE, 36
K----AGLIN, 86
KAEDING, 88
KAEMPF, 107
KAEMPFF, 22

KAGELIEN, 82
KAHL, 96
KAHLE, 62 88
KAHUND, 33
KAISER, 27 32 40 54 84
KAMMERLAUDER, 35
KAMP, 65
KAMPER, 112
KANSCHELBACH, 65
KANTZ, 103 104
KAPELL, 74
KARSTEDT, 106 110
KASENS, 48
KATTLEMAN, 44
KATTLEMANN, 22 30
KATTLEMEYER, 19
KAUFMAN, 77 106
KAUTZ, 106
KEAAS, 88
KEBE, 54
KECH, 60
KEE, 1
KEEFER, 50
KEFER, 60
KEFFER, 42
KEFFLER, 64
KEFSTER, 113
KEGFER, 86
KEHLENBRINK, 64
KEHLINBRINK, 39
KEHR, 21 50 59 63 72
  73 87 94 97 98 100-
  104 108-111 113 115
KEILMAN, 74
KEINEY, 27 29-32 36
KEINKULLER, 104
KEISCHER, 24
KELESCHMANN, 29
KELINDIERST, 20
KELLER, 24 66 77 96
  107
KELLIAN, 15
KELLNER, 44
KELMANN, 80
KEMICH, 87
KEMPER, 15 50

KEMPLE, 37
KEMZEY, 32
KENKEAD, 20
KENNEY, 15 16
KENNY, 13
KEOH, 100
KEPLER, 35 107
KEPPER, 69
KERBY, 21
KERLEY, 4 7 17 26 31
  48 69 84 90
KERLY, 41 64
KERMANN, 68
KERN, 104 105
KERRELL, 91
KESKER, 31
KESSLER, 71
KETCHUM, 61
KETTELMANN, 111
KIAKLI, 97
KIEBETZ, 20
KIELMAN, 44
KIENTS, 88
KIESHL, 103
KILEAN, 97
KIMZEY, 23 27 29 31 33
  40 41 43 45
KING, 67
KINGCADE, 18 55
KINGKADE, 22 115
KINGLEY, 40
KINKEAD, 19 77 85 93
KINKLE, 103
KINNAMEN, 69
KIOKER, 79
KIRCHNER, 56 57
KIRCHOFF, 74
KIRKLAND, 85
KIRLEY, 10 12
KIRN, 13
KISO, 40
KLAGES, 95
KLANS, 72
KLARING, 37
KLASENER, 89
KLASNER, 101

KLASSNER, 96
KLAUS, 68 75 77 92
KLEE, 42 71 111
KLEIN, 25 34 37 43 53 75
KLEINDIENST, 84
KLEINDIERST, 18
KLEINSCHMIDT, 46 78
KLEINSHMIDT, 81
KLENG, 30
KLENHAUS, 90
KLENKE, 103
KLEONIGHAUS, 88 89
KLEONINGHAUS, 91 92 94
KLICK, 64 101 105 110 113
KLIEDUNST, 97
KLING, 93
KLINGE, 66 67 70 73 76 84 87 88
KLINGER, 66 97 101
KLINK, 87
KLOCKENBERGER, 47
KLOENINGHAUS, 91 95 98
KLOGGES, 103
KLOPNER, 109
KLOPPER, 103
KLOSNER, 35
KLOSSNER, 104
KLOTT, 42 50 91
KLUMAS, 37
KLUNKE, 72
KNEISEL, 23 26
KNGKADE, 22
KNIEF, 91 95 103
KNOCHE, 53
KOBUSH, 106
KOCH, 53 56 91 93
KOCHE, 93
KOENIG, 74 105 108
KOESTER, 76
KOHL, 22
KOHLAGE, 69
KONE, 87
KONEKE, 42
KONIG, 78 108 112

KONING, 92
KONOKE, 41 44 45
KOONAY, 89
KOPPE, 72 76
KOPS, 46
KORSTEDT, 114
KOSENBERGER, 106
KOTHOFF, 45
KOTTER, 76
KOTTES, 41
KOTTHOFF, 34 48
KOTTWITZ, 102 105
KOWING, 22-24 27 28 31 34-40 43
KOZAK, 73
KRABEN, 44
KRAG, 20
KRAMANS, 103
KRAMER, 41 48
KRAMME, 110
KRAMPE, 97
KRASK, 62
KRATTLE, 36 57 107
KRATTLEY, 42
KRATZHELLER, 54
KRAUP, 42
KREAMER, 66
KREATLY, 37
KRECH, 35 102 103 106 107
KRECKER, 45
KREIGER, 103
KRESSEY, 83
KRETER, 46
KRETTI, 25
KRETTLE, 49
KREUTJER, 62
KRIEB, 91
KROBER, 72
KROMER, 53
KRUGER, 51 81 86
KRUSE, 107
KRUTTLY, 95
KUBITZ, 94
KUCK, 60 100
KUEBLER, 106 107

KUENSTER, 88
KUGGE, 103
KUHFUSS, 49
KUHL, 78
KUHLEM, 51
KUHLEMANN, 59
KUHLENCAMP, 94
KUHLHOELTER, 113
KUHLMANN, 110
KUHN, 59 66 68 101
KULEN, 83
KULMAN, 59
KUMMEL, 112
KUNZELMANN, 46
KUPE, 52
KUPER, 76
KUPPER, 32 33
KUSCHEL, 46 50 65 75
KUSCHER, 62
LABAUBE, 22 35
LABERS, 51
LACEY, 38 42
LACY, 65 84
LADD, 9
LAIN, 48 53
LAMANCE, 46
LAMBERT, 54
LAMBET, 78
LAMBETH, 13 102 114 115
LAMPBETH, 92
LAMS, 29 43 48 104
LANDBERG, 67
LANDENDORFER, 98
LANDEOCHER, 84
LANDWEHR, 71
LANE, 7 14 17 56 81 84 85 99 108
LANG, 56
LANGE, 55 80 83 90 91 101 114
LANGENBERG, 64 72 90
LANGENBERY, 92
LANGENBORY, 63
LANGENDOEFFER, 17
LANGENDOERFER, 99

LANGENDORFER, 19 29 43 96 111 112
LANGHORST, 106
LANIZ, 56
LANQUILLION, 41
LASEN, 92
LATCAR, 76
LAUBERT, 101
LAUER, 73 95 105
LAUGHLEN, 13
LAUGHLIN, 1 6 11
LAURA, 104
LAURIE, 68
LAVEN, 10
LAYTON, 49
LEA, 84
LEACH, 24-27 31 33-42 45-48 50-53 55-57 59-62 67-70 73 75 77-79 85-88 93 95 103-105 109 111-113 115
LEE, 24 29 31 36 37 41 44 45 60 70 71 82 87
LEECH, 17 18 22 32 65
LEEPER, 72
LEHNHOFF, 88
LEIMBERGER, 93
LEIMER, 93
LEIMKUELER, 109
LEIMKUHLER, 51
LEIST, 80
LEME, 15
LEMMER, 75
LEMMON, 88
LEMMONS, 52 57 100
LEMON, 2
LEMONS, 78 110 111
LENENBERGER, 38
LENICKE, 111
LENK, 37
LENOX, 3
LENSING, 76
LEONARD, 58
LEONHARDT, 20 43
LEOPOLD, 15-27 30-33

LEPEL, 60 62 64 114
LESSEL, 37
LESSELL, 21 30 34-36 38-45 48 105
LETCHER, 83
LEVI, 59
LEVY, 80
LEWECKE, 57
LEWIS, 31 92 102 115
LICHTENSTEIN, 98
LICKLIDER, 30-35 37 38 40-42 44 47 57 65
LIELE, 111
LIEMKUELER, 113
LIEMKUHLER, 73
LIESMEIER, 110
LIETHER, 66
LILLMAN, 103
LIMMULE, 77
LINCOLN, 62
LINDEMAN, 61
LINDEMANN, 75 78
LINK, 66
LINKE, 34
LINNEMANN, 63
LINZ, 98
LIPPE, 101 103 114
LIVELY, 1 10 18-21
LOBEL, 79
LOCKHART, 38 73 86
LOELLER, 113
LOFTON, 14 19
LOGSDON, 6
LOGSTON, 2 27
LOHENUT, 86
LOLK, 107
LOMPE, 103
LONGENOTTI, 58
LOOBY, 43
LORBUR, 56
LOSTER, 102
LOVING, 14
LOWERY, 14
LOWS, 52
LOYD, 9
LUCAS, 18 20-26 32-37

LUCAS (Continued) 39 42-44 48 68
LUCHSEGER, 84
LUCY, 69
LUDWIG, 29
LUEBBE, 47
LUEDERS, 87
LUENBURG, 104
LUETTHAUS, 110
LUHRING, 62
LUKEKINGS, 18
LUMKUELER, 108
LUNDSFORD, 1
LUPPOLD, 43
LUSTER, 41 65 68 70 74 104
LUTHY, 62
LUTNER, 98
LUTON, 68
LUTY, 38
LYRUNA, 71
MACCHISNEY, 20
MACKDADE, 41
MACKFEE, 32
MADE, 99
MAEAR, 60
MAECKLY, 92
MAGDALENE, 48
MAGGE, 36
MAHAN, 60
MAHANEY, 41 45 51 55 56 59 62 66 69 70 76 77 101 103 114
MAHANY, 90 95 115
MAHL, 114
MAHONEY, 32
MAHRIE, 91
MAIDE, 98
MAIER, 44 66 91 104 109
MAILAND, 90
MAKEL, 61
MALONE, 10
MAMATH, 105
MANGENMEYER, 31
MANN, 22 60

MANNARING, 74
MANSUR, 39
MANTZIS, 74
MARGAIN, 74
MARGRAVE, 17
MARGRAVES, 2-9 15
MARIE, 71
MARIS, 90
MARKEL, 35
MARKSFIELD, 29
MARKUM, 11
MARNER, 73
MARRIE, 2
MARROTT, 32
MARSCHNER, 63
MARSH, 36 104
MARTIN, 10 13 16 66 89 111
MARX, 35 44 59
MASEY, 110 113
MASIE, 63 65 67-69
MASON, 6 8 10 18 50 66 72 74 83 111 113
MASSEY, 5
MASSIE, 3 7 9 10 15 24 44
MASTENEM, 82
MAT-----, 19
MATHAEWS, 68
MATHEW, 97
MATHEWS, 16 43 50 51 60 69 70 78 90
MATHIE, 19
MATHIS, 51
MATLOCK, 35
MATTEWS, 12
MATTHEW, 97
MATTHEWES, 112
MATTHEWS, 15 46 91 95 97 98 103
MATTIX, 37
MATTOCK, 51 68
MATTOCKS, 24 37 53 67 70 77
MAUPIN, 19 44 62 67 104 105 112

MAUR, 78
MAXWELL, 14 17 20 21 23
MAYER, 72
MCAFEE, 15 54
MCALLISTER, 114
MCBRIDE, 5 9
MCCAMMENT, 78
MCCANN, 42
MCCARTHY, 47
MCCARTY, 64
MCCONNEL, 96 101
MCCORD, 7
MCCOURTNEY, 75
MCCRACKEN, 16 20
MCDANIEL, 16 74 78 90
MCEWIN, 13
MCFARLAND, 9
MCGEE, 6 10
MCGOUR, 6
MCGOWAN, 8
MCGOWEN, 47
MCGOWN, 27
MCGUFFY, 83
MCHANY, 23
MCHUTTON, 21
MCINTIRE, 86
MCKENNEY, 31 32 39 56
MCKENNY, 96
MCKINEY, 23 104
MCKINNEY, 9 11 24 79 90 102 105
MCKINSIE, 70
MCKNIGHT, 13 72
MCLAUGHLIN, 84
MCMAHAN, 46
MCMANNIS, 22
MCMANNUS, 12
MCMEAN, 55
MCMILLAN, 88
MCMILLEN, 45 115
MCMILLIAN, 30 34 70
MCMILLIN, 66
MCMILLON, 31
MCNIGHT, 6 11 13
MCNITE, 12

MCQUALITY, 106
MCQUIEN, 105
MCTILTON, 15 16 17
MCWILLIAMS, 70
MEEKS, 35
MEGAN, 40
MEIER, 31 38 39 42 46
    61 70 72 88 89 95
MEIN, 98
MELIES, 81
MELLER, 31
MELLIER, 45
MELON, 28
MELTEN, 98
MELTON, 72
MENAPANA, 66
MENAS, 9
MENGES, 22
MENNAHOUSE, 69
MENNYPENNY, 46
MENZ, 52
MEPTEMAKER, 73
MEREDITH, 32 39
MERIDETH, 103
MERIDITH, 84 85
MERPHY, 90
MERRELL, 35
MERRY, 27
MERTEER, 1
MERTENS, 18 52 107 109
MESCHLER, 30
MESSMEYER, 114
METGLER, 72
METLOCK, 78
METTENDORF, 63
METZ, 23
MEYER, 41 42 45 58 59
    65 67 77 79 81 84
    88-90 92 95 100 108
    110 111
MEYERS, 75 83 84 86 93
MEYOR, 15 50
MICHAEL, 80
MICHAELS, 113
MICHE, 72 74 76-85 87-
    89 96-98

MICHEL, 26 42 76 115
MICHELS, 35 54 110 112
MICKS, 103
MIDDLECALF, 10
MIDGATE, 76
MIDLOCK, 3
MIEGEL, 43
MILLER, 4 6 8-15 19 20
    25 26 30 33 38 43 44
    52 53 55-57 61 73 74
    87 92 97 102 106
MILLIGAN, 68
MINER, 52
MINHORSE, 82
MINOR, 22 24 25 43 46
MISKER, 112
MISLLER, 111
MISNER, 82
MISON, 45
MITCHEL, 27 33 52 65
MITCHELL, 91
MITTENDORF, 96 105 115
MITZEL, 41
MOCHEL, 93
MOECKLY, 94
MOELLING, 114
MOLAND, 20
MONCA, 25
MONGUMERY, 64
MONIG, 107
MONNIG, 24
MONTGOMERY, 2
MONY, 45
MONZEL, 26
MOODY, 8 10 89
MOONEY, 4
MOOR, 45
MOORE, 13 16 17 37
MOPPIN, 31
MORELAND, 14
MORELOCK, 29
MORGAN, 34 72 103
MORIK, 50
MORLOCK, 86
MORMAN, 11 13
MORRIS, 8 9 12 13 45

MORRIS (Continued)
　51
MORRISY, 44
MORROW, 1 3 5 6 8 9
MOSCH, 48
MOSEBY, 26
MOSELY, 80
MOSHEL, 45
MOSS, 30
MOSSES, 36
MOTHAUSHER, 107
MOTHER, 51
MOTSCHENBACKER, 25
MOUSEHUND, 35 40
MUELLER, 58 60 83 107
　110 111 113
MULENHAHN, 26
MULHAUS, 112
MULLER, 22 31 32 44 45
　66 67 75 81 89 94
　103 107 109
MULLIGAN, 42
MUNDENGIR, 58
MUNDEWEILLER, 64
MUNDWELLER, 65 67
MUNDWILLER, 42 77
MUNSEL, 68
MUNZANMARIR, 57
MURPHY, 7 8 43 44 57
　58 60 64 65 67 68 71
　72 74 77 81 89 95
　114 115
MURRAY, 1
MUSCAT, 54
MUSKAT, 86
MUSKRAT, 66
MUSTER, 108
MUTGEN, 71
MUTH, 46
MUTSCHENBACH, 63
MYER, 64
MYERS, 6 34
NAAS, 62
NAEGELIN, 25 98
NAEGLIN, 30
NAGEL, 32

NAGLIN, 22
NAHNER, 110
NANCE, 3
NAPE, 114
NAPEAR, 9
NAPIER, 13 17 41
NARYHAM, 99
NASKERMAN, 57
NASSE, 87
NAUGH, 67
NAUGHS, 69
NAUGLE, 82
NAUPER, 64
NAYLEN, 100
NEAL, 69
NEARM, 61
NEBEL, 102
NECKERMANN, 39
NEELY, 97
NEESE, 83
NEFF, 33
NEHEMEIER, 72
NEHMEIER, 71
NEIDAV, 86
NEIDHARDT, 102
NEIDHART, 72 79 92
NEINERT, 80
NEISMEGE, 67
NEISON, 51 52
NEITHARDT, 33
NEITZER, 105
NEIWALD, 34
NELSEE, 80
NELSON, 47 107
NEMYDT, 6
NEPYEAR, 19
NESE, 103
NESTEL, 45 49-57 59-61
　63 64 66-68 71 72
　74-77 80 81 84 86 87
　89 92 93 95-97 99
　101-114
NEUHAUFER, 80
NEUMAN, 42 72
NEUMANN, 79
NEVENHAHN, 30

NEWBERRY, 2
NEWMANN, 19
NICHOLAS, 1
NICHOLI, 105
NICHOLS, 14 114
NICKERMAN, 74
NICKLES, 7
NICKS, 82
NICOLES, 12
NIEBRUEGE, 113
NIEDERMEIER, 60
NIEHOFF, 93
NIENHAUSEN, 90
NIERMANN, 97 101
NIETHAMMER, 77
NIEWALD, 47 90 108 114
NISCHE, 56 105
NOBLET, 14
NOE, 48
NOGDT, 60
NOLDE, 43 58
NOLLING, 72
NOLLTING, 60
NOLTE, 62 63 64 67 100
NOLTENMEYER, 101
NOLTEUSMEIER, 93
NOLTING, 111
NOONAN, 95
NORDMANN, 64
NORE, 53
NORIMMER, 101
NORTHCUT, 19
NORTMAN, 83
NORTMANN, 85
NORWOOD, 50
NOVAK, 78
NOWACK, 106
NUBRUEGGE, 115
NUEHMANN, 109
NUGLE, 69
NUHOFF, 58
NULLMEIER, 110
NULLMEYER, 53 57
NULLMIER, 34
NUMWALD, 69
NUREMBERGER, 33

NURRE, 98
NURRENBERG, 31
NUSBIT, 31
NUTHARD, 112
NUTTY, 74
O'NEAL, 4
OBENHAUS, 92
OBENNABRENBROCK, 39
OBERKROM, 52 83 85 86
OBERMEIER, 59
OBERMIER, 34
OBERSTREET, 36
OCHSNER, 54
OCLASCHLAGER, 36
OETERER, 74
OETTERER, 87
OGESCHKI, 52
OLIVER, 69 74 88
OLPEL, 105
ONCKEN, 34
ONEKEN, 68
OPNER, 112
ORME, 9
ORMES, 9
OTT, 33 38 54
OTTEMEIER, 109
OTTERMAEIER, 112
OTTLEB, 25
OUSLEY, 95
OUTMANS, 92
OVERKROME, 47
OVINSON, 1
OWEN, 4 6 95
OWENS, 1 4 9 12 36 68 85
OXNER, 31
OZESCHIEN, 98
PALKOWICH, 43
PALMER, 23 39 55 56 102
PAMISON, 2
PANDE, 76
PANKEY, 32 94
PANNELL, 14 17 20 38
PAREE, 84
PARHAM, 25 85

PARKER, 106
PARKHAM, 55
PARKS, 7 8
PARSON, 17
PARSONS, 17 21 22 29 38
PASCH, 111
PASCHEL, 77
PATTEN, 90
PATTERSON, 4
PATTIE, 13
PATTY, 6 13 17
PAULMAN, 21 22
PAULMANN, 32
PAUSAULL, 15
PEARCE, 3
PEBION, 34
PEHR, 35
PEITZMEYER, 16
PELMER, 94
PELTER, 34
PENKINS, 95
PENNING, 31
PENNINGTON, 36 41 100
PEPE, 103
PERKINS, 7 11 26 37 45 47 84 95 114
PERRY, 4
PERRYMAN, 60 63 66 68
PETECHE, 91
PETER, 78
PETERS, 68 71 73 77 80
PETERSON, 19 32 45 46
PETRUS, 80 112
PETRUSCHKE, 106
PETTERSON, 108
PETTY, 5
PETUCH, 92
PFANTECH, 80
PFANTSCH, 89
PFATENHAUR, 76
PFEIFER, 30
PFIEFER, 108
PFOTEUHAUSEN, 113
PFOUTCH, 34
PFOUTENHOUR, 32

PHARLY, 21
PHELPS, 98
PHILIP, 109
PHILIPP, 29 32 91
PHILIPS, 5 26 30
PHILLIP, 30 76
PHILLIPS, 12 13 23 76
PIBBONS, 104
PICKER, 74 79 81 105 106 108 110
PICKERING, 16
PICKLER, 78
PIDRERK, 68
PIENIER, 55
PIERPOINT, 102
PIERSON, 90
PIFFER, 90
PIGMAN, 26
PILANT, 84
PILLAT, 25
PILOT, 96
PINNEL, 24
PINNELL, 6 7 9 10 21 114
PIPER, 8
PITCOCK, 72
PITOWEZYK, 97
PLAMPKE, 88
PLASKE, 72
PLATTNER, 49
PLENZINGER, 28
PLOUGHMAN, 50
PLUMER, 110
PLUMMER, 18
PLUST, 110
POCH, 25
PODJADKE, 108
POE, 4 5
POESCHAL, 47
POESCHEL, 33
POGUE, 25 26
POHLMAN, 54
POHLMANN, 114
POHREN, 114 115
POINTER, 2 4 8-10 16 115

141

POLL, 39
POLLE, 52
POLMANN, 107
POLSTON, 108
POMMER, 22 23 29 30 35 60
POPE, 43 48 64
PORSCHEL, 62
PORTER, 15
POSEY, 12 15
POTTER, 41 48 49 53 55 58 61
POTTIY, 70
POWELL, 46 47 49 58 61 70 73 84 89
POWERS, 16
POYNTER, 8 21
PRAGER, 33
PRAGERS, 17
PRAT, 92
PREUSS, 90
PRICE, 5 18 50 52 113
PRIEL, 24
PRIEP, 57
PRINCE, 54
PRIOR, 5 7 48 52
PRIP, 60
PRISE, 46
PRISS, 87
PRISZ, 108 113
PROLLER, 28
PRUDOT, 106
PRUIT, 61 73
PRUITT, 85
PRYER, 65
PRYOR, 1 3 7-11 15 17 25 42 46 51 57 69 70 77 94 100
PUCHTA, 58 77 114
PULLAM, 71
PUMMEL, 5
PUTMAN, 61
PYATT, 12
QUICK, 14 107
QUINN, 81
RABENAU, 95 97-99 102

RABENAU (Continued) 104 107-109 112 114
RABENS, 55
RABERTTSON, 70
RADDEN, 21
RADKIN, 114
RAHLE, 109
RAHN, 44 51 53 55 57 86 91 94 96 97
RAHNS, 48
RAMEY, 112
RAMSAHL, 93
RAMSELL, 36
RAMSEY, 12
RAMSON, 39
RANSCHENBUSCH, 47
RANSELL, 35
RANTER, 99
RAPP, 113
RASCHE, 63
RASCHER, 81
RASHER, 81
RATGEB, 38
RATLIFF, 53 57
RATTLER, 12
RATTLES, 13 17
RATTLIF, 108
RAUSCHENBUSCH, 56
RAUSCHEUBUSCH, 54
RAUSS, 39
RAUSTHER, 103
RAY, 5 59
READ, 43 46 49 51 52 59 60 64 74 88
READER, 34
REAVES, 61 83
REBSAMEN, 67 94
REBSUENER, 106
RECKER, 34
RECKERS, 34
RECKETS, 17
REDMAN, 1
REED, 2-4 6 7 13 22 23 27 30 36 38 42 46 47 51 53 60 61 66-68 73 74 76 78 80 81 83-85

REED (Continued)
  87 109 110
REEDLER, 47
REEFO, 68
REHMERT, 113
REHMI, 60
REHNE, 30
REICHERT, 91 99 109
REICKERT, 97
REIDIGER, 74
REIF, 100
REIFSTECK, 59 84
REIFSTOECK, 64
REITEMEIER, 57
REITEMEYER, 98
REITEMEZER, 86
REITH, 33 44 93
REITZ, 115
REMART, 63
REMBOLD, 101
REMERT, 73
REMMERT, 34 96
RENFRO, 7
RENFROW, 29 88
REPHTO, 13
RETEMEYER, 67
RETHEMEIER, 95
RETKE, 109
RETKIN, 53
RETZHOFF, 84
REUDIIGER, 104
REUGGER, 62
REUTTER, 30
REVE, 79
REVIS, 4
REYNOLDS, 31 33 43 63
  65 66 75 76 85 102
RHADINE, 83
RHASDES, 90
RICH, 45
RICHARD, 27 77 100
RICHARDS, 74
RICHARDSON, 6 20 24 39
  42 43 48 60 63 68 70
  74 98 100-102 109
  110

RICHE, 32
RICHEY, 12
RICHIE, 12 24 42 43 48
RICK, 31 56 63 65
RICKETTS, 53
RIDEN, 14
RIDENHOUER, 54
RIDENHOUR, 14 22 26 34
  42 64 68 86 94 96
RIDENOUR, 33
RIDFENSTAHL, 39
RIEBSAMEN, 79
RIEFENSTAHL, 35 37 38
RIEGER, 113
RIEK, 48 69
RIETER, 99
RIGHT, 5
RILES, 75
RILEY, 64 80
RINEHART, 44
RINGEISEN, 109
RINWORD, 40
RITCHEY, 38 71
RITCHIE, 14 50 51 55-
  57
RITHIE, 58
RITTER, 70
RITTERBUSCH, 96
RITTERBUSH, 53
RIVCHERT, 103
RLAUS, 72
ROARK, 19 32 95
ROBENAU, 105
ROBERSON, 52 65
ROBERTS, 99
ROBERTSON, 2 4 6 10 21
  26 41 59 65 70 79 84
  114
ROBESON, 83
ROBINSON, 12-14 31 37
  66 100 111
ROBISON, 27 36 70 72
RODEN, 19
RODER, 64
RODERS, 31
RODGERS, 10 12 15 17

RODGERS (Continued)
    22 81
ROEDEL, 104 106-108
    112
ROEDERL, 104 105
ROEMER, 107
ROESCHELL, 33
ROESCHER, 49
ROESKE, 22
ROGERS, 6 8 17 20 21
    23 27 36 39 48 59 60
    66 87 101 105 114
ROHLFING, 71 103 107
ROHREBACKER, 17
ROISTE, 115
ROLAND, 29
ROLLFING, 60
ROLOFF, 89
ROMANEMSKI, 61
ROMANENSKI, 61 62
ROMANOWSKE, 70
ROMANOWSKI, 58
ROMMEL, 65
RONNEBERGER, 52 59 79
RONNEBURGER, 102
RONNENBURGER, 99
ROOK, 21 38 40 45 53
    55 60 61 64 66 67 75
    77
ROOKS, 41
ROSE, 77
ROSENBERGER, 26
ROSER, 37
ROSLIK, 73
ROST, 63
ROTHELE, 93
ROTHEMEIER, 84
ROTHERMEYER, 102
ROTHETE, 98
ROTHFUCHS, 79 110
ROTHKEN, 72
ROTHMEIER, 54
ROTHSCHAEFER, 114
ROTTHOFF, 21
ROUPET, 65
ROUPOT, 112

ROUSCH, 35
ROWARD, 2
ROWARK, 12
ROWLEY, 73
ROY, 11
ROYE, 9
RUBE, 75 79 81
RUBENAU, 93 104
RUBSAMAN, 92
RUCHERT, 102
RUDEGER, 33
RUDEMEYER, 34
RUDGER, 91
RUDIGAR, 51
RUDIJER, 52
RUDOLF, 39
RUDOLPH, 58
RUEDEGER, 36
RUEGGE, 47
RUEGGER, 49 97
RUFFNER, 44
RUGGE, 46 69 114
RUGGER, 63
RUGGESICK, 27
RUHLE, 43
RUHLMAN, 53
RUMSFORD, 87
RUNELS, 38
RUNNOLLS, 94
RUPE, 75 77 79 81-86
RUPP, 79
RUPRECHT, 40 61
RUSCHEL, 73
RUSH, 91
RUSSEL, 38
RUTHEMEIER, 113
RUTHERFORD, 9 14 23
RUTS, 61
RUTT, 94
RYAN, 46
SABERFIELD, 7
SADERWERTH, 97
SAGE, 9
SAIL, 99
SALADIN, 33
SALLY, 4

SAMPSON, 8
SAMSE, 94
SANARTT, 11
SANDBERG, 73 75
SANDBERGER, 76 79 80
  92 93 96 98 99
SANDERS, 35 46
SANDS, 101
SAPHNEANSHAUSEN, 71
SASMAHAUSER, 91
SATTERFIELD, 42 43 52
  53 68 72 94
SATTLER, 58
SAUL, 92
SAWYERS, 62
SCAGGS, 8 14
SCANLEN, 88
SCANTH--, 80
SCANTLIN, 63
SCENBYE, 86
SCHACK, 54
SCHAEFER, 34-37 43 59
  88
SCHAEFFER, 50 51
SCHAEPERKOTTER, 95
SCHAERMANN, 92
SCHAFER, 20 42 43 50
  54 68
SCHAFERKETTER, 63 65
SCHAFFERCOLTER, 86
SCHAFFNER, 54 110
SCHAIBEL, 50
SCHAIBLE, 50 52-58 60
  63-65 68 71-73 75 79
  81
SCHAILBE, 72
SCHAMNBURGER, 63
SCHANOT, 29
SCHAPPENHORST, 89
SCHARF, 39
SCHARFENBERGER, 53 62
  100
SCHAUCH, 67
SCHAUENBERG, 36
SCHAUMBURG, 109
SCHAUNBURG, 88

SCHEICHAUM, 80
SCHEIDECK, 50
SCHEIDECKER, 38 67
SCHEIDEGGER, 85
SCHEIDIGGER, 69
SCHEIFFER, 102
SCHEIRBAUM, 89
SCHELLING, 107 108
  110-113
SCHENKER, 35
SCHERBAUM, 92
SCHIBLE, 69
SCHIBLER, 69
SCHICKERLING, 47
SCHIEDECKER, 60
SCHIEFER, 29 67
SCHIERBAUM, 97
SCHIERMAN, 45
SCHIETZ, 86
SCHILDMACHER, 112
SCHINDEL, 75
SCHINDLER, 29 39 62 84
  91
SCHIRER, 27
SCHLENDER, 30
SCHLEUDER, 52
SCHLOEMER, 67 88
SCHLOMANN, 42 105
SCHLOTTOCH, 98
SCHMATSLE, 106
SCHMEIDER, 96
SCHMIDT, 30 34 41-43
  45 48 51 56 60 67
  82-86 99 103-105 113
  114
SCHMIPF, 60
SCHMITT, 24 70
SCHMITZ, 46 98
SCHNAPPERS, 44
SCHNEIDER, 23 33 39 48
  53 83 88 101 106
SCHNEIDEWING, 72
SCHNELL, 40
SCHNELLER, 84
SCHNETH, 103
SCHNIDEKER, 47

SCHNIEDER, 80
SCHNOFR, 53
SCHOCKLEY, 54 70 101
SCHOCKLY, 73
SCHODEL, 23
SCHOENIGOETZ, 43
SCHOERNT, 79
SCHONING, 45
SCHORER, 115
SCHRACK, 28
SCHRADER, 26 83
SCHRAKE, 41
SCHRAM, 41 63
SCHRAMME, 83
SCHRECK, 63 115
SCHREIMANN, 73
SCHREYMAN, 69
SCHRIEBER, 19
SCHRODER, 28 46
SCHROEDER, 77 109
SCHUBERT, 20 48 66
SCHUCK, 77 87
SCHUFER, 17
SCHUH, 99
SCHUK, 76
SCHULER, 75
SCHULSE, 14
SCHULTE, 57 73 108 110
SCHULTMIER, 86
SCHULTZ, 66
SCHULZ, 79
SCHULZE, 58
SCHUMUCKER, 104
SCHUNEMEIER, 57
SCHURBAUM, 85 87
SCHUREMANN, 50
SCHURMANN, 39
SCHUSTER, 37
SCHUTH, 109
SCHUTT, 102
SCHWARR, 84
SCHWARTZ, 43
SCHWARTZEL, 101
SCHWARZ, 102
SCHWEDER, 90
SCHWEIGHAUSER, 45 59

SCHWEPPE, 96
SCHWER, 78
SCHYGUDIA, 60
SCLATTERY, 46
SCOEMER, 16
SCOTT, 10 11 13 15-17
  23 66
SCRIBNER, 16 53
SCUBNER, 33
SCULDTHEIST, 17
SEALS, 10
SEARCY, 17
SEAY, 12 14
SEBO, 98
SEEMS, 102
SEGER, 113
SEIDLER, 30
SEIFER, 93
SEIFERT, 66
SEIMS, 95
SEISL, 95
SEIST, 73
SELBY, 12
SELEE, 94
SELKER, 112
SELLERS, 39
SEMKEN, 30 31 105
SEMKER, 35
SEMKIN, 23 31
SENGENBERGER, 97
SENN, 36 49
SENNOR, 84
SERCE, 89
SERCY, 14
SERVING, 73
SETZER, 24
SEVERS, 36
SEWEL, 26
SEWELL, 42
SEXTON, 84
SHAEFER, 23 24
SHAFFERKOLTER, 86
SHAMBURG, 29
SHAW, 8
SHEA, 78
SHEIBECK, 102

SHEIREL, 102
SHELTON, 23 37 38 40 44 49 52
SHEMY, 8
SHENEY, 83
SHERALD, 27
SHERER, 83
SHERMAN, 14 66
SHIBLER, 69
SHIES, 28
SHIRRELL, 104
SHIVERE, 13
SHIVERS, 3 4 6 14 47 61
SHOBE, 1 2 5 9 18 20 22 29
SHOCKLEY, 4 5 7-9 11-13 15 16 22 24-27 30 32 33 35 40 46 47 49 51 55 57 68 69 78 82 92 94 102
SHOEMAKER, 17 43 87
SHOENNER, 109
SHOKLEY, 22
SHOMMBERGER, 80
SHONGER, 29
SHONNGERS, 18
SHOOKMAN, 9
SHORNIWAUD, 60
SHURLS, 9
SHURMAN, 46
SHURMANN, 28
SHURRELL, 10
SHUTZ, 112
SIEDLER, 63
SIEDMEIER, 101
SIEFERT, 63 79
SIEGER, 102
SIEGMAN, 91
SILBERMAN, 72
SILLYMAN, 73
SILVER, 108
SIMENS, 74
SIMERS, 57
SIMMONS, 48
SIMON, 1 2 6

SIMONS, 96
SIMPSON, 8 10 11 14 19 20 25 27 46
SINCLAIR, 3
SINKLER, 2
SIRE, 74
SITTON, 24 51
SKAGGS, 90
SKILES, 94
SKINNER, 36
SKYLES, 50 53 55 63
SLAGGS, 1
SLEIGER, 83
SLEVE, 76
SLINKMAN, 62
SMALLWOOD, 78
SMITH, 3 6-12 14-21 23-27 33 35 36 40 45-48 51-53 57 58 60 61 63 69 73 74 78 81 82 85 86 88 90 94 95 97 105 109 115
SNELSON, 18
SNITHEN, 17
SNYDER, 67
SOHIVARY, 112
SOHLOTTOCH, 102
SOHNS, 95
SOHUCK, 108
SOLINS, 95
SONDERS, 66
SONDERWORTH, 95
SONNTAG, 102
SONTAG, 109
SORREL, 35 51 58
SORRELL, 15 20 30 72 114
SORRELS, 23 101
SOUDE, 85
SOUDER, 27 33 54 85 108
SOUDERS, 34 37 38 40 44 50 64 66 67 69 78 82 86-90 92-94 96 99
SOUDERWERT, 37
SOUDRE, 87

SOUNTAG, 53
SOUSE, 52
SPAIN, 12-16 18
SPALDEN, 52
SPALDIN, 41
SPALDING, 27 102
SPALLDING, 68
SPALTE, 81
SPANDING, 87
SPANHAUZEN, 31
SPARTE, 88
SPAULDING, 33 45
SPECKALS, 64
SPECKHALS, 58 81 113
SPECKHOLS, 100
SPICHTING, 29 31
SPIELMAN, 37
SPILLMAN, 42
SPINDLER, 43 54
SPOHRER, 101
SPORER, 101
SPRENGER, 108
SPURGIN, 64 65 68 70 88
SRINK, 75
STADFORD, 31
STADTHORDER, 75
STAEMMER, 81
STAFFFORD, 35
STAFFHORST, 22
STAFFORD, 25 26 35 39 60 96
STANGE, 44
STANTON, 40
STAPLETON, 66
STARK, 4 110
STARKEY, 1 2
STARLING, 32
STAUDE, 104
STAUFFER, 110
STEAKE, 56
STECK, 68
STECKLIN, 82
STEEN, 21 28 43 56 62 75
STEFFEN, 78

STEIGER, 36 58 75 90 106
STEIN, 15 58 81 95 112
STEINBECK, 89
STEINER, 64
STEINHAUSER, 48
STEINMETZ, 86
STEINMEYER, 111
STEINMITZ, 73
STEKE, 100
STENDRIDGE, 20
STENE, 104
STENTER, 43
STEPENSON, 67
STEPHAN, 73 79 108
STEPHENS, 29 36 38 46 115
STERLING, 36
STERN, 86
STETS, 112
STEVENS, 21 70 73 99
STEWART, 5 16
STIEF, 24
STILES, 14
STINEMAN, 94
STINES, 39
STITES, 15 17-20 22 23 26 32 33 41 45 46 100
STOCK, 57 59 75 82
STOCKER, 73
STOCKLIN, 39
STOEHR, 39
STOEKE, 21
STOEPPERMANN, 30
STOHLMANN, 102
STOHR, 48
STOKENBLOKEN, 82
STOLLER, 51 100
STOLLON, 45
STOLTMANN, 51
STONE, 85 90
STONER, 36 58
STONNER, 23 71 93 107
STOPPLEMAN, 72
STORCH, 92

STORCK, 99
STORK, 60 63 113
STORY, 63
STOTARED, 89
STOVEAK, 54 55
STOVEALL, 16
STPEHEN, 104
STRACK, 81 111
STRADER, 16
STRADFORD, 40 54
STRAHENER, 70
STRAIN, 24 42 50 55 58 78 94
STRALLNER, 71
STRANK, 110
STRANTON, 87
STRAPNER, 79
STRASNER, 82
STRASS, 69
STRATFORD, 97 108
STRAUB, 45 54 58 62 101 105
STRECH, 100
STRECKER, 17 99
STREHLY, 30 105
STREIN, 17 18 20 33
STRICK, 50
STRICKER, 26 31 77
STRIEN, 7
STRINGER, 4 9
STROBEL, 47 100
STROKMEIER, 42
STRUBE, 112
STRUCKER, 80
STRUESEL, 100
STRUMP, 33
STRUMPT, 97
STUART, 1 3-5 8
STUDDY, 96
STUEHLINGER, 22
STUMP, 22 36 60
SUBER, 84
SULLENS, 2 23
SULLIAVAN, 38
SULLINS, 57 60-62 66 70 74 75 78 80 85 86

SULLINS (Continued) 93
SULLIVAN, 22 27 32 40 43 45 46 49 53 56 60 66 70 72 83 87 90 98 102 104
SUMTAG, 45
SUNDAYMIRE, 55
SUNKEL, 27 42 107
SURGEY, 58
SURL, 89
SURRATT, 10
SUTES, 82
SUTHERLAN, 36
SUTTER, 36 110
SWAFORD, 2
SWANSON, 27
SWEICHAUSER, 31
SYFERT, 96
TABOR, 12
TABOUR, 6
TACKEITT, 41
TACKET, 7 12 16 32 55
TACKETT, 3 4 46 54 89 91 94 97 98 101 102 104 105
TAK, 105
TALBERT, 36
TALON, 66
TAMMER, 80
TAMSCH, 65
TAMUSCH, 62
TANKEK, 33
TANNER, 83
TAPPE, 72 89
TAPPMEIER, 42
TARBER, 68
TAYLER, 27
TAYLOE, 87 95
TAYLOR, 5 7 8 12 14 16 18 38 40 60 65 74 77 94
TAYOR, 86
TEGE, 74
TEGGE, 63
TEHOTTE, 40

TENGE, 22
TENISON, 43
TENNERSON, 11
TENNURE, 20
TERILL, 15
TERRELL, 92 97
TERRILL, 17
TERRY, 8 78 85-88 91
TEUBNER, 48
TEULLINGSR, 71
TEUPNER, 28
THEE, 106
THERIEN, 48
THEUERLYEN, 84
THEYES, 22
THIEPAN, 76
THOFERN, 47 50
THOMAS, 48 62 74 77 83 85 110 115
THOMPSON, 6 9-11 13 14 16 62 73 76 85 114
THOMSON, 12 40 45 47
THOPERN, 60
THROCKMORTON, 4
THURKON, 57
TIES, 58
TIGERT, 4
TILTY, 96 111
TIMKEN, 67
TIMKER, 69
TIMMER, 107 109
TINDEL, 79
TINNAL, 46
TINNERMEIER, 104
TIPPET, 59
TOBBE, 62
TOBEL, 78
TOCHAPPLE, 43
TODD, 42
TODTMAN, 89
TOEDEMANN, 97
TOELLE, 91 92
TOFARN, 24
TOLDTMAN, 84
TOLLE, 83 103
TOMAECHKE, 99

TOMASCHKE, 102
TOMPSON, 56
TOON, 112
TOPPE, 65
TOWNLY, 7
TRACHT, 47 105
TRAIL, 98
TRAUTWEIN, 19 39 99
TRAVESTER, 101
TREASE, 89
TREIVER, 60
TROMER, 39
TROUTMAN, 16
TROVER, 69
TROWER, 18 45 66
TRUPE, 74
TSCHAEPLER, 52
TUCKER, 30 33 35 36 41 43 56
TUELLE, 85
TUERK, 37 39 40 42-44 46 47 50-54 56-58 60 61 64 66 68 72
TUERKE, 54
TULK, 69
TULLEY, 81
TULYER, 69
TUNING, 103
TUPPE, 86
TURNER, 13 67
TURPIN, 2
TYGERT, 3
TYREE, 92
UBMEIER, 89
UFFELMANN, 109
UHALL, 21
ULENSMAN, 82
ULEY, 81
UMRATH, 42
UNCHY, 81
UPHOFF, 97 106
USLER, 44
UTHE, 109
VAGEL, 74
VALENDARN, 91
VALENDORN, 49

VALENTIN, 110
VALETTE, 44
VALLET, 15
VANDERGRIFF, 27
VANDERLIPPE, 70 71 76 92
VANLEY, 58
VAUGHAN, 7 9 43 50 51 93 110 111
VAUGHN, 13 16 67 78 81
VAUN, 7
VAZELPOHL, 100
VEACH, 2 6 19
VERAGUT, 30
VIEMAN, 115
VIEMANN, 26
VILINGE, 77
VINCENT, 4
VINEYARD, 5
VINSON, 11
VOGEL, 48 50 76 77 82 100
VOGLSANG, 72
VOGT, 19 25 34 37 71 84 103
VOHLGEMOUTH, 48
VOIGHT, 78 98
VOLD, 71
VOLIZEN, 76
VOLK, 29 113
VOLLERTSON, 24
VOLLMAN, 41
VOLLMER, 102
VONART, 32
VONBECK, 106
VONBEHREN, 20
VONBERN, 91
VONBOAPEN, 85
VONHARD, 108
VORK, 23
WACHTER, 74
WACKER, 55
WAFRI, 49
WAGNER, 21 22 26 47 80
WALDECKER, 50 68 71
WALDEN, 3

WALDO, 1 2 3
WALKE, 71
WALKER, 4 5 6 24 52 81 111
WALLACE, 10 13 14 16 35 74
WALLENSTEIN, 54
WALTERS, 21
WALTON, 11 19 26 27 41 51 68 69
WARD, 10 11 20 46 52
WARDEN, 3 53 61 98
WARDER, 99
WARE, 27 78
WARNARE, 21
WARREN, 27 77
WARRIN, 13
WASELOH, 106
WASHAM, 9
WASHINGTON, 99
WATER, 48
WATERMANN, 103
WATKINS, 2
WATSON, 16 55 61 111
WATTRON, 67
WATTS, 27
WAUSEHUND, 74
WEATHERFORD, 9 14
WEBER, 29 31 37 51 52 55 65 77 82 91 94 100 110
WEDEKING, 75
WEDLING, 77
WEELY, 91
WEENNLENGER, 82
WEHKING, 69
WEHMEIER, 75 78 82 91 110
WEHMISE, 100
WEHMUELLER, 113
WEHMUELTOS, 67
WEHRLI, iii
WEIDEMAN, 61
WEIDEMANN, 75 111
WEIDERMAN, 93
WEIDERMANN, 96

WEIDMANN, 66
WEIFSER, 100
WEIGEMAN, 69
WEILNLAYED, 89
WEILSEL, 109
WEINDMEIER, 111
WEINLAND, 23
WEIP, 50
WEIPAL, 59
WEIR, 8-11 14 18
WEISER, 102
WEISS, 47 48 93
WEIST, 81
WELHELMI, 103
WELL, 23
WELLER, 33
WELLNER, 34
WELSCHE, 70
WELSH, 43
WELTE, 80
WELTING, 67
WELTON, 2 26
WEPELHORFT, 55
WERLI, 77
WERLY, 26
WERNER, 103 112 115
WERREN, 108
WERTHMEIN, 95
WESELOH, 108
WESELSH, 113
WESEMAN, 63
WEST, 12 20 39 108
WESTHOBS, 14
WESTHOLD, 105
WESTHOLZ, 91
WESTLOCK, 101
WETHE, 92
WETTLOCK, 105
WEYMANN, 18
WHEAT, 64 88
WHEEL, 105
WHITACER, 38
WHITE, 23 25 26 53 56
   66 77 95
WHITLEY, 12-14
WHITLOW, 85

WICK, 100
WICKELL, 105
WICKER, 31
WICKS, 99
WIDMER, 87
WIEMAN, 47 91
WILAMS, 21
WILBER, 85
WILBURN, 87
WILD, 102 113
WILDE, 84
WILE, 51
WILHELME, 80
WILKENING, 88 89 91
WILKERSON, 68
WILKINSON, 69
WILL, 33
WILLAIMSON, 1
WILLARD, 88
WILLCOX, 21
WILLEMAN, 91
WILLEMANN, 105
WILLENBACH, 97
WILLIAMS, 3 7 15 18 19
   24 31 33 40 47 54 56
   75 87
WILLIAMSON, 70
WILLMANN, 105
WILLS, 21
WILLTEN, 85
WILMS, 54 109
WILSON, 5 10 15 32 40
   46 76 101
WILTING, 54
WINDOLF, 43
WINDOLPH, 68
WINN, 20 23 32 35 51
   77 81
WINTER, 36 72 75 106
WINTERS, 34
WISEMAN, 12 13 38 65
WISEMANN, 20
WITMANN, 30
WITTCOCK, 99
WITTE, 71 106
WITTEN, 24

WITTENBACH, 85
WITTENBUCK, 85
WITTICH, 39
WITTMAN, 22 97
WITTMANN, 26
WITTRICK, 115
WITTROCK, 112
WITZEL, 106
WITZSTEIN, 30
WOERT, 64
WOGLER, 75
WOHLGEMUTH, 46
WOHLT, 38
WOLKING, 79 103 110
WOLLBRINK, 90 92
WOLLEMADE, 75
WOLLSCHLAGER, 48
WOLTER, 57
WOLZ, 39
WONNEL, 70
WOOD, 8-11 45 46
WOODRUFF, 104
WOODS, 8 32 82
WOODWARD, 86
WOODY, 10 15 17
WOOLLAM, 41
WORTHMANN, 108
WOVLSCHECK, 94

WRATTLES, 1
WRIGHT, 18 67 103
WROTON, 47
WUNZ, 101
WYATT, 1 2 4-6 14 16
   44 60
YARNIER, 103
YATES, 4
YEAGER, 35
YEATS, 21
YELLY, 54
YOUNG, 13 83 87 97
YOUNGEBLUT, 100
YOUSE, 94
ZAHL, 60
ZEITZ, 62
ZELLS, 32
ZENNON, 89
ZEUGGEN, 42
ZIMMER, 99 100 105
ZIMMERLE, 75
ZIMMERLEY, 59
ZIMMERLI, 84
ZOFENER, 106
ZORN, 113
ZUMOLT, 36
ZUMWALT, 32 107
ZUMWOOD, 107